Visual Information Systems:
The Power of Graphics and Video

VISUAL INFORMATION SYSTEMS:
THE POWER OF GRAPHICS AND VIDEO

RICHARD H. VEITH

G. K. Hall & Co. • Boston, Massachusetts

VISUAL INFORMATION SYSTEMS:
THE POWER OF GRAPHICS AND VIDEO

RICHARD H. VEITH

Copyright © 1988
by G.K. Hall & Co.
70 Lincoln Street
Boston, Massachusetts 02111

Book design by Barbara Anderson

Book production by John Amburg

Copyediting supervised by Michael Sims

Library of Congress Cataloging-in-Publication Data

Veith, Richard.
  Visual information systems.

  (Professional librarian series)
  Bibliography: p.
  1. Information display systems.   2. Information
storage and retrieval systems.   I. Title.   II. Series.
TK7882.I6V445   1988   005.74   87–31265
ISBN 0–8161–1861–2
ISBN 0–8161–1881–7 (pbk.)

CONTENTS

LIST OF TABLES AND FIGURES

PREFACE

In preparing this book, a word that comes to mind is "viewmaster" (with no reference to the company of that name). The computer systems used for information retrieval have become viewmasters, using "master" in the sense of ruler or governor. Computers control our access to massive amounts of stored information to such an extent that we can find only what the viewmaster shows us and can see it only in the way that the viewmaster recreates it.

Admittedly, calling the computer a viewmaster is an exaggeration, but only a slight one, because information data bases are becoming so enormous and retrieval techniques are becoming sufficiently complex that most of us are indeed at the mercy of the combination of hardware and software that we *must* use in order to glimpse any part of a data base. The focus of this book, however, is more on "view" than on "master," as people, such as information systems designers and developers (and everyone who chooses one system over another), are really the creators of the view. Moreover, the importance of the view is increasingly being recognized, not only for its effect on information retrieval but also because of the rapidly growing number of persons who need to use one view or another.

To put the subject in context, this development of computer as viewmaster is extremely recent historically. For thousands and thousands of years people have been accumulating information—written and drawn records—on tangible media stored in visible locations. Yet now we have billions upon billions of records stored in an invisible way on media that in many cases are also invisible to their users, such as those stored on a remote computer system's disk packs and magnetic tapes.

Even in the short history of the computer itself, however, the rise of huge informational data bases is a recent one. The computer was originally seen as a device for performing mathematical calculations, and the roots of these devices can be traced back a few hundred years—to mechanical calculators in the 1800s such as Babbage's analytical engine, before that to the 1600s and Pascal's adding machine, or even back to an Iranian device for calculating built in the 1400s. In this century, various devices for tabulation, calculation, and mathematical analysis were being perfected in the first half of the 1900s, with the beginnings of an electronic computer appearing in the early 1940s. At the midcentury mark, electronic computers had just begun to emerge from the embryo of World War II research and development, and were still primarily seen as calculating or "computing" machines.

At the same time, information storage and retrieval techniques were being automated with entirely noncomputerized methods, such as microfilm and edge-notched cards. In the latter system, for example, spaces along the edge of an index card for a document were reserved for specific key words, or topic terms, relevant to a collection, and each space might have a hole in it. If one or more rods were inserted through one or more holes and used to lift the deck of cards, some cards would fall out because that hole (or holes) had been notched through to the edge. The cards that would fall would identify documents matching the search request. The exciting information storage technology of the time, though, was microfilm in various shapes and sizes. Microfilm was promoted as the most likely way to accommodate the growing mass of recorded information that was beginning to concern information professionals.

It was also around this time that some information professionals did begin to see the computer as a device to automate part of the processes of information storage and retrieval. In 1950, Claire Schultz and Robert Ford at Sharp & Dohme Company used an IBM 101 Electronic Statistical Machine to search files of literature references, in what was, according to Schultz, the first-ever use of a stored retrieval program and punched-card equipment to search for information with the ability to combine search terms using the logical operators AND, OR, and NOT.[1] Within a few years, methods for computerized information retrieval were being discussed seriously, and reportedly the first paper to describe a computerized re-trieval system using postcoordination (i.e., the system can find a group of items matching a set of search terms even though this group of items was never recognized as a related group before) was delivered in 1954 at an IBM "computation" semi-nar.[2] By the end of the 1950s, large-scale systems for infor-mation storage and retrieval were being attempted.

During the 1960s and through the 1970s there was a gradual shift from batch-search information systems to on-line interactive systems, and as the 1980s began, the quantity of computerized information and the number of persons using that information started to multiply dramatically. The change can be described in various ways, and the statistics can be staggering. In the United States, commercially available data bases in 1979 numbered about 500 and contained a collective 150 million records; by 1986 there were over 3000 such data bases holding 1.7 billion records.[3] The number of customers for just thirty of the largest of these data bases rose from virtually none in the early 1970s to over 1.5 million by mid-1986.[4] (In France, where telephone customers can choose to receive a computer terminal to access on-line telephone directories and other data bases, the number of terminals installed since the early 1980s is over 2.3 million and growing steadily.) Within the United States federal government, reputedly the owner of the largest collection of computer equipment in the world, the number of microcomputers alone jumped from 2000 to over 150,000 from 1981 to 1986, and many of these microcomputers are used to access the 3.5 billion records—according to esti-mates by congress' Office of Technology Assessment—in thou-sands of data bases (of which over 4200 are open to the public).

Moreover, these figures for government and commercial data bases represent only a fraction of the total volume of in-formation that is now stored on, and consequently accessible through, computer systems, whether the systems are super-computers, mainframes, superminicomputers, minicomputers, microcomputers, or personal computers.

The shift from "normal" information system proce-dures—and document-creation procedures as well—that pre-vailed prior to the 1960s to the computerized methods of today has been so pronounced and yet so taken for granted that it is easy to miss the essence of the change; namely, that it is not the volume but the access method that has changed most. A good example is in the field of chemistry, where an abstracting service, Chemical Abstracts, attempts to summarize the world-wide production of chemical literature including patents. The service was begun in 1907 and by 1938 had published over a million abstracts. In less than half that time, the second million abstracts had been published by 1951, and this increased rate was, of course, accomplished without computers. A decade or so later, Chemical Abstracts began a shift to computerized systems and by 1984 had published over ten million abstracts, with the number growing now at a rate of about half a million per year.

The key point in this example is not, however, the increased production rate of abstracts, but the fact that every abstract published since 1975, and many from earlier years, can be searched for and displayed on the remote terminal of a chemist just about anywhere. This is especially true as the Chemical Abstracts service is part of an on-line scientific and technical information network, STN International, supported by organizations in Europe and Japan as well as the United States. Over seven million abstracts can be searched interactively, and those that match the search restrictions can be displayed in a matter of minutes. Given the volume of abstracts and the availability of computer terminals, it is increasingly likely that chemical researchers will use the computer to sift through abstracts and patents. In fact, researchers may not even have access to printed versions of all these materials, let alone have the desire and the time to wade through them. Therefore the chemical researcher does not really see the volume of the data base but uses some search methods to narrow the result down to something manageable, seeing only what the computer—the viewmaster—presents.

Obviously, not all recorded information has been reduced to computerization, and some people will gladly argue that 95 percent is still on paper. As the statistics show, however, and ignoring conjectures about the rate of change or the difference between augmentation and replacement (paper will not be replaced completely), the trend toward increasingly more computerization of information is equally clear.

In addition to this trend, two more themes must be introduced. The first is that the shift to computer data bases has meant a very real change in the whole concept of accumulating recorded information, especially in this transitional period when most recorded information is still presented on paper or other visible media prior to or concurrent with computer storage. That change, often overlooked, is the fact that the computer system relatively rarely recreates stored information as it looked originally when it existed on paper. The characters are the same, but the font is the font of the display system, and lines and formats may not be the same at all. Therefore the reader has lost not only the ability to see written information in proximity to other pieces of information as they originally existed (e.g., articles together in the same paper or magazine, or books together on a shelf), but also the ability to see the physical appearance of the original publication. In the short span of a decade or so, information seekers have lost a whole set of visual cues normally brought into play when going to information recorded on paper, or even on microfilm.

The other theme behind this book is that, once again, a change is coming, and it is just beginning. It is the use of graphics and video information systems to recreate the visual cues, and to go beyond that to new visual aids and computer-generated visual orientations. While video and computer graphics have been around just about as long as the computer itself (longer, in the case of video), it has until recently not been technically and economically feasible to endow information systems with high-quality graphics and video displays for the great majority of users. That is no longer true. I am writing this, for example, using a microcomputer, a Macintosh, that displays a page on the screen pretty much as the page appears on paper, and I can switch to a larger view of the stored documents in which I can rearrange the location of documents relative to each other. Of course, this is not a complete visual representation of a paper system. My microcomputer display does not show a full page at a time, and the identifying picture of the document is only an "icon" that is the same for all other documents in my system. When I use the telephone to dial into a remote data base, I do not see pages of information as they appear on paper unless the pages were also created on a system compatible with my microcomputer.

Nonetheless, the graphic and video capabilities of information systems are beginning to proliferate on a large enough scale to permit their use as tools in the information-retrieval process. Such display mechanisms can reintroduce visual cues, provide the currently "lost" element of visual orientation, and provide even new and unusual visual representations that go beyond anything possible in traditional paper-based systems. It is often said, for example, that creativity stems from the ability to formulate mentally new and different associations, often in a nonlogical and even subconscious process. If information systems can not only present stored information visually but also dynamically rearrange and reassociate items in a visual way, we might "see" things we might not have seen otherwise.

As we continue to expand our use of computer systems for both storing and gaining access to recorded information, the computer remains the viewmaster. The computer system controls the way we can find information and the way we can see what we have found. Now as graphics and video capabilities become integral parts of computerized information systems, the viewmaster does not have to be as restrictive as in the past. In fact, the viewmaster can now provide views that replicate the centuries-long traditions of paper-based systems and can even provide views that would not be possible in the real world of physical paper. The individuals who study, design and create information systems are now fashioning the way the viewmaster's views will work.

That is where this book begins. The size and reach of digitally stored data bases is undeniably expanded, it is recognized that we do need better ways of finding information within these galaxies of binary digits, and graphic and video tools are now available that will support a solution. The visual tools can recapture some of the visual dimensions of information storage and retrieval that existing retrieval systems lack. More important, and the focus of this book, visual tools can add features that go beyond a repackaging of thousands of years of traditional information searches. Some observers, for example, expect computer graphics dramatically to increase individuals' ability to comprehend computer-stored information and the relationships among items.

This book provides an analysis of computer graphics and video within information systems, leading to suggestions for systems development. The first chapter serves as an introduction and presents a scheme for categorizing the varied ways graphics and video appear in information systems. The second chapter looks at the reasons behind the importance of the visual dimension by summarizing the physical, physiological, and mental fundamentals of light and vision. The following chapters then examine types of graphic displays, the use of graphics and video in image-based systems, and the use of graphics to organize the basic screen display. The final chapters look ahead to the ways computer graphics and video can facilitate access to computer-stored information and spur creativity in the information retrieval process, summarizing design guidelines and anticipated developments for the systems that are the subject of this book.

NOTES

1. Claire K. Schultz, "Through the Looking Glass," *Bulletin of the American Society for Information Science* 7 (December 1980):30–31.

2. Frederick G. Kilgour, "New Information Systems," *Bulletin of the American Society for Information Science* 6 (February 1980):13.

3. Martha E. Williams, "Transparent Information Systems Through Gateways, Front Ends, Intermediaries, and Interfaces," *Journal of the American Society for Information Science* 37 (July 1986): 204–14.

4. "Online Subscriber Count Tops 1 Million," *IDP Report*, 26 April 1985, 1–5. See also, "Online Password Counts Rose 22% in '85," *Information Industry Bulletin*, 16 January 1986:1–3.

ACKNOWLEDGMENTS

Over the years, many people have helped me to become acquainted with the various topics related to this work. While it is impossible to list all of their names, I do remember and fully appreciate their contributions.

I am also grateful to the individuals at the many organizations who responded to my requests for information and photographs. Organizational credit is listed with each photograph, and citations for other material appear in footnotes. I realize that some people made a considerable effort to assist me and, although their names may not appear in the credit lines or citations, I thank them.

On a personal note, I particularly want to thank Peter Cawley of CNR Partners and Paul Gandel of AT&T Bell Laboratories for taking the time to read drafts of the manuscript and offer cogent suggestions. For providing a general atmosphere of interest in most, if not all, of the areas covered by this book, I am indebted to Michael Shaw, a colleague at Volt Information Sciences. I also greatly appreciated the encouragement, enthusiasm and guidance of Karen Sirabian, the editor on this project.

Finally, I sincerely thank Bonnie Storm for her help and support during the long process of putting this book together.

1

ELEMENTS, TOOLS, AND OBJECTS

This book is an investigation into the impact of graphics and video technologies on computerized information retrieval systems. Graphics and video capabilities are relatively recent additions to computer systems in general use, and the proliferation of these capabilities in and with information systems is likely to change the systems themselves as well as the way we think about computer-stored information.

As we begin to recognize the contributions of the visual, nonalphanumeric dimensions of the retrieval process, we can see the potential for a major advance in the art and science of information retrieval. During the next several years, it is quite possible that this addition, or reintroduction, of visual elements to information retrieval will contribute substantially to better use of computerized information systems, including all manner of data base systems, wider use of such systems, and more creative results.

The background for this book is that in the history of computerized information systems, words and pictures have not been close companions. The past constraints of technology led designers to create computer systems that were based almost entirely on the manipulation and presentation of keyboard characters. Computerized information retrieval systems, specifically, came to employ a variety of procedures based on words and phrases to allow a searcher to find a string of text or a reference to documents without using any visual cues or spatial orientation. Great efforts have gone into devising methods of taking the words and phrases of information seekers and matching their requests against an invisible store of information (a data base) to determine if the system can produce any items that seem to answer the searchers' questions. If the search was indeed successful, the resulting reference, data, or text would usually be presented as computer-generated type on a screen or paper; that is, the typeface would be that of the computer system used for retrieval, not the typeface or anything else resembling the original document.

Using a computer for information retrieval in this manner has become such a common practice that it is difficult to convince people that the process is missing something. Yet something is indeed missing, and that is the whole set of visual, nonverbal perceptions and associations that we employ every day as we view our environment. When the retrieval systems that are in use today were being developed, there were technical and economic constraints on visual display techniques. Recently, however, the technology of computer graphics and display systems has permitted the reunion of the visual with the verbal. Computerized systems at many levels can now produce pictures or graphics along with words, with all the benefits of both means of conveying meaning.

This is a remarkable development in a number of ways. For one thing, there can be a duplication of print capabilities, including the visual elements of the printed page such as arrangements of text with pictures and varied fonts. More than that, some new capabilities have been added to the information retrieval process, such as the use of pictures as tools (as symbols for actions, for example, or to provide a synthetic spatial orientation) and the appearance of pictures as the objects of a search, and even the dynamic presentation of pictures such as animated graphics or motion video. These topics—the merging of graphics with text, the employment of graphics and video as visual tools, the presence of graphics and video as the objects or products of an information search, the incorporation of motion in information retrieval systems—and the implications of all this are key issues for the design of future information retrieval systems.

Graphics Growth

Computer graphics have been around since the earliest days of the computer itself, but the economics of the relevant technologies, as well as technical limitations, more or less mandated the strictly alphanumeric systems that we have become accustomed to—until recently. Credit for being the first computer system to use a video display terminal is given to the Whirlwind I, active around 1950, but progress in the use of the video display terminal for graphics designs was slow for a decade or two.[1]

Finally, by the end of the 1960s it became possible to recognize a computer graphics industry as such, especially with the development of the storage tube. According to Carl Machover, a graphics industry pioneer, it is impossible to overstate the importance of the storage tube to the history of graphics systems.[2] The storage tube, particularly the direct-view type, is a form of video display tube that does not need to have the screen display continually refreshed as other screens do; instead, a wire mesh inside the tube can maintain an image for minutes or even hours before a refresh cycle is required. The storage tube today is no longer in the mainstream of computer graphics, but it offered for a time the primary feasible way to maintain a line drawing on a video tube. The storage tube not only made computer graphics possible, but also was considerably less expensive than previous means.

As computer graphics developed during the 1970s, large-scale graphics systems began to provide impressive capabilities for computer-aided design, among other things. Graphics software began to be improved, making it easier for nonprogrammers to create images. By the end of the 1970s and the beginning of the 1980s, graphics and video components began to become commonplace outside the world of the larger computer systems. Two things occurred at roughly the same time; the technologies supporting video display processing became more affordable and more available, and the phenomenon of the microcomputer brought computer processing power to hordes of users in the business marketplace and to a lesser extent in the home. It has been said that the beginning of the boom in graphics can be traced directly to a 1978 move by IBM that lowered the price of computer memory by 40 percent, thus more readily satisfying the high memory requirements of computer graphics.[3]

The emergence in the mid-1980s of a broad range of graphics products and a greater interest in the graphics or visual side of computer displays encouraged speculation about the magnitude and importance of this interest. One observer wrote that "the availability of inexpensive and sophisticated graphics may turn out to be as powerful a force for change as the microcomputer itself."[4] Another stated that "today's graphics 'happening' is as important an event as the birth of the digital computer."[5] Other articles have made note of graphics pouring into the office, graphics as the fastest growing segment of the computer industry, graphics saving time and money, a flood of computer graphics software, and the like. While some of this is certainly overstatement, it is nonetheless true that graphics and video technologies have a lot to offer to users of computer systems, whether or not various implementations grow in the way and at the speed that might be forecast.

The remainder of this chapter is an overview of topics in succeeding chapters, and throughout, broad concepts are mixed with details of technologies. While the emphasis is on conceptual understanding, the technical aspects are also included, as the systems under discussion are bounded by the technologies that make them possible. In the field of information systems, technical constraints, or techno-economic constraints, are a powerful influence on system design and acceptance.

Categorizing the Contributions

The first step in understanding the potential magnitude of the change in the way computerized systems present information is to categorize the ways in which graphics and video are, or can be, part of the retrieval process.

In fact, several different relevant developments in the computer industry have attracted widespread attention and can be seen as distinctly different phenomena. In the broader context of visual or nonverbal dimensions, topics such as the use of icons (defined later in this chapter) and the use of interactive video are related. They are both relatively recent additions to the field of computerized information, they both present pictures instead of words and thus evoke nonverbal responses, and they both signal a possibly substantial change in the way information systems are built and used.

There are, then, at least three major aspects to "visual's invasion" of formerly text-and-number systems, and the rest of this chapter defines and describes these as a way to understand and appreciate the scope of visual information systems in general. The three major aspects are (1) the set of basic visual elements in computerized retrieval systems; (2) the way in which the elements, alone or in combination, can be used as tools in the retrieval process; and (3) the appearance of the visual elements as the components of the object of the retrieval process. These three categories can in turn be divided into subcategories, as follows:

1. Elements: color, form:graphics, form:video, and motion
2. Tools: symbols for actions/objects, spatial orientation, attractiveness, and transformation
3. Objects: stored pictures/graphics, dynamic creations

This breakdown is offered as a procedure for analysis and not as a statement that these are exclusive categories into which everything must fall. There are always exceptions to general classifications. Ignoring for the moment some of the finer distinctions and concentrating on the basic differences among elements, tools, and objects, it is possible not only to recognize the contributory roles of each, but also to see how new relationships might be formed.

Elements

The three elements of color, form, and motion are presented here as four elements based on a distinction between graphics and video, which is explained below. Before getting into that distinction, though, some general comments can be made about the relationships among all the elements. While color, graphics, video, and motion are certainly not mutually exclusive, each does describe a major way in which a visual dimension can be expressed, and none is a necessary ingredient of another. Color is often part of both graphics and video, but it has indeed been used alone (with text) as a form of emphasis or even for spatial orientation. Similarly, both graphics and video can exist without color. In addition, motion or animation can be part of a graphic design or an element of a video display, but both can exist without motion, and motion can be implemented without either, as discussed in the following sections.

COLOR

Color as a distinct element, that is, as an addition to an otherwise monochromatic display, can be used to highlight text, to categorize text or numbers, to increase the speed of recognition of a colored portion, to provide spatial orientation, or simply to increase the attractiveness of a display. For example, screen displays might have basic text in one color, titles and keywords in other colors, columns of numbers in alternate colors to improve readability, and a background color to indicate a major subsection of a data base. In practice, however, it may not be a good idea to have such a multitude of colors on a single screen for an essentially textual display.

The value of color in retrieval systems, or the value of specific ways of using color alone, is still under debate and often hard to separate from other visual elements. That is not surprising, as the effects of color perception in general are only approximately understood. Rudolf Arnheim's respected text on visual perception devotes a chapter to color, pointing out that each person may react differently to given colors, and that different uses of the same color produce different reactions in the same person.[6]

In addition, color is actually composed of hue, saturation (the purity of a color), and brightness, and each of these affects perception individually. Attempts have been made to correlate colors with generalizable reactions, such as a warm feeling, but it is not always clear whether brightness, for example, might not be more of a contributing factor to psychophysical reactions than hue. Experiments on the distinctness of colors (where objects in different colors may seem to merge with each other) have shown that brightness and saturation are, in these cases, more important than hue. Arnheim found no difficulty in saying, though, that color is a less efficient means of communication than shape, such as the shape of letters on a page. In fact, if our alphabet were composed of different colors rather than shapes, Arnheim argued that we would be limited to about six values, as that is about the number of different colors that can be distinguished, recognized, and reliably identified as different from each other by the general public.

For video displays, the perception of color is further affected by the physical construction of the display system, the technology employed, the current settings or adjustments of color controls on a given display device, and even by the location of the viewer relative to the screen. The study of color as a distinct element is therefore a complex combination of technology, visual perception, and subjective reactions. In the recent past, as information systems that use color have been developed for general consumer use, researchers attempted to discover the distinctive contributions of color alone, and practitioners developed rules of thumb for the use of color in screen design.

The effects of the display technology on color were highlighted in a study of one of the first general-purpose consumer information services to employ color as a fundamental element, the Prestel service in England.[7] The system uses television sets as the display devices and provides up to six colors (plus black and white). The study confirmed that, first of all, even though the coding for each of the six colors was standardized, the exact shading of a color varied from one manufacturer's television set to another, and varied with the age of a set. Also, the perception of the contrast of the background with the color of text was dependent on ambient lighting. Moreover, the value of color as an addition to text was considerably affected by personal preferences. Of course for some individuals, such as those with some form of color blindness, colors may have little or no value. Given all these problems, the study nevertheless made some recommendations: the best Prestel colors for text (out of the seven possible, including white) on a black background were green and yellow; putting headings in a color other than the following text was useful, but paragraphs in different colors were confusing; different colors for rows in a table were liked best when done with at least three rows per color; colored text was liked least when the colors were used inconsistently or the meaning of a color change was not obvious; and no more than four colors should be used for text for a given screen.

All of these recommendations have to be evaluated in context, however. The study covered one particular system that produced only a fixed set of six colors viewed on color television sets, and comparisons were only in terms of that implementation of six colors. Other systems, with the number of possible simultaneous colors varying from a dozen or so to millions, have caused a whole new set of conclusions to be drawn about the number of colors to use, the ways to use color, and subjective reactions to specific colors and combinations.

The task of distinguishing the specific contributions of color for video displays of information continues to be a research goal. A series of studies on the design of teletext screens, for example, led to the conclusion that, among other things, the effects of color on readability of a screen should be recognized as entirely apart from aesthetic appeal.[8] When the researchers used a memory test to see if the addition of color helped persons to recall words, there was no significant improvement. On a subjective scale, however, subjects tested responded that the addition of color made the screen increasingly cheerful, exciting, and interesting.

More recently, some researchers concentrated on the use of color in certain tasks such as decision making using newer graphics technology with higher resolution and better color. Experiments by Izak Benbasat and co-workers involving business graphics and based on only three colors, suggest that color is helpful under time constraints and during the learning period in general, but in other situations its benefits depend upon the person viewing the display.[9] Specifically, among the individuals tested, some normally had difficulty differentiating parts of a complex display, but with the appropriate addition of color, they could perform as well as the others.

The suggestions for the use of color in information systems continue to accumulate: use only three to seven colors; use blue for backgrounds and large areas, but not for thin lines or small shapes; avoid placing contrasting colors together, such as red with green, because this can cause afterimages and illusions of shadows; remember that colored areas of greatly different sizes, although created with the same color, may not appear to be the same color; be wary of using colors that are close to each other in value to differentiate information, because changes in ambient lighting can change the perception of hue, brightness, and saturation; and use brighter colors for older viewers.[10]

Thus the presence of color combines all the ambiguity of general perception with the specific discrepancies caused by the process of producing color for a video display, which is explained in more detail in Chapter 2. As a general statement, however, there are two common ways of passing a color signal to a computer monitor. The better monitors take separate red, green, and blue signals (i.e., RGB monitors) to create the color picture, while others use a composite color signal, and some are designed for both inputs to fit different configurations. Composite video signals are a combination of individual color and brightness signals; for television systems in the United States, for example, a composite television signal is transmitted as a mixture of one luminance level and two chrominance levels that are based on RGB values. A television receiver must be able to interpret that signal and determine the original red, green, and blue levels fast enough to drive individual color guns. If a color change is too abrupt, such as at the edges of thin text, the color will suffer, as a television receiver processes the luminance portion of the signal before the chrominance.

In short, color is a distinct, identifiable element of the visual experience even though the effects of its use are varied and sometimes ambiguous for both psychological and technical reasons.

FORM: GRAPHICS

As a prelude to identifying graphics as an element of visual information systems, it might be helpful to explain the difference between what is meant by "graphics" and what is meant by "video." In computer systems today it is generally understood what graphics are—they are lines and objects generated by the computer in some fashion—and what video is—it is the replay of images originally captured by a television camera. Computer graphics often have a limited number of colors or have a cartoonlike look to them, while video displays have a continuous range of colors and look more real. As many television and movie viewers know, however, it is no longer possible definitively to tell the difference among a computer-generated display, a computer-enhanced display, and a "real" camera-input display. Moreover, in a given instance, it may not matter much at all whether a display on a computer screen was initially created by camera input, by an artist at a digital tablet, or by a programmer at a keyboard.

For discussion purposes, however, there is a broad category of computer graphics, and another somewhat smaller category of computer-controlled video systems, and it will be helpful to consider the contributions of each. Therefore, the topic of computer graphics is presented as a distinct element, apart from video, that has brought its own recognizable set of features to computerized information systems.

Another reason to distinguish graphics and video is that each, as generally implemented, is technologically different and this difference has led to different means of use. As a simple example, a computer data base of chemical information may contain thousands of digitized graphics of chemical structures, while a video-based system may contain dozens of short video segments, stored in analog form on a videodisk, demonstrating chemical reactions. (The spelling of "videodisk" tends to vary by industry, with a final "c" implying analog video and a final "k" implying digital data; but with the growing use of optical media of different types for mixed applications, the final "k" is becoming more common and is the form chosen here for all applications.)

In the example just given, the end product in each case could also have been done the other way. The chemical structures could certainly have been stored as analog still frames on the videodisk, and the chemical reactions could have been demonstrated with a series of digitized graphics screens. The way in which each system is created can easily affect how it is used. The information system with digitized graphics can be used on line by way of telecommunications terminals located just about anywhere, while the videodisk-based system is most likely used by someone sitting at a workstation that includes a microcomputer and the videodisk player, because the transmission of the video segments would require a transmission line with a television-wide bandwidth and two-way capability that is not normally available over long distances.

Therefore, accepting the value of talking about graphics apart from video, it must be noted that the subjects of computer graphics and computer video do overlap, and computer graphics alone is a multifaceted topic, as will be seen in Chapters 3 and 4. The label of computer graphics can be applied to simple plotting and graphing functions as well as to the most complex algorithms for generating pictures of realistic surfaces with all the apparent properties of a physical equivalent. The techniques for generating the graphics can vary considerably too, from using alphanumeric characters for "drawing" objects to dividing the screen into minute areas, or pixels, each with its own set of color and display values.

Many issues in computer graphics, while perhaps relevant in the sense that they portend better displays or different types of displays, are beyond the scope of an investigation of the graphic elements of information systems. A recent national conference on computer graphics, for instance, covered such arcane topics as anisotropic reflection (the way some surfaces scatter light more in some directions than in others), hemi-cubes (a procedure for calculating imaginary reflections), fillets and chamfers (ways in which the surface edges of objects meet), quaternions (four-coordinate systems), and fractals (a mathematical concept in which a small amount of information can generate infinite nonsmooth surfaces).[11]

Without delving into the particulars, these techniques and others are concerned with two basic topics in computer graphics: producing more realistic images, including nonreal scenes, and producing the images in more efficient ways that require less time and less computer power. It is this work that has helped to make it possible to add the visual dimension to information systems and to build better ways of mixing the nontextual graphic elements with traditional computer-generated text.

For our purposes, the primary interest is in graphics as either a tool in the information retrieval process or as the object of a retrieval process. As argued throughout this book, the use of graphics to create retrieval tools, if exploited, can be expected to provide a very substantial improvement in our ability to use large information systems.

The appearance of graphics as part of the objects contained within an information system cannot be ignored either, as this too affects how we react to, and are able to use, information stored by computer. One way, often overlooked, that graphics capability is part of an information object is in the display of merged text and graphics, not only as a preliminary step to a print product but also as an alternate product in its own right. Computer systems to combine text and graphics in a page format have been used in automated publishing. Versions of such systems are increasingly available to the general public as desktop publishing systems and even used in situations where the page display may not be copied to paper at all. As the capabilities of these systems become part of information retrieval systems, the retrieved product is no longer a string of text produced by a simple character generator in the display device, but perhaps is an actual facsimile of a document page whether or not the page ever existed in paper form.

Systems for merging text and graphics that produce page displays that are exact renditions of what could be printed on paper pose a bit of a classification problem. Should they be placed in the graphics category or in the video (still frame) or image category, or somewhere else? Functionally, it does not seem to make much difference. An information system that retrieves complete reproductions of a printed page could be doing so whether the page was stored as analog video, digitized video, or digital files created by an automated page-production system. The only thing that might be different would be the actual hardware used. This area of text/graphics systems where the display is indistinguishable from a video still frame is discussed again in Chapter 4.

It may help to remember, though, that the retrieval of page images—stored on film rather than as computer text/ graphic files or digitized images—actually predates either graphics or digitized video and led to some of the first concerns with techniques for finding information. One of the early suggestions for an automated retrieval system was that the system be a desk-size device for holding hundreds of millions of microfilm images. This oft-cited suggestion, made in 1945 by Vannevar Bush, Director of the U.S. Office of Scientific Research and Development during the Second World War, was based on the recognition that a mechanism was needed to store and retrieve the growing accumulation of written records[12] (and perhaps on the assumption that the retrieved ought to look like the original). Bush was worried about the "growing mountain of research" and the fact that while methods for creating written and photographic records had improved immensely, the methods for accessing recorded information had not changed since the "days of squared-rigged ships." He suggested a microfilm-based system because he was impressed with developments at that time in photocells and photography. (He was also impressed with the new computing machines, but saw them as just that, machines to perform arithmetic calculations especially for business applications—he could see no large market for machines to do advanced analysis.)

Regardless of the fact that Bush extolled microfilm over computers, his main argument was that new procedures were needed for finding information placed in storage. The human mind operates by association, and therefore a retrieval system ought to include a procedure for selection by association, as well as traditional cataloging and indexing. A user of Bush's desk-sized device would be able to link items together in a trail of associations, and would subsequently be able to flip through a stored trail as fast as flipping through a book. Trails could intersect, in a "mesh of associative trails," and these could be transferred from one machine to another. Bush did not really explain how the associative trails would be displayed, but today's computer graphics techniques would handle the job well.

Over forty years later the essence of Vannevar Bush's concern is still valid: information retrieval systems need some way to take advantage of all the human dimensions of seeking information. Computer graphics, used as a tool in the retrieval process, can provide some of that by presenting a nonverbal, flexible view of the associations among the stored records.

FORM: VIDEO

The addition of video to information retrieval systems, as a form identifiably apart from graphics, is another development that has probably been tinkered with for about a long as either has existed. It has only recently become more feasible as the relevant technologies have become concurrently less expensive and more available. Laser videodisks, in particular, are well suited for retrieval systems incorporating video because the video, whether motion or still frames, can be stored with each displayable frame accessible in less than a second or two. Microcomputers, or personal computers, can be used to control the searching of a "videobase" and the user of the system can be treated to standard motion video with sound, still frames with sound, slow or fast motion video, still frames alone, a choice between two audio channels, and superimposition of computer-generated screens, to name the more common features.

As indicated by the description of elements, tools, and objects, each of the elements identified can be used to create both tools and objects. Video is often assumed to be the object of an information system; for example, a request for information on a particular hotel could be met by the display of a two-minute video segment showing and describing the location, rooms, service, facilities, and so on. Video can also be a tool in the retrieval process itself. For example, it can be used to provide spatial orientation within a data base. The Sony Corporation, makers of videodisks and videodisk players, once produced on videodisk a sample "videobase" about Hawaii, with information linked to locations. The viewer begins an information search with a still-frame map of Hawaii and can choose information on specific geographic areas as shown by numbers on the map. The information about a tourist attraction, hotel, or the like is subsequently presented as a short motion video segment. Thus on this disk video is both a tool—the map providing a spatial arrangement for finding information—and the object sought. The various means of providing spatial orientation are discussed in later chapters as some of the ways visual elements enhance information retrieval, but it should be noted that video procedures for orientation are certainly not limited to information systems about physical places.

Video can also be used to augment the attractiveness of a system, including instructions on using a particular system. Information systems designed for use in public places incorporate video segments telling the viewer what the system is all about and how to use it. In computer systems, video segments might be used as an alternative to the ubiquitous and often incomprehensible error messages. Instead of a written error message or error number, a video segment could be shown of a kindly person explaining the problem.

Earlier, a distinction was made between graphics and video, and while it is apparent that the territory of each is generally understood, it is also clear that the distinction rests somewhat on the technology used for each. The technology, in turn, affects the ways systems are built and used. For example, setting aside the current existence of digital or digitized video, for most of video's history the video signal has been an analog signal. Put simply, a traditional video camera generates a continuous signal as electrons systematically scan, in a horizontal fashion, a light-sensitive surface in the camera. The strength of the signal, which can be depicted as a squiggly line with peaks and valleys, thus continuously varies, with the peaks indicating the bright portions of a horizontal slice of a scene.

It is important to mention the nature of an analog video signal because that has affected the way that video has been used within information systems. With an analog video signal, it has not been easy for retrieval systems automatically to identify objects within a video frame, or even to find specific video frames themselves. For example, if a television picture showed a house, it could be extremely difficult for a retrieval system sequentially to read the continuously varying signal of horizontal scan lines and determine at what point it has found slices of the house and what parts of the signal are not part of the house.

Digitized video, on the other hand, is much more amenable to image processing, such as by scientists and technologists working on "machine vision," robotics, and artificial intelligence. In these areas, ways have been devised for computers to essentially recognize objects seen by its "eye," a video camera or a scanner, after the video input has been digitized. Systems have in fact been built that produce a certain level of recognition such that the computer can take appropriate action. As a simple example, one of the earlier of such systems could distinguish among blocks of different shapes and colors and could pick up the right object upon voice command. Today, machine vision systems in factories can identify shapes, measure distances and sizes, determine the orientation of objects and any motion, and detect a certain amount of surface shading.[13] More often than not, however, the current vision systems used in manufacturing are designed for specific tasks where the need to recognize what is seen can be restricted to a relatively small range, because that is about the extent of capability of affordable systems.

Along the same lines, vision systems are being developed to analyze series of pictures, such as in the case of radiology images. At the New York Hospital-Cornell Medical Center and elsewhere, work has been under way for several years to develop intelligent data base systems so that radiology images can be scanned by computer and classified according to measures that human researchers would use if looking at each image.[14] Subsequently, the images can be searched by the same criteria. The need for this kind of image-processing system has arisen because of the very rapidly increasing number of radiology images generated by new techniques such as computerized tomography, digital radiography, and magnetic resonance imaging.

Another aspect of digitized video is that it is not stored in the same manner as analog video. In digitized video, a video signal that started out as a continuous analog signal is converted to a stream of discrete points. Each point can be stored as a number, or set of numbers, and the quantity of points can equal or exceed the ability of the human eye to tell one from another when they are converted back again to points of color in a video display. For digital computer systems, which already treat everything as numbers stored as bits, or binary digits, a video frame that is a series of numbers stored as bits is just another string of bits, and can be handled accordingly. Therefore a digitized video still frame can be stored on the disk packs of a mainframe or on the floppy diskette of a personal computer, treated as a record within a data base, and retrieved as the object of an information search, or even displayed as a tool to be used in the retrieval process.

Having said earlier that the mechanisms for processing and storing analog video, as opposed to digital video, have affected the construction and use of retrieval systems, it should be added that the same storage material can be used whether the signal is analog or digital. Magnetic tape is an example of a medium that is used widely for recording both analog and digital signals. Videodisks are also used for digital data as well as analog signals. The effects of using one process or the other are not always the same, however, at least not yet. Using certain digitizing techniques, if each frame of a color television picture were converted to digital form and stored on a videodisk, it would take more space than the same sequence of frames stored in analog form. To view the frames in real time, that is, at thirty frames per second, the computer processing the digital stream would have to be larger and faster than might otherwise be necessary, while on the other hand, the hardware needed to view the analog signal is readily available. Analog and digital processes still have their own roles to play in retrieval systems, and do not yet produce completely interchangeable results.

Although the technologies of computer graphics and video are used here to distinguish the basic form of the visual aspect of information retrieval systems—each technology is both widespread and a major component of various information systems that have a visual nontext dimension—other technologies might have to be considered. Film has been mentioned, even though film, and especially microfilm and other microforms, can be functionally equated with either video still frames or static computer graphics. Another example is holography, which can provide not only pictures and pictures that can move, but also pictures in three dimensions such that you can walk around so as to see the sides of an image just as if the real object were there. Holographic information retrieval systems, although still pretty much in the embryonic stage, provide the additional element of real depth. Two-dimensional screens can depict depth and can do so convincingly, but holographs and any similar technology provide a third dimension. Even though computer graphics systems can rotate computer-generated objects to show the sides and back of an object, these are still two-dimensional displays that simply do not (yet) reproduce photographic detail as holograms do. The subject of holography and holograms is referred to again in Chapter 7.

MOTION

The final element in this classification is motion. Both graphics and video can involve motion or not, depending upon the system and the implementation. The concept of motion in video is obvious. The uses of motion in graphics are probably almost as obvious, although the techniques for achieving motion or simulating motion in computer graphics displays can be considerably diverse.

Highlighting motion as an element, however, brings out its contribution, namely, that it is relative to the viewer. For information retrieval systems, motion can be used to signify that information is being brought from one place to another, that the viewer is moving within the space occupied by the data base, or that the information object is shrinking or expanding relative to the viewer. Motion can also be expressed without the use of graphics or video. Retrieval systems that are menu based and designed as inverted trees can give a user the impression that, as each menu choice brings up a more detailed menu, the user is moving "deeper" within the data base.

The element of motion, therefore, can be used as a tool to express spatial orientation, whether or not graphics or video is involved. An example, well known to many computer afficionados, that does not involve graphics or video is the game

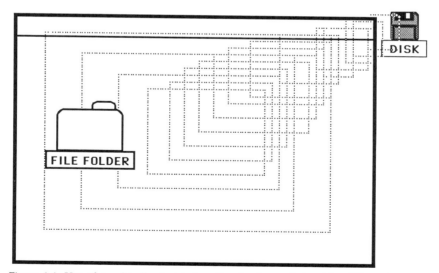

Figure 1.1. Use of graphically depicted motion to show relationships. When the disk is "opened," a series of rapidly expanding rectangles appear, followed by a solid rectangle that becomes the surface for icons representing the contents of the disk, such as a file folder icon.

Adventure. The game begins with a simple statement that you are at the end of a road, outside a small house. As you type in commands to move in different directions, you can find a cave and explore it for treasure, with the computer verbally describing your surroundings at each step. An added twist to the spatial orientation is that in the cave, tunnels can turn, and one move south does not mean that you can return to the exact spot by going north on the next move. The game has a real sense of spatial orientation and relationships that, as explained in the following chapters, can be exploited to provide information seekers with better procedures for exploring the massive amounts of information that have been reduced to invisible digital states.

Motion that moves the display of information objects or collections themselves, while the viewer or user remains static, has also been used. One example of a suggested motion is in the procedure for accessing diskettes, opening file folders, opening files, and the like on some microcomputers and workstations. When the desired object is selected, such as by moving a pointer to a picture of the object, graphic lines are quickly drawn in an increasingly wider pattern that looks as if the object is expanding or opening up (Fig. 1.1). Similarly, when you are done with a file, it shrinks back into the file folder, and the collection of file folders can shrink back into the diskette. This use of motion, expanded upon in Chapter 5, not only adds to the attractiveness of the system itself, but also reinforces the notion that information items, or data, are located within other entities and that you can find things by opening up these entities.

In a way, the graphic expanding and shrinking of objects on a display screen is merely a further development of the concept of motion from earlier menu-selection systems. If a graphic object is "opened up" to reveal an additional set of objects, this is pretty much the same as if a menu choice is made and a subsequent list is presented. The graphic procedure may be more understandable, and even more capable given the additional visual cues, but it is only a progressive development, not an entirely new concept. On the other hand, recognizing the value of the motion element, as used in a system capable of graphics, can lead to a better understanding of how graphic tools can improve our grasp of relationships.

The three elements of color, form and motion, with form

divided into graphics and video, have been presented here in a sequence that is a rough indication of the technical capabilities of a system. Systems can incorporate some color usually more easily than graphics, especially complex graphics; graphics are usually easier to implement than video, that is, video within a computerized system; and still frames, especially digitized ones, may be easier to manage than motion video. That is only a very general way of looking at the elements, and the order of presentation does not necessarily imply increasing sophistication. Some quite sophisticated systems do not use color at all, and some rather simple retrieval systems are built around motion video segments stored on a videodisk. Moreover, the first and last elements—color and motion—may seem somewhat different at first glance, as they might be thought of as subelements of graphics and video. As explained above, however, both color and motion can exist alone without always being components of graphics and video, and it is this recognition that gives them their place as distinct elements.

Tools

The previous sections described the major elements of what can be called the visual dimensions of information retrieval systems. As was mentioned, these elements, alone or in combination, can be used to create retrieval mechanisms that provide better, easier, or more attractive ways of finding information in data bases. In other words, they can be used to create retrieval tools.

The nature and importance of using graphics and video as information system tools comes up again throughout this book, particularly in Chapter 5, and therefore only brief summaries are presented below in the process of categorizing the tools.

ICONS: ACTION/OBJECT SYMBOLS

The word usually associated with the use of symbols to denote actions or objects in computerized systems is "icon." According to the dictionary, an icon is an emblem or symbol or pictorial representation. In computer displays, it is generally a small line drawing of some recognizable object that, supposedly, readily indicates what will happen when a pointer is moved to select that picture (Fig. 1.2). For example, a drawing of a file box might indicate a filing system, a file folder could represent a collection of files, an open eye in a video system might mean camera input, and a trash can may be the place to drag files to get rid of them.

The addition of icons to computer display screens has been attributed to work done at various places, including Xerox Corporation's Research Center in Palo Alto, California, beginning about 1970 or 1971. It was there that researchers developed systems using icons as well as other techniques that are now also becoming popular. For about a decade, icons were used in only a relatively few expensive systems. Then in 1983 Apple Computer, Inc., brought out the Lisa, and in 1984 the Macintosh. It was the latter that finally made icons an accepted part of the computer environment. Given that success, other companies began marketing software to use icons on systems that

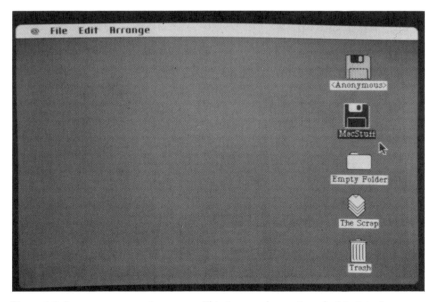

Figure 1.2. Icons on a computer screen. This is an early version of a Macintosh screen. A disk labeled "MacStuff" has been selected, and this is indicated by reverse video. (Courtesy of Apple Computer, Inc.)

had not been designed for them, such as Digital Research, Inc.'s GEM (Graphics Environment Manager) software for IBM microcomputers.

In practice, the use of icons provides a shorthand way to express the functions and objects available to users, and in a more attractive fashion than words or phrases. The disadvantage of icons is that they might actually convey less information to a user than the word or phrase they are meant to replace. Although this topic is covered at more length in Chapter 5, it is worth recounting the experience of one software reviewer with a new program. In the package being examined, the icon representing the action of clearing the screen was a disk being thrown into a garbage can, while the icon for deleting a record from the disk as well as from the screen was a disk with an arrow pointing to a garbage can. Such a fine distinction in meaning was not immediately obvious to the reviewer.[15]

When used properly, icons can become a sort of language with pictograms, the manipulation of which represents nouns, verbs, and phrases. Recognizing icons as language might seem like a return to the practices of ancient times. After all, writing developed from the use of pictures to symbolize objects and actions. As well-described in the authoritative account by Oscar Ogg, the beginning of the use of alphabets dates back nearly 50,000 years to the drawings on cave walls.[16] Pictures evolved into picture stories and gradually evolved into symbols that would be drawn by different artists in the same way to mean the same thing. In virtually all civilizations around the developing world, pictures and symbols to indicate objects and ideas predated alphabets. Eventually, symbols came to be used to indicate the sound of the word associated with a picture as well as the object depicted, and the sound could be for a syllable or even for a single letter. The Egyptians used all of these methods at the same time. A drawing of an eagle could mean "eagle," with a human face it could mean "soul," it could mean the sound of the letter "a," or it could be the letter "a" itself (Fig. 1.3). In fact, the Egyptians apparently used symbols for letters in some of the earliest examples of their hieroglyphics, and actually made more and more use of pictures for complete ideas and objects as time went on. In another part of the world, the Mayans also used pictures for objects, syllables, and words,

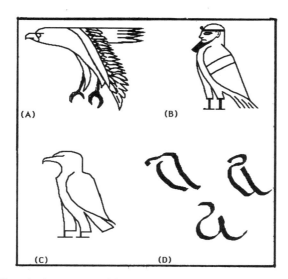

Figure 1.3. Hieroglyphs, icons, and letters. In Egyptian writing, icons for things, concepts, and sounds all coexisted. A drawing of an eagle could represent an eagle itself (a), or with a human head it could represent the soul (b), or still looking like an eagle it could stand for the "a" sound (c). Eventually, the drawing of the eagle icon evolved into the letter "a" (d). (Adapted from Oscar Ogg, *The 26 Letters* [New York: Van Nostrand Reinhold Co., 1983]).

using several pictures for the same sound, and apparently mixed and matched them to create clever puns.[17]

Two of the major difficulties with picture writing, explained by Ogg, are that the reader must already know something about the message in order to understand the picture, and the quantity of pictures required to convey all thoughts can be considerable. These same problems can befall icons used in sophisticated state-of-the-art computer systems. More often than should be the case, some modern icons are completely incomprehensible. Nevertheless, when carefully constructed they can be useful, and represent a primary tool for information retrieval made possible by the addition of graphic capability to computer displays.

SPATIAL ORIENTATION

Perhaps more important than icons, the elements of color, graphics, video, and motion can be used alone or together to provide a sense of spatial orientation. In this era of widespread computer systems, where all manner of information has been coded into electromagnetic states, it is hard to imagine that for a very long time recorded information was maintained in a visible form and stored in a visible physical location. This property of being visible and spatially oriented can be an important factor when searching for information.

Historically, as the quantity of written information accumulated, classification procedures were established so that persons could go into an area and find what they were looking for, aided by a catalog or listing of items paired with location references. The ancient library of Assurbanipal at Nineveh, going back about 2500 years, had a catalog listing the contents of all alcoves and cubicles, which were identified by a sign above each.[18] The individual tablets within an alcove were arranged by subject or type and contained an identification tag. In fact, for at least 4000 years we have been storing information in visible form and amassing the media in large collections. Some of the ancient examples are the Sumerian library at Telloh with some 30,000 tablets, the Babylonian library at Borsippa, Egyptian libraries at Gizeh and Thebes, Greek (later Roman) libraries at Pergamum in present-day Turkey and at Alexandria, Egypt, with a combined total of over a million papyrus rolls, and several dozen public libraries in Rome, not to mention all the private collections that existed in these civilizations.

Thus for a very long time written records have been gathered into collections both large and small, but the words, pictures, and symbols could be seen existing on a piece of material, in a volume, on a shelf, in a room. Then during this century, technology provided ways to shrink copies of written material to such small sizes that the writing has to be viewed through a machine, such as a microfilm reader, in order to be readable. Yet that was not a great leap from previous practice. The primary difference was only that more copies of pages could be contained in smaller physical spaces.

With computerization and the storage of information as minute electromagentic states on some visibly blank material, a major change did take place in the storage and retrieval of written records. Incredibly vast amounts of data are stored in extremely small spaces, and the space on the storage medium has no relationship at all to our understanding of what might be coded on that medium or where it might be located. In fact, our only avenue of access is through a computer system. On top of that, this avenue of access has been in terms of words—no pictures to trigger recollections or associations, and no spatial orientation to jog the memory or correlate information.

Now, however, the elements of the visual dimension can be used to provide spatial orientation as a tool for finding one's way within a data base. This does not mean the graphics have to depict the placement of chapters in a book or books on shelves. After all, one of the advantages of computer retrieval systems is that there does not have to be any relationship at all between the physical order of bits on a digital storage device and what is retrieved and presented together as a related set. Instead, the retrieval system can use a variety of procedures to search through a data base and find items that match a given search request, and each new request can generate a new set of relationships. As a practical matter, however, the order of bits on the storage medium may indeed have a relationship to the order of the items themselves, as in large systems when searches of related items are expected often, it can be helpful to store such items together, even with high-speed computer systems.

Spatial orientation in information systems, then, is largely synthetic. It also can be dynamic, that is, generated in response to the pattern of searches or the known preferences of the searcher. In this way spatial orientation can provide the image of relationships that would be impossible in real space, and can even provide alternate spatial orientations to give the user literally a new way of looking at things.

In the 1960s George Miller studied the emergence of the new computerized information systems, and wondered, "Where in the world is the information?"[19] By this he meant, where exactly will the information items be located, since spatial orientation is such a fundamental part of our millennia-old practices of recording and storing information. Moreover, Miller added, we also often impose a spatial orientation or relationship on things or concepts that do not have a "real" spatial existence, such as the taxonomic trees of biology and similar methods of organizing knowledge. He went on to speculate about some of the ways in which automated systems might be built to maintain a form of spatial orientation, such as electronically storing photographs of real bookshelves: the photograph could be called up on a television screen and enlarged until the viewer could read the titles of the books, with the extra benefit that the viewer could point to a desired volume and the television screen would then display the title page and table of contents. News and other information regarding actual places could be organized in a system that used real geography to locate information. Spatial references could be invented for just about any collection of information, with options for the user to reorder the invented environment according to taste or preference. While the techniques might differ, ideas such as these are at the heart of current work on display arrangements that treat the computer screen as an electronic desktop or file cabinet.

Spatial orientation can also be accomplished without graphics or video, as mentioned previously. Words can be used to set the scene and indicate the movement from one location, fictitious or otherwise, to another. A computer bulletin board service, for example, called the Caves of Aptos, is organized as a series of underground caverns, with rooms for users to leave messages, rooms to play games, and rooms to keep programs available for down-loading or copying by the users, all of whom are able to dial into the system from their own personal computers. A similar example is a computer service of health information organized as a medical center. The Adventure game, referred to earlier, is probably among the best and most well-known computer programs using words to provide spatial orientation. Some researchers have suggested that Adventure specifically be used as a model for designing more mundane computer programs, such as those for word processing and text editing.

Among other things, the game provides "orientation," while many users of commonplace computer applications programs experience "disorientation."[20] In Adventure, the player starts with a few sentences providing a brief description of where he or she is located and can then move off in any direction. Because it is a game, the player is likely to move quickly in whichever direction seems most promising. In many applications programs, however, new or infrequent users may not be able to decipher where they are in the program or how they get to the process they want to use.

The addition of visual elements to computer systems not

only adds some of the valuable assets of precomputer spatial orientation, but also brings the capability for imaginative ways of generating synthetic spatial relationships. Much work has been done in the field of information science to develop associative procedures to determine which strings of text (documents or document references) are most relevant to each other or to an information request, as explained in Chapter 6. Some of these techniques can be considered as part of the larger effort to develop artificial intelligence and knowledge systems. These same techniques can be used to generate synthetic spatial relationships, especially dynamically generated relationships as the system "understands better" the intent of a user's request. It is interesting to note that Miller's question—Where in the world is the information?—has been remembered even to the extent of being the title of the first chapter of a 1984 book on the human-computer interface.[21]

ATTRACTIVENESS

An often neglected aspect of computerized information systems is the design of the presentation format—how the retrieved information is presented to the user. For a long time, the technology of affordable computer terminals provided a format consisting of mediocre computer-generated text on paper or screen. It probably did not help much that the creators of these systems were constant computer users themselves who accepted the limitations of these displays as perfectly adequate. Now the technologies of computer display systems have improved, and the user population has expanded to such an extent that it is advisable to include "attractiveness" as a tool for improving usage of information systems.

Writing and publishing have a long tradition of care and concern for the design and appearance of all parts of the finished product, from the style of the written character or typeface of the printed character, to page layout, cover design, and binding. Over centuries, an immense amount of effort has been expended to establish not only readable but also eminently attractive character styles. Writers and copiers who took pride in their work considered the attractiveness of the finished product to be one of the purposes of doing the job.

It has also been argued that the style of characters bears a direct relationship to the technology, that is, to the tools used for writing or printing. The earliest Greek letters, for example, were square and sharp because they developed during the days of stone and wax tablets, while Roman letters became more rounded and graceful as the use of wide-point pens and parchment became commonplace.

As printing developed in Europe in the fifteenth century with metal movable type, technology once again affected the product. (The Chinese probably used wood blocks to print designs on paper as early as the second century, but did not begin using movable type, as blocks of wood, until between the eleventh and thirteenth centuries.) One of the first and primary contributions of the printing process to presentation format was the standardization of a relatively few styles of type that combined the best features of the many handwritten styles. In fact, according to Oscar Ogg, since the introduction of italics at the beginning of the sixteenth century, no new style of type has been accepted for standard use, although variations on existing styles continue to appear. A second contribution, if it can be called that, of early print technology was that the pen no longer influenced the shapes of characters. Nonetheless, printing itself soon came to be considered an art form too, and there was no decrease in the amount of effort, by those who cared, that went into creating the most pleasing as well as useful typefonts.

At each new advancement in the means used to create print products, it seems that there is an initial period during which more attention is given to exploring and exploiting the technology than to examining how the product is affected by the technology. Sooner or later, however, the less utilitarian, or the more artistic and creative, side of the technology is recognized and improvements are made in the attractiveness of the product. We are now at that stage in the display of text on computer screens and computer printouts. On video display screens, especially, more thought is going into the design of character sets that are still readable and attractive given the limitations of the video display. As displays with better resolution become more common, more care can be given to the design of character sets. At the upper end of this scale are the systems that are designed to display on video screens and to print on paper high-quality character sets that cannot be distinguished visually from traditional print.

Attractiveness as a tool for information retrieval goes beyond the design of character sets, albeit one of the goals of information systems should be a character display that is easy and pleasant to read. The elements of color, graphics, video, and motion can readily be used to enhance systems beyond the appearance of the text alone.

Some might question the classification of attractiveness as a tool of information retrieval. How does that feature of a display help a user find information in the same way that symbols or spatial orientation might? The answer is that while an attractive display may provide no more hard facts than an unattractive one, the former is more usable because of subjective reactions on the part of the user. The user may simply like the attractive system better, appreciate it more, use it more often, and feel that it is easier to use. Consequently, in a general sense, attractiveness fulfills one of the definitions of tool as a means to an end.

The importance of including attractiveness as a tool made possible by color, graphics, video, and motion is to ensure that it is not overlooked in the design of information systems. It is an important element that should be understood in its own right. On the other hand, cost could be a concern, and as the need to minimize cost is felt, the attractive features of a system may be the first to go. After all, if the information is the same in black and white, why spend money to add color? Part of the reason for the question is that color and graphics capability currently makes the display device more expensive due to the additional hardware and processing required and to the numerous standards for graphics, while the hardware for monochrome alaphanumeric displays is less complex and text is almost always coded by just one or two standards.

The value of attractiveness, therefore, might be measured in monetary terms and people's willingness to pay, but there is always room for more study of the many and subtle ways this feature can influence and affect the use of information retrieval systems.

TRANSFORMATION

In addition to providing an attractive setting, graphics and video can be used as tools to transform and summarize information that is held or acquired in nongraphic form. Especially in the area of data analysis, computer graphics have been used for years to translate sets of numbers into visual representations, whether bar charts, graphs, scatter plots, pictograms, or something similar. Graphics are used not only to translate information from one representation to another but also, in many cases, to summarize, since hundreds or thousands of numbers can be represented by a single picture. One can compare items visually at a glance, instead of reading through long tables of numbers. In fact, much of the whole area known as business graphics is essentially centered on the use of graphics as a tool to translate and condense numeric information. As the users of statistical packages know, the production of plots and graphs is one of the key features of these packages as a way to convey information that would be hidden in tables of numbers.

This particular use of graphics as a tool may be the most common and perhaps the least exciting. In recognizing this function of the visual elements, however, it becomes possible to see that the transformation activity does not have to be limited to data analysis and business graphics. In the traditional world of information retrieval, where systems respond with numbers to indicate the quantity of records that match a search and even to indicate the likelihood that certain items answer the information request better than others, there is room for graphics to be used to translate the numbers into something more visually striking. A system that employs color could mark the display of a group of answers with colors to indicate the individual items that the searcher is most likely going to want to read first, for example, with red for the most likely. Bar charts have been used to indicate the relative quantity of records in different related categories and other similar summaries.

Pushing this function farther, some of the visual elements might be used to transform text rather than numbers. In the same way that graphics are used to summarize relationships among large sets of numbers, they could also be used to summarize in a single picture the relationships among items in large text files. How this might actually be accomplished is not yet clear from the record of current information retrieval systems, but it is a logical step to explore for future systems and is discussed again in Chapter 7.

Objects

The final aspect to consider in assessing the role of graphics and video in information systems is their role as the object of a search. This can be done in a variety of ways, some of which were mentioned previously, such as collections of digitized images, motion video on a videodisk, and even the filmed pages in a computerized microfilm retrieval system. The graphic or video as the object of an information request is probably the most likely thing to come to mind when the subject is mentioned together with computerized retrieval. Examples of such systems can range from the use of ordinary text eventually to retrieve an image, whether a still frame or a video segment, to systems built around the fact that every screen presented to the user is a graphic, to systems in which a graphic is not in fact stored as such but is generated dynamically in response to some user action.

One particular class of systems in which the graphic is the object of an information search that is of special interest here is that used for real geographic maps, because of the potential for navigating synthetic space. The concept of spatial orientation can be implemented using some of the same concepts and techniques used in creating, storing, retrieving, and manipulating real maps.

Several map retrieval and generation systems are in use, from systems where maps are stored in nonelectronic form to those in which the maps themselves are just strings of bits in an interactive computer system. The midrange might be the systems that store the coordinates for all the maps that the systems might be expected to generate, so that the appropriate one can be assembled for display purposes. An example is an insurance company system that stores the coordinates for states, counties, and sales districts, and in combination with a statistical package and demographic and sales data, can generate a map for geographic areas that meets the criteria of a search request. Sections of the display can be shaded to highlight individual districts, counties, or states, and displays can be shrunk to the district level or expanded to the multistate level. Near the high end of the range of such systems would be interactive graphics systems for mapmaking, such as those used by transportation agencies and cartographers, and image processing systems for converting airplane and satellite photographs to computer-enhanced maps.

At the lower end of the range of these systems are ones that are used more or less simply to retrieve maps stored as such, but some map retrieval systems can be quite complex and innovative. One of the more fascinating is the set of mobile map systems being developed for trucks and automobiles. Major auto manufacturers are at work on systems that will contain tens of thousands of individual maps in a computer in a truck or car, with a display device that indicates the vehicle's movement across the map, perhaps using reference signals from the motion of the vehicle or from an external source such as a satellite. Prototypes have already been built, but it is not expected that these systems will begin to appear in cars until the 1990s or later.

Another unusual example is the "movie map" created by the Architecture Machine Group at the Massachusetts Institute of Technology (MIT) in the late 1970s and early 1980s, and mentioned again in Chapter 4. Part of the system involved putting 50,000 slides and movie frames of Aspen, Colorado, on a videodisk. The movie frames were photographed by a specially equipped truck that could capture one frame every nine feet as it drove through Aspen. Slides were also taken of building interiors and exteriors at several times of the year, and photographs from earlier years were found. When all the frames were assembled on a videodisk, the complete system included a touch-sensitive monitor with left and right, back and forward arrows. By pressing the arrows, a user could "drive" through Aspen, and the motion on the screen appeared only slightly discontinuous. Users could also stop and "go into" buildings, and look at the buildings in different seasons and different years, for all the buildings where the necessary slides and photographs had been gathered and stored. Moreover, the system included some frames of real maps of the city, including an aerial map, a street map, and a detail map, and users could zoom up and down. While moving through the city, the monitor also displayed at the top a few lines indicating the major streets in Aspen so that the traveler's progress could be tracked in a different color on this abbreviated line map.

The movie map tends to cloud the classification process, but, except for the line drawing dynamically indicating movement through the city, it is merely an elaborate way to retrieve video still frames stored on a videodisk. With some qualifications, it is still useful to group the systems in which graphics and video are the objects of the retrieval process into two main classes: stored objects and dynamically generated displays.

STORED PICTURES/GRAPHICS

This category, which contains the bulk of retrieval systems that produce or reproduce some images as the object of a search, can be broken down into two broad subdivisions to highlight the contributions of graphics and video. The first subdivision contains those systems that use normal alphanumeric interaction with the user to establish what is being sought in order to provide the graphic or video. The second group contains those systems that are completely graphic or visual, where even the interactive process with the user is in terms of screens composed of graphics and color, or even video.

From the perspective of the information systems designer, the second group, where each screen is a visual display, holds considerable promise for improving the retrieval process. Assuming for the moment that we are talking primarily about systems that use display terminals rather than printers, each step in the process can be viewed as an orchestrated display. This means that visual concepts can become an important part of the entire system design, for all of the reasons given previously.

Throughout this chapter, the word "screen" has been used to refer to a given display at a terminal, and the implication might be that each screen is stored as such in the computer system. This is indeed true in some instances, but in others, the elements comprising a given display are stored as separate entities and assembled on demand. Furthermore, a given display might change only in part, as new elements replace existing areas of the screen. This brings a refinement to the notion of visual elements as the objects of a system; namely, that system designers must think of screens as objects to be carefully constructed and designed even though the complete screen is only assembled as the result of a user's actions, and may be composed of screen parts that can appear in any number of combinations. This leads to the next category, dynamic displays.

DYNAMIC CREATIONS

Some information systems with graphics capability can generate displays completely independent of any graphic stored in the system. A simple example might be a design that is the result of a mathematical function that might continue drawing until the viewer does something to stop the action. Other examples involve the use of a stored volume of data to generate charts and graphs.

As noted earlier, this area is becoming quite common. The computer has available to it a set of numbers, and a program or function that tells it how to build a chart or graph in answer to a given request. In some systems the numbers can be pretty dynamic themselves, such as a stock market information system that graphs the value of stocks over time, with actual values fluctuating according to live trading on the stock market floor. From mainframes to microcomputers, graphics programs are available to generate charts and graphs and plots and pies based upon some set of numeric values, as well as hybrid systems in which the graphic-generating capability is in the microcomputer and the numbers are drawn from some distant mainframe or on-line service. In addition to the chart-drawing capabilities, there may also be whole libraries of pictures and symbols, to be chosen, sized, and inserted into a finished document.

According to some reports, this area of dynamic graphics known generally as business graphics is a potentially huge market in the process of opening up.[22] Other estimations state variously that the sales of business graphics hardware and software will grow from $500 million in 1982 to $6 billion in 1990, and that the number of microcomputers used in offices for graphics will grow from 400,000 (14% of the total) in 1985 to 2 million in 1987, to involve 50 percent of all business micros by 1990.[23] A 1984 review article by several University of Minnesota researchers engaged in a six-year study of management graphics likened the impact of graphics on business as a succession of waves, with the first, or introductory, wave already past.[24] The second wave is just building, and it is this wave that is of central concern to this book, namely the integration of business graphics with data bases. In other words, this will involve the employment of graphics as an integral part of information systems, including systems that produce numbers, as a means to enhance the information and as a tool to access the information, including transforming it, as mentioned previously.

The dynamic generation of screen displays does not have to involve only the creation of graphs and plots of numeric data. In fact, a microcomputer connected to a display device can be instructed to draw just about anything upon reception of instructions to do so. Depending upon the sophistication of the terminal, the resulting display could be quite complex. It is also possible that the instructions from a computer, based upon some information request, could involve the addition of motion, such as instructions to take an image and rotate, flip, spin, or split it, or use it to create an animated sequence. Again, the resulting display would not exist in storage anywhere, and would only exist while being viewed.

Another large class of sometimes dynamically generated graphics is within the set of CAD/CAM/CAE systems (computer-aided design, computer-aided manufacturing, computer-aided engineering). Since the 1970s, these systems have become increasingly impressive. Designers can create products on a screen, manipulate and alter them endlessly, and when done cause the stored data to be transferred to a computer-controlled machine actually to build the product. In the past, designers saw only line drawings of objects, albeit in three dimensions. More recently, screen images can be displayed with solid, textured surfaces, and designers can even test different colors and different lighting conditions on the computer-drawn image before making a final decision.

The dynamic generation of displays is not limited to computer graphics. An information system may also involve live video input from one or more cameras depending upon the purposes of the system. A simple example is the manufacturing, transportation, or security system in which an attendant sits at a console and selects among computer responses and specific camera inputs to track what is going on. A more complex example would be systems that do store static video images, but are able to manipulate the video in real time to produce "special effects" such as those seen on television, with images that seem to bend, twist, shrink, expand, multiply, merge with other images, or fly across the screen. The resulting display is a dynamic creation and thus may not be actually stored as such, although it is based on a stored object image. (In television production, the output of special effects systems is almost always stored once the desired effect has been achieved.)

As is true for much of computerized graphics, it is only since about 1979 or 1980 that the equipment to produce video special effects has become available outside of very specialized applications, and in the years since, the capabilities of the special effects machines have increased enormously. The special effects, or digital effects, capabilities that once required fairly large and expensive systems are now being included in single microchips or small chip sets. Thus it is increasingly feasible that the dynamic generation of video effects can be accomplished at the user level.

Depending upon the circumstances, there can be quite a fine line between a display that is generated dynamically and one that is stored in the computer, especially for graphics. Some computer graphics are in essence always generated dynamically, as some display processor interprets a string of code that is a set of drawing instructions. The distinction that is being made here is based on the way in which the set of instructions is stored. If the instructions are in effect treated as a unit and contain the code to build one particular image, we can consider that equivalent to a stored graphic or stored image. If the instructions are a general set, designed to produce different images depending upon some immediate action by a user or other outside influence, the resulting display from each activation of the instructions can be classed as a dynamic display.

The intention behind this categorization of stored images and dynamic displays is not only to recognize how each is used, but also to see how each might be used in new and different ways, including in combination. A common area of combination is a display in which parts of the screen do not change while other parts of the screen react dynamically. For example, a system can display a heading and border design common to all screens in a certain section, while the text area of the screen changes as new information is found. In systems that provide windows, where different sections of the screen are marked off to display different activities, the parts of the screen are divided obviously, some of which may react dynamically while others do not. As graphics manipulation software and hardware become more sophisticated, the graphics effects and animation capabilities of large expensive systems will migrate to smaller systems, including the terminals used for information retrieval.

Summary

The visual, nonalphanumeric aspects of present and future information retrieval systems are many, and their potential benefits great. To study these features and how they might develop further, a set of basic elements has been identified. The categorization also shows how these elements, alone or in combination, can be used as tools for retrieval or can constitute the objects of an information search. Color, form (as graphics or video), and motion can be used as symbols for actions, as means of providing synthetic spatial orientation, as ways to improve attractiveness, and as means of transforming stored data or information. The same visual elements also come into play when graphics and video, in both static and dynamic forms, represent the objects of an information search. In the recent past, due to technical improvements and economic changes, the use of graphics and video as tools and objects in information systems has begun to increase tremendously.

2
Basic Visual Processes

All of our senses help us to know what we know, and our language indicates awareness of the contributions of each sense as well as of the composite nature of the result. Yet of the five senses, sight is arguably the predominant one, and definitely complex.

In information systems with display terminals, the sense of sight can be called upon not only to read words, but also to comprehend pictorial displays that are an integral part of the functioning of the system. There is an increasing appreciation of the value of the visual, nontextual dimension of information systems, and the basis for that appreciation lies in understanding the natures of the processes involved, from the relationship between the structure of the eye and the construction of display devices, to the effects of visual stimuli reaching the brain. This chapter concentrates on what might be called the mechanics of the processes, such as the arrangement of rods and cones in the retina, the photons that affect the rods and cones, the devices that generate the photons, and the combined effect on the cerebral hemispheres.

It is a mark of the complexity of the general topic, however, that there is much that we still do not know about sight, perception, and the brain's grasp of visual input. Nevertheless, current research from the genetic level on up is providing more evidence for the power as well as the intricacy of the visual, and in this case nonverbal, experience.

The Visual Experience

When we see, the conscious result is based on a set of processes. When we look at video display terminals, the experience is the sum of processes from the physics of light and the mechanics of the video terminal to the physiology of the eye and the brain and the psychology of perception. These factors can be grouped into four general areas in which the activities that comprise the visual experience can be located: the source or point of generation (or reflection) of light; light itself; the reception of light by the eye; and the processing of the visual signals by the brain (Table 2.1.) Each of these sets of activities contains many variables affecting the total experience, and each is obviously a substantial subject in its own right. It would be impractical to try to treat each topic in depth in a book devoted to one particular implementation; however, an understanding of the basics of the processes can lead to better designs for that one implementation, namely, visually oriented information systems.

One statement that can be made at the outset is that vision is almost an artificial experience. What we see and how we see it are functions of all the factors in each of the areas outlined in Table 2.1, and anywhere along the way something can subtly or drastically change what the total visual experience will be. In the world of words and language, it is fairly easy to demonstrate that a word denoting an object is not the object

Table 2.1: Components of the Visual Experience (Selected Topics)

a DEVICE creates LIGHT which activates		EYE RESPONSES	that trigger	BRAIN FUNCTIONS
phosphors	spectrum	rods		pathways
photons	quantum	cones		cortex
electrons	wavelength	fluids		optic chiasma
raster scan	intensity	optic nerve		hemispheres
refresh	electromagnetic	sensitivity		associations
frequency	frequency	inhibition		memory
resolution	phase	focus		neurochemical
vectors	polarity	photochemical		neural nets

itself, and a similar lesson can be applied to vision. The perception of an object is the result of a series of processes that trigger a response in the brain. The response, the consciousness of sight, may not merely misrepresent the underlying physical source, we might even legitimately "see" something that is not really there due to the psychophysical nature of sight.

The pertinent parts of the visual experience, for the purposes of this book, are the display source such as the video terminal, and, at the other end, the brain's processing of that visual input. It is at the source, after all, that we are able to create the visual designs, and it is the ultimate impact in the brain that we want to exploit.

The topics in this chapter do not follow the strict sequence of events from light generation at the display device to assimilation in the brain. Instead, the structure of the eye and the nature of light are presented first, as these factors influenced the historical development of display technologies and help to explain why display devices are created the way that they are, thus providing the foundation for the subsequent topics. For each of the topics, the primary concentration is on those aspects that contribute to the value of visual displays in information systems.

Sight and the Eye

The gross structure of the eye is deceptively simple and fairly familiar. Light enters through the cornea and lens and is focused on the retina, where a photochemical reaction takes place that is eventually interpreted as an image. A visual sensation can also be experienced by applying pressure on the eyeball and even by electric stimulation. These are far from the experience of seeing, however, unless at some future time we are able to create "real" visual images with direct electrical stimulation of the optical system.

STRUCTURE OF THE EYE

For normal sight, light must pass through 5 layers of the cornea, the aqueous fluid between the cornea and the lens, 2 layers of the lens enclosing lens fibers, the vitreous mass between the lens and the retina, and 9 of the 10 layers of the retina before it hits the approximately 125 million rods and cones in the retina, which in turn feed only about 1 million fibers in the optic nerve.

All of the layers of the eye can be grouped into essentially three coats or shells enclosing the lens and the fluid within the interior of the eye, as depicted in a nonproportional manner in Figure 2.1. Only brief summaries of these layers are included here, as this material is available in standard texts.[1]

The outermost coat or shell includes the sclera and cornea. The sclera is the portion around the bulk of the eyeball, and the cornea is the transparent portion. The cornea itself has five layers, but the middle layer, the substantia propria, constitutes about 90 percent of the mass of the cornea.

The middle shell controls the reception of light, because light passes through the opening in the shell, or pupil. The shell consists of a membrane around the inside of the sclera, the grooves, ridges, and muscle fibers that control the lens (called the ciliary body), and the five layers of the iris. The iris

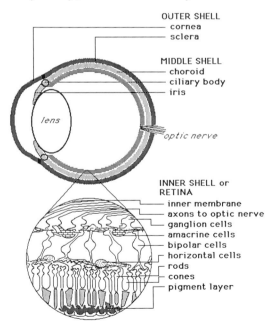

Figure 2.1. Structure of the eye. The three major shells enclose the aqueous humor between the cornea and the lens, the crystalline lens, and the vitreous humor in the interior of the eye.

has the central opening, the pupil, that widens or narrows depending upon the relative absence or presence of light.

The innermost shell is the retina, but before light reaches the retina, it has already passed through the transparent and fluid portions of the eye that actually bend or refract the incoming light, just as water affects the direction of a light beam. Between the cornea and the lens is the aqueous humor (a term that dates back to the 1600s) that is maintained at a constant pressure and is recycled about once an hour. The lens, formally known as the crystalline lens, is also transparent and is composed of lens fibers. The lens is able to be slightly reshaped by muscle fibers so that it becomes more or less curved in order to focus light on the retina. As we grow older, the lens loses some of this ability to be reshaped.

Filling the inside of the eyeball, between the back of the lens and the retina, is the fluid known as the vitreous—or glasslike—humor (another seventeenth-century term). Normally, this fluid is clear, but sometimes floating specks that are cells or remnants of cell structures cast shadows on the retina. By the time light reaches the retina, it is as if we are seeing through water.

Finally, the third and innermost shell is the retina, a thin membrane composed of ten functional levels throughout most of the structure. The most significant layer within the retina contains rods and cones. Although it might seem a little backward, the light-sensitive rods and cones are at the back of the retina membrane, behind the nerve cells that form the transmission path from the rods and cones along the inner layer of the retina to the optic nerve.

RODS AND CONES

Rods and cones are special cases of the branching portion, or dendrites, of neurons. Generally speaking, rods are rod-shaped and cones are cone-shaped, or a bit thicker at one end. Both are actually defined more by their function than by their shape, however. Some cones, as mentioned below, are more rod-shaped than not. The rods and cones connect bipolar cells that in turn connect to the ganglion cells that form the optic nerve.

Within the retina, there are also horizontal connections among the rods and cones as well as among the ganglion cells. These horizontal connections contribute to the processing power of the photoreceptors of the rods and cones.

The rods are by far more numerous, but less important individually, in that unlike some cones, many rods must share transmission paths out of the eye. There are about 120 million rods, mostly in the periphery, with fewer near the center of focus and none at all in the fovea, the exact center of focus. Rods respond to levels of light—but not to color—and especially well to low levels. The sensitivity to low light is due to the presence of the visual pigment rhodopsin (visual purple); under bright light, the amount of rhodopsin is decreased. When low light returns, however, rhodopsin is regenerated in the rods as long as vitamin A is present, as our eyes adjust to moving from light areas into the dark. The fact that rods are absent in the center of focus explains why it is easier to see things in low light when not trying to stare at them directly. The fact that the 120 million rods feed into only about 1 million ganglion cells in the optic nerve also helps in low light, because even though the light reaching an individual rod is not enough to trigger an impulse at the ganglion cell, the sum of the reactions of a group of rods feeding a single ganglion cell can be enough to cause the cell to react.

Cones are the photoreceptor cells that are responsible for our color vision and ability to see detail. There are only five to seven million cones in each of our eyes, and they are concentrated in the back part of the eye, particularly at the center of focus, the fovea, where no rods exsit at all. The approximately 30,000 cones in the relatively tiny fovea itself are actually rather rod-shaped, and each is connected to a single bipolar cell that in turn communicates with a ganglion cell.

All cones are not alike, in that some respond better to certain light wavelengths, or colors, than others (the wavelength of light, which can be measured in billionths of a meter, is explained later in this chapter). At least since the early 1800s, for example, we have known that some cones respond particularly well to red light, some to green light, and some to blue light. Put differently, red-sensitive cones absorb light best at about 560 nanometers (560 billionths of a meter), green-sensitive cones react best at about 530 nanometers, and blue-sensitive cones at approximately 420 nanometers. The visual pigment in rods, in contrast, responds best to wavelengths between 495 and 505 nanometers. There are also fewer blue-sensitive cones than red- or green-sensitive ones. The ratio of blue cones to rods, for example, is said to be about 1 cone to 200 rods, while the ratio of red and green cones is put at 1 cone to 30 rods.

The long-standing theories of red-, green-, and blue-sensitive cones have been more recently confirmed by investigations of the DNA structure of red, green, and blue pigment genes. This leads to the suggestion that some persons also have a hybrid fourth color gene, not counting rhodopsin.[2] On the basis of these and related studies, it is possible that the genes for rod pigments and those for cone pigments evolved from a single ancestor somewhere between 1 billion and 500 million years ago, and that also during that time the blue pigment gene similarly evolved. It is only within the last thirty or forty million years that the red/green pigment gene evolved into two separate gene sequences. Now, possibly through an evolutionary process of recombination of the green pigment genes, there is a suggestion of a hybrid gene for a class of cones that would absorb light best at a wavelength between red and green.[3] In fact, some persons have normal color vision in that they see all colors, but yet see them a little differently than most others do. Theoretically, over the course of millions of years, humans could wind up with four types of cones: red, green, blue, and reddish green.

A final note on cones and color is that color perception is based on wavelength (ignoring intensity for the moment) when the duration of the light stimulus is sufficiently long. If the burst of light is very short, it will appear white despite its "true" color given its wavelength.

MOTION AND DURATION

The photochemical reaction of rods and cones is subject to adaptation. A continuing stimulus to a given set of photoreceptors causes the photochemical reaction to diminish and we no longer see the object of the stimulus. So that this does not normally happen, the eye is continually moving. This not only allows the rods and cones to react to variations in stimuli, but also allows the fovea in effect to scan the field of view to create a focused image.

Actually, three different types of involuntary eye movement have been identified. Drifts and tremors are two types that are aptly labeled. Drifts are slow and smooth movements, while tremors occur at a frequency of about fifty times per second, producing an eye movement across about one-fourth of the visual angle of a drift. The third class of movement is the saccades, which are sharp jumps that might occur three or four times per second, and are responsible for directing the fovea to the area of interest. Reading, for example, is done in a series of saccades. These sharp jumps are also known as rapid eye movements (REMs) and are used to identify a stage of sleep.

In addition to these types of eye movements, there are the more voluntary movements, such as the eye following a moving object, adjusting to near or far objects, and adjusting for head motion when we wish to keep an object in focus as the head moves.

Related to the necessity for changing the stimulus on the eyes is the fact that once a stimulus is received, the photochemical reaction does not dissipate as fast as the stimulus might disappear. This persistence, or afterimage, can be extremely short, or it can be noticeably long if we have stared at an object. As is discussed in later sections, knowledge of the persistence effect was central to the development of such devices as movie projectors, television screens, and video display terminals.

A COMPLEX CASCADE

In sum, the physical side of light reception by the eye is an intricate, unfolding story that has been presented only briefly here. The act of seeing begins with what is actually referred to as a cascade of reactions at the molecular level even before a neural signal is transmitted to the brain. In short, a great deal of activity takes place in the eye before signals even leave the retina.

With this summary of eye structure as a background, we can now review the physics of light and the way light is created by display devices.

The Nature of Light

Vision begins with light, and the reactions of the visual pigments in rods and cones are determined as much by the complex characteristics of light itself as by the biological nature of the receptors. A lot is known about the nature of light, but it can be surprisingly difficult to describe, as light has a dual personality. It behaves according to both classic electromagnetic wave theory and quantum theory at the same time, yet it is easier sometimes to invoke only one or the other theory to explain a particular feature.

PHOTONS

To start from the perspective of quantum theory, a photon is the basic unit of light, a quantum of radiant energy. In this theory, a quantum is a quantity (a very small quantity), or an increment, or distinct part or parcel. A photon is also described as a discrete particle that carries a quantum of energy. The number of photons in a light ray is related to the intensity of the light, and the amount of energy in a single photon depends upon the frequency of the light.

The word "frequency" indicates that the movement of photons can be interpreted as a classic wave pattern. Like ocean waves, this brings in the notions of length (such as the distance from crest to crest of breakers at the shore), as well as frequency (such as how many waves hit the beach in a minute) and speed (length times frequency, with the speed of light being a constant 300,000,000 meters per second). Light is, in fact, only one part of an entire spectrum of electromagnetic waves, near one end of which are cosmic rays and near the other end are electrical power frequencies, with visible light and television and radio wavelengths in between. As Table 2.2 portrays, frequency and wavelength vary inversely; very high-frequency waves, such as x-rays, have very small wavelengths, while low-frequency waves, such as alternating-current (AC) electrical power, have long wavelengths.

Returning to quantum theory, the energy of a photon can be absorbed, but only as a complete package; that is, either all of the energy is absorbed or nothing at all. At the same time, a high-frequency photon has a lot more energy than a low-frequency photon.

Perhaps a good example of the wave/quantum nature of light is that provided by David Falk, Dieter Brill, and David Stork in their excellent explanatory text, *Seeing the Light* (their book is also the basis for other parts of this section).[4] Assume you have a completely walled-in area of a certain size and you heat the interior walls to a given temperature. The walls would eventually emit radiation in the visible range—they would glow—and the light would be entirely due to the temperature. While the radiation would be across a broad band of frequen-

Table 2.2: The Electromagnetic Spectrum (Selected Segments)

approximate wavelength in nanometers (billionths of a meter)		approximate frequency in Hertz (cycles per second)
1	x-rays	300000000000000000
250	ultraviolet	1200000000000000
400	violet light	750000000000000
460	blue light	650000000000000
490	cyan light	610000000000000
530	green light	570000000000000
600	yellow light	500000000000000
650	red light	460000000000000
10000	infrared	30000000000000
300000000	radar	1000000000
5000000000	television	60000000
270000000000	radio	1100000
5000000000000000	electrical power (AC)	60

cies, there would be much less on both the short-wavelength end and the long-wavelength end, with peak radiation in a middle area of the band. The diminishing radiation in the longer-wavelength range can be attributed to the fact that it would be increasingly difficult to fit the longer wavelengths within the volume of the enclosed area. The explanation for the diminishing radiation at the other end of the band—shorter wavelength and therefore higher frequency—is that in quantum theory more energy is required to "make" a photon as the frequency increases. Therefore, for a given temperature, there will be a drop-off in photons at the short-wavelength/high-frequency end of the relevant band of frequencies, as higher-energy photons would be beyond the energy level established by the temperature.

PERTINENT WAVELENGTHS

Falling back on the depiction of light as waves, we can specify the wavelengths that are responsible for vision. Visible light for humans has a normal wavelength range somewhere between 360 and 830 nanometers. As mentioned previously, different wavelengths in the visible spectrum correspond to different colors as we see them. Ultraviolet light, which we cannot see because it is absorbed by the eye's lens, has a wavelength shorter than about 400 nanometers, and infrared light, which we also generally cannot see, has a wavelength longer than 830 nanometers. There are exceptions, of course, to these approximate boundaries, and sometimes the boundaries can be extended. At the short-wavelength end, in the ultraviolet range, a human eye would react to wavelengths as short as 300 nanometers if the lens was surgically removed. At the long-wavelength end, a source of sufficient intensity would permit some human eyes to see in the 1100-nanometer infrared range.

Not all living things respond to the same range of wavelengths. Among a number of examples, insects can see in the ultraviolet range where wavelengths are shorter than those that trigger our rods and cones. Some reptiles respond to wavelengths longer than those in our visible range, that is, they "see" heat.

PHASE AND POLARITY

Several other elements are included in the definition of light, such as phase and polarity, that affect vision and can be factors in the design of some display devices, as will be seen later.

The phase of a light wave can be described relative to a point in time or relative to another wave. Because waves are depicted as having crests and troughs, when the crest of one wave occurs at exactly the same time as the trough of another wave, they are one-half cycle, or 180 degrees, out of phase. If they met each other in this out-of-phase condition, they would tend to cancel each other out. On the other hand, if two waves are in phase, the wave energy is additive and the resulting crest would be larger than either wave alone. For light waves, the meeting of two wave fronts from two side-by-side slits, fed by a single source, can be seen against a backdrop as an interference pattern with alternating bands of light and dark.

The interference pattern can also be produced from the particle or quantum theory point of view, demonstrating again the dual wave/particle phenomenon. If photons are emitted one at a time from a single source, they can be forced to follow two separate routes before reaching a sensitive medium where any pattern could be detected. (Inexplicably, physicists believe that a single particle actually can follow both routes simultaneously.) If enough photons are transmitted, the pattern would be a wave interference pattern, as each photon would follow one of the multitude of paths possible for a wave of photons, and as the sensitive medium collected the evidence, the cumulative result would be identical to an instantaneous light wave.

The polarity of a light wave refers to the direction of the electrical field that is associated with light. As light travels, an electrical field is established that is perpendicular to the direction of the ray of light. This field might be horizontal or vertical relative to the direction of the light, or it might be somewhere in between, or it might change too often to exhibit any given perpendicular orientation. In the last case, the light is unpolarized. If the light is polarized at an angle between horizontal and vertical, it is said to be composed of two waves in phase with each other but with one polarized horizontally and the other vertically. Sunlight is generally unpolarized, but because molecules in the air produce a scattering effect, and because light can be reflected, sunlight can reach us at right angles to the sun itself, and this light is polarized.

A polarizing filter can be used to permit light of only one polarization to pass through because electrons in the molecules of the filter can be moved in the direction of a given electrical field to absorb the energy, and thus the light, associated with that field or polarity.

EFFECTS OF LIGHT

In addition to the responses of our photoreceptor cells to visible light, other cells in our bodies react to electromagnetic radiation both within and beyond the visible spectrum, and especially in the ultraviolet range.

For instance, evidence exists that exposure to ultraviolet light can injure the cornea, although it is somewhat uncertain whether the damage occurs primarily in the range of 280 to 315 nanometers or 315 to 400 nanometers.[5] On the other hand, natural ultraviolet light is instrumental in our bodies' production of vitamin D_3. Ambient light in general produces biological rhythms, and, of course, we can feel heat that we cannot see because our bodies do react to wavelengths that are not short enough to trigger a photochemical reaction in our rods and cones.

The effects of electromagnetic radiation from video display devices has been debated for years, but no clear danger has emerged. In the latter half of the 1960s, considerable concern was expressed about radiation from color television sets, which operate at higher energy levels than do black-and-white sets. Some laboratory experiments with plants seemed to indicate effects such as excessive growth and roots growing in unusual directions, even though black photographic paper placed between the plants and the television set presumably blocked all visible light.[6] In other experiments with white rats, the effects of exposure to television radiation included first hyperactivity and then lethargy, even though the rats were similarly shielded. Furthermore, a television set placed fifteen feet from a rat breeding room, with two walls between, seemed to reduce drastically the breeding results, and the breeding program only recovered after the television set was turned off.

That early concern with color television led to additional studies that confirmed higher than expected levels of radiation in some sets. Therefore legislation was passed limiting the acceptable radiation levels.

The effects of radiation on reproductivity are still being argued. A University of Michigan study completed in 1986 concluded that pregnant women who use video display terminals less than twenty hours a week show no more than an average risk of miscarriage.[7] The study was unable to say as much for women who use video terminals for more than twenty hours a week, however, because the difference that did appear was not statistically significant. As this is being written, the National Institute of Occupational Safety and Health is beginning a study, first proposed in 1982, to investigate the effects of video terminals on pregnant women.

An unresolved debate continues about other effects of constantly looking at light-emitting terminals, such as blurred vision, headaches, and other discomforts. Some researchers have related abnormal glare or focus problems indirectly to feelings of discomfort, in that the glare seems to reduce the number of normal eye blinks, which in turn is the apparent cause of the discomfort.[8]

Visual Display Devices

Within the environment of information retrieval systems, the light that reaches the eye is usually generated by some visual display device. These devices are constructed to take advantage of what is known about the nature of light as well as about the eye's response to and the ultimate perception of light. More to the point of this book, the visual display device is probably the largest single determining factor in the visual quality of an information system. Therefore, with the preceding sections as a base, this section surveys the range of display devices and how they technically accomplish the generation or reflection of light. Often, however, the technical concern is not over what light is actually generated, but what the overall impression is in the eyes of the viewer.

As one example from prevideo days, most of us are familiar with the fact that when we look at a role of movie film in our hands we see a series of individual frames. When the frames are shown in rapid succession, although still individually, through a projector, we see a motion picture. This is because the eyes' photoreceptors, under the relevant lighting conditions and speaking generally, retain an image for about one-fiftieth of a second. Movie film is projected at a rate of twenty-four frames per second, but each frame is actually shown either two or three times in succession, so that the eyes are presented with up to seventy-two frames per second. This is too fast for us to distinguish the individual frames, although it does not mean that it is impossible for human eyes to perceive better quality at faster basic frame rates. High-definition film systems have been demonstrated at thirty frames per second, and even at sixty frames per second, with a noticeable improvement.

Video displays are also presented as a series of discrete frames, although frames may be composed of fields that may be interlaced or noninterlaced, and fields may be composed of dots that are actually presented sequentially rather than all at once. Other visual displays such as liquid crystals, discussed later, use entirely different techniques.

VIDEO TUBES

While it is certainly possible to produce graphic designs on computer terminals that print on paper, including terminals that print only characters, it is the relatively recent flood of video displays that makes it not only possible but feasible to add graphics and video to interactive information systems.

The most common video display techniques used in computer systems are known as either raster-scan or vector displays, and both use the cathode ray tube, or CRT. The picture tube in the average television set is a CRT, as is the tube in many computer terminals, although such a terminal might be called a VDT (video display terminal). The history of the CRT can be traced back at least to the mid-1800s when various researchers and inventers were experimenting with the elements that would become part of the tube. By 1878 the English physicist William Crookes managed to create an image in a primitive picture tube, and not long after that, Thomas Edison's work on the incandescent lamp led to the discovery of the "Edison effect," which made the vacuum tube and the CRT possible. Edison discovered that when a current was passed through a filament inside a vacuum, such as a glass bulb, the filament not only produced light by heating up and glowing but also produced an invisible cloud of electrons impelled away from the filament.

This effect of electrons streaming away from a filament was refined by later researchers to create the vacuum tubes of early radios, oscilloscopes, televisions, computers, and other electronic gadgets. In the vacuum tube, the part that emits the electrons is called a cathode, which can be either the heated filament itself or a metal sleeve that fits over the heater filament. In the simplest form of the vacuum tube, the negatively charged electrons are attracted to a positively charged plate within the tube.

In the cathode ray tube, the emitted electrons are formed into a beam, or ray, and "shot" toward the inside surface of the face of the tube under the control of deflection systems that can direct the beam to a point or sequence of points. More specifically, the electrons are emitted from the cathode in no particular direction, but pass through an opening in a control grid that provides some focus, with the number of electrons passing through determined by the electrical potential of the control grid. The electrons are then first accelerated and ultimately finely directed by either electrostatic or electromagnetic means such that the beam converges to a pinpoint on the inside surface of the CRT.

We see the effect of the electrons hitting the inside face of a CRT because the inside face is coated with phosphor particles, which glow for a small bit of time when hit by the beam of electrons that, in some CRTs, is focused to hit a spot of about 1/100 inch (0.256 millimeters). This is a result of the fact that when electrons hit a phosphor, energy is absorbed in the phosphor molecule for a short time. As the molecule returns to its normal state, photons are emitted that travel to the retinas.

The duration of the photon emission, or the phosphor glow, and what type of glow it is depend in part on the type of phosphor used. Phosphor coatings have been made from combinations of calcium, cadmium, and zinc, and produce either colorless (white) or colored displays with a variety of glow-timing or persistence. In fact, persistence can vary from less than one-millionth of a second to several seconds or more, although generally a phosphor reaches its peak intensity and begins to fade in less than one-tenth of a second. Within a half-second, the phosphor may have dropped to at least one-third of its peak intensity. The type of phosphor chosen for a cathode ray tube depends on how the tube is expected to be used. If a display has to change quickly, a long-persistence phosphor would not be desirable, as an individual phosphor speck might still be glowing when it should already be dark. A display that does not change quickly, on the other hand, could use the long-persistence phosphor because the electron beam would not have to return to an individual location as quickly just to keep that spot glowing.

Color television CRTs actually use three versions of a phosphor: red, green, and blue. Table 2.3 shows that a red phosphor, P22-R, emits photons with a peak wavelength of 625 nanometers, compared to our red-sensitive cones that peak at about 560 nanometers; the green phosphor P22-G has a peak wavelength of 535 nanometers, compared to a peak sensitivity of 530 nanometers for our green-sensitive cones; and the blue phosphor P22-B peaks at 440 nanometers, compared to approximately 420 nanometers for our blue cones. These phosphors have different persistence rates of 1.0 millisecond, 0.06 millisecond, and 0.022 millisecond, respectively. Monochrome video terminals for computer systems use a variety of other phosphors, such as P31 and P39 for green displays, P134 for amber displays, and P171 and P188 for white displays. In each case, a particular phosphor is chosen to match its characteristics with the variables of the electronic components so that the desired type of display is produced.

One of the main concerns in creating CRT displays that are to be read (e.g., in information systems) is the perception of flicker. Flicker is a complex phenomenon in that it is a function of phosphor size, persistence, electron beam size, frame display rate, colors, and contrast, in addition to other factors

Table 2.3: Selected Phosphor Types

phosphor	peak wavelength (nanometers)	decay to 10% (milliseconds)
P1	525	24.5
P2	543	.1 - .035
P4	560	.06
P7	n.a.	400
P12	n.a.	210
P16	385	.00012
P20	560	.05
P22-B	440	.022
P22-G	535	.06
P22-R	625	1
P22-G-LP	525	150
P28	n.a.	600
P31	n.a.	.038
P39	525	150
P42	520	10
P43	544	1
P44	540	1

n.a. = not available

Adapted from: Conrac Corp., Raster Graphics Handbook; and other sources.

such as the size of the screen, ambient lighting, viewing distance, and the sensitivity of a person's eyes.

Perceived flicker cannot be totally explained by simply relating phosphor persistence and refresh rate to the rate of photochemical reactions in the retina. For instance, the intensity of the viewed display affects the retina's ability to discern separate images, and the intensity is that of areas of color, not just dots of color. Furthermore, the cones in the retina adapt at different speeds to different colors. Under appropriate conditions, we can detect individual video frames being refreshed at rates anywhere from 20 to 100 per second. Both greater intensity and higher degrees of contrast can increase the chance that a flicker will be perceived. Thus large bright areas can appear to flicker even though darker areas of the same display do not, and sharp contrasts that coincide with horizontal scan lines (explained below) can also appear to flicker. As described in the next section, a standard television frame is actually composed of two interlaced fields where the combined effect is not perceived as flickering even though each field alone would flicker.

RASTER-SCAN CRTS

Phosphors produce the waves of photons that initiate photo-chemical reactions in the retina, but the major factor affecting CRT display quality is not the phosphor type but the method of controlling the sweep of the electron beam that is focused on the phosphor-coated screen. In CRT terminology, the two primary methods are raster-scan and vector-refresh (or simply vector) systems.

A raster is defined as that area inside a cathode ray tube that is scanned by the electron beam, and the pattern is basically horizontal. The beam alternately sweeps from left to right and then right to left in a blanked-out mode, starting at the top and continually descending. The scan lines, therefore, are not exactly horizontal, and when the beam is blanked to move from the right side back to the left side to begin a new line, this horizontal retrace is actually more horizontal than the visible portion. In practice, however, the lines can be referred to as horizontal. It is this characteristic of the raster-scan display, a series of horizontal lines, that leads to a pervasive concern with resolution, especially for CRTs used in computer displays. Therefore, much of the discussion in this section touches on the relationship between resolution and raster scan.

Camera Input   In television, scanning is a fundamental procedure at both the camera and the receiving ends. Although technology continues to change, a traditional video camera contains a camera tube that is a CRT. External light is focused on the outside front of the tube, which is coated with a transparent conductive film such as tin oxide. From inside the tube, an electron beam scans a photoconductive coating in the same manner as mentioned above. A video signal is produced at the front of the tube as electrons are displaced by the photons of the external light, and are replaced by the internal scanning electron beam, yielding a current that is proportional to the external light at each point. For color, the red, green, and blue levels are individually detected, although color cameras may achieve this with either a single tube or with three tubes.

A more recent type of camera, the solid-state imaging camera, accomplishes the same effects without the use of a picture tube. Instead, the light-sensitive surface is a type of semiconductor chip known as a charge-coupled device (CCD). The surface is composed of an array or matrix of "photosites" that react to photons. The energy of a photon is absorbed within a "depletion region" sandwiched between a material with excessive numbers of electrons and a material with a minimum of electrons. The absorbtion creates a charge within the depletion region that can actually be shifted from each photosite to a position where the charges for an entire row of photosites can be converted to a video signal. For color cameras, there are red-, green-, and blue-sensitive chips.

The resolution of CCD cameras is determined by the number of photosites, or picture elements; Hitachi CCD cameras used for surveillance have a picture element matrix of 510 (horizontal) by 492 (vertical). For CCD cameras used in non-television applications, such as those that digitize document images, a CCD array can be used more than once to build up the total image. An Eikonix camera for scanning documents uses a precision stepping motor to move the CCD array, and in four to thirty seconds can create a 4096 × 4096-pixel image.

One of the factors affecting the development of CCD cameras has been the difficulty of creating the image-detecting chips without defects. Chips with too many defects are unsuitable for use in broadcast cameras, but might be used in lower-quality surveillance cameras. Techniques are also available to mask a certain number of defects, such as filters or the use of an additional memory chip to keep track of, and compensate for, photosites that are defective.

A television signal also contains synchronization pulses so that the activity in the camera is duplicated in a receiver. That is, the picture is recreated at exactly the same time in the television receiver, with the electron beams in the camera and the receivers sweeping along at the same speed in the same direction at the same time. For recorded video, of course, the display is no longer in step with a live camera, but synchronization pulses for horizontal and vertical control must still be provided.

Interlace Scanning   The electron beams in both television cameras and receivers do not, however, simply trace horizontal lines starting at the top of the picture tube. During the development of CRT technology, it was determined that problems could be avoided if the rate at which a screen was scanned was related to the rate of the power source—60 hertz in the United States—while not trying to complete a frame too much faster than could be detected by the average eye. Some early television systems tried scanning at a rate of thirty frames per second with the scanning pattern being strictly sequential, but because the photoreceptors in the eye can adjust, under sufficient light, to changes at a rate of about fifty times per second, the result was a noticeable jerkiness or flicker. To improve the result without increasing the scan rate, interlaced scanning was developed.

In the interlaced method, the electron beam skips every other horizontal line that would normally be scanned until it reaches the bottom of the screen, then jumps back to the top and scans the skipped lines. Consequently, even though the same number of total lines are being scanned, a top-to-bottom sweep is accomplished every one-sixtieth of a second, constituting a field, and the eye does not usually detect a flicker, that is, a flicker due to scan rate, even though a complete frame is still being generated at a rate of only thirty per second. A television frame is composed of an odd field and an even field. As television in the United States was developed with 525 scan lines per frame, each field contains 262.5 lines. As the electron beam completes the odd field, it begins the first half of line 263, then jumps at midpoint back to the midpoint of the first line of the even field. The number of scan lines, 525, was not chosen because of any unyielding physical principle. In fact, in non-broadcast monitors as well as in broadcast television in other countries, different numbers of scan lines are used. As television technology has improved, high-definition television systems (HDTV) have been created that use a much higher number of scan lines per frame, between 1000 and 4000, or a higher scan rate, 80 to 100 fields per second. A proposed HDTV standard sets the number of scan lines at 1125 but keeps the frame rate at 30 per second.

Vertical Resolution   In video displays for computer systems, the interlacing of scan lines can be omitted, as the computer CRT does not need to adhere to the constraints of broadcast television, and it is motion video that is most helped by interlacing. If the total number of scan lines is held to about 525, the frame rate becomes 60 per second; but there are only 262 lines in the frame instead of 525, thus giving a vertical resolution of just 262 lines from the top of the screen to the bottom for any size screen. The change from an odd number of lines to an even number is explained by the fact that one of the ways to create noninterlaced scanning on a monitor designed for interlaced scanning is to eliminate one scan line, making an even number. Without the extra line, the scanning beam begins the second field at the same spot as the first field, thus making each field a complete frame.

For reading text on a CRT, the reduction in vertical resolution is judged to be more than compensated by the increase in perceived stability. As most CRTs do not display all scan lines in the viewable portion of the screen (some are blanked out while the electron beam flies back to the top of the screen and others are just above the top edge) it is common to speak of vertical resolution of about 200 lines for graphics displays on a CRT of the type generally used for television in the United States. A vertical resolution of 600 to 1200 lines or more is practical with monitors that are not normal television sets.

In raster-scan CRTs, vertical resolution in absolute terms is fixed by the number of horizontal scan lines. The perceived resolution is also determined by the width of each scan line and by the distance between the eye and the screen. All other factors being equal, a small monitor will appear to have better vertical resolution than a large monitor, because the number of scan lines per vertical inch is greater in the small monitor. If the electron beam in the larger monitor is adjusted to produce broader scan lines, or the eye is moved farther back, however, the perceived resolution will change. The larger monitor might even appear to have better resolution—again assuming the number of scan lines is the same—despite the fewer number of scan lines per vertical inch at the monitor surface.

Horizontal Resolution   Horizontal resolution in raster-scan CRTs is determined at one level by the speed, or frequency, with which the horizontally sweeping electron beam can vary its intensity, or in other words, the bandwidth of the display signal. For broadcast television in the United States, the bandwidth is limited to 4.2 megahertz within a 6-megahertz channel. Using a rule of thumb that each megahertz supports about 80 horizontal image points, the horizontal resolution is about 335 points and cannot be any better given the bandwidth.[9] Videocassette recorders typically use an even smaller bandwidth of 3 megahertz, resulting in a horizontal resolution of only 240 points. For computer terminals, however, the bandwidth is often much higher; some sample rates are 18, 20, and 50 megahertz. The higher bandwidths accommodate not only greater horizontal resolution but also greater vertical resolution with an increased number of horizontal scan lines.

Horizontal resolution should not be confused with the horizontal scanning rate, which is sometimes given as a measurement of a monitor's performance. The horizontal scanning rate is a product of the number of fields per second and the number of lines per field. A television display that has 262.5 lines per field and 60 fields per second has a horizontal scan line rate of 15,750 per second, or 15.75 kilohertz. A computer terminal with 370 lines per field and 50 fields per second would have a horizontal scan rate of 18.5 kilohertz.

In addition to the bandwidth limitations, resolution is also affected by a number of other factors, such as the size of the focused spot of the electron beam. This size is usually set to be approximately the same as the vertical distance between scan lines, which varies with the size of the screen and the number of scan lines. Normal spot sizes in monitors used as computer displays are on the order of 0.2 to 0.5 millimeter in diameter when measured at half brightness. In contrast, the spot size of dots used in high resolution computer-driven plotters is about 0.056 millimeter, or one-tenth the size.

Color Mask   Yet another determinant of resolution in color monitors is the size or type of color mask. The color of color television is produced by three different beams of electrons streaming from the cathodes, or "guns," at the back of the CRT. Using a number of different techniques, the beam from the blue gun is focused on a blue phosphor, the red gun is focused on a red phosphor, and the green gun on a green phosphor. The net effect is a spot of color of the appropriate mix of red, green, and blue.

One technique is to use a metal mask, or shadow mask,

with holes such that the beams from the three color guns converge to a single point at the hole and then diverge slightly to hit their respective phosphors. Actually, each phosphor is hit primarily by one beam and by the fringe, or shadow, of the other two beams. Other techniques involve a mask with slots or metal strips instead of holes. The Sony Trinitron, for example, contains a single three-beam electron gun, and a mask of thin, vertical metal strips. A newer mask technique, called the flat tension mask because the shadow mask is stretched or "tensioned," permits thinner masks and even better color resolution.

Thus to some extent the resolution of the color monitor is affected by the physical holes or slots in the color mask, as well as the spot size of the electron beam. The spacing between holes or slots depends on the size of the screen as well as the color technique used, and is similar to the spot size of the electron beam, varying from 0.2 to 0.6 millimeter. This compares fairly well with the limits of our eyes given normal viewing distances, but there is room for improvement. Our eyes' ability to distinguish detail is based on the distance between a light source and the retinas, and on the intensity of the light and the overall lighting condition. For a normal reading distance (about eighteen inches) the lower limit on detail is about 0.13 millimeter. For very close distances, the smallest point that can be seen is about 0.004 millimeter in diameter.

The physical size of the phosphor dots themselves is also a factor in resolution, although the dots are normally matched to the limits of the electron beam and, in the case of color, the shadow mask.

As raster-scan CRT technology continues to be refined, new ways of producing the scan are being developed. To increase the resolution without increasing the scan rate, at least one company has created a CRT with a ten-beam gun that produces a frame of 2500 scan lines every sixtieth of a second.[10] For information systems incorporating standard television video, the display device must still adapt to, and is constrained by, the characteristics of that video signal. Similarly, for information systems using digitized video or images stored as a matrix of pixels, the display is restricted to the amount of computer memory devoted to storing the screen data, as discussed in Chapter 3.

VECTOR CRTS

Unlike raster-scan CRTs, the image in refreshed-vector CRTs is not created by a fixed pattern of scanning. Instead, the electron beam can be deflected from any point to any other point, tracing a line in a given direction, that is, producing a vector.

A display on a vector CRT is composed of points and line segments, and any image can be generated subsequently, whether lines or curves, drawings or text. There is essentially no practical limit to the resolution beyond the size of the electron spot as it hits the phosphors and the size of the phosphors, although the better vector-drawing systems have an addressable resolution of about 8192 × 8192, compared to current high-resolution raster displays of 1024 × 1024. In vector systems, a curved line is just as finely drawn as a horizontal line or a vertical line, which is often not the case with raster-scan CRTs. Like raster-scan CRTs, the electron beam must retrace the entire pattern fast enough, in a continuous cycle, to keep the phosphors glowing. The capability of the vector CRT to produce an image is related to the number of vectors that can be drawn during each cycle. For example, a typical rate is 150,000 "short vectors" in one-sixtieth of a second.

As is the case with other types of CRTs, the type of phosphors used would be chosen to persist just long enough to match the vector-refresh rate. A text written in 1973 lists the most common phosphors used for computer displays as the P7, which fades by 10 percent in 30 milliseconds, and the P31, which fades at a much faster rate, 0.038 millisecond.[11] The 1985 *Raster Graphics Handbook* lists three newer phosphors—P43, P44, and P45—for use in visual displays that decay by 10 percent in 1 or 2 milliseconds, and the P22-G_{LP}, which is a long-persistence phosphor used in some color graphics terminals that takes 150 milliseconds to lose 10 percent brightness.[12] Improvements in phosphor technology go hand in hand with improvements in vector-drawing technology; as the latter permits more to be drawn faster, the former must produce the appropriate emission and decay characteristics.

In the past, most CRTs used as computer terminals for the display of graphics were vector CRTs and were monochrome. More recently, vector CRTs with color capability have become common. The color can be produced using several different methods. One method is very similar to raster-scan devices in that red, green, and blue color guns are used, with the electron beams tracing vectors rather than horizontal scan lines. Another method uses two different phosphor layers on the inside of the CRT, such as a layer of red-producing phosphors on top of a layer of green-producing phosphors. A single electron beam is then used, and by varying the strength of the beam it will strike only the red layer, or the red layer with only a portion of the green layer, or it will strike the green layer as hard as the red layer. In the last instance, the resulting green light dominates. Otherwise, either a mixture of red and green or only the red appears. Similar effects can be produced with a single layer of phosphor material that is made up of particles successively coated with different types of phosphors, or with a single layer of different types of phosphors that are substantially different from each other in terms of the energy level at which they respond to the electron beam.

Although raster-scan monitors are increasingly used for computer displays, vector CRTs traditionally have had a substantial advantage for computer graphics where the displayed image is created by calculations of points. This is because the memory and processing requirement in vector systems is only to keep track of and manipulate end points of vectors rather than pixel data for every possible pixel. The end points are then used by either analog or digital vector generators to create the signals that deflect the beam along the desired path. Therefore, whether a computer is calculating a complex image or is continually recalculating real-time movement, a vector CRT can require less memory and less processing power than a raster-scan CRT.

A shift to raster CRTs, however, has followed dramatic drops in prices for memory chips and processor chips. By 1985, raster CRTs outnumbered all other types of CRTs used for high-resolution graphics.[13]

STORAGE TUBES

Storage tubes, an older and now declining technology, are CRTs that are able to maintain an image for a certain period of time before the phosphors have to be rewritten by the electron beam. While for conventional CRTs the electron beam must return about fifty or sixty times per second to each spot that is to be visible, for storage tube CRTs this amount of time can be measured in hours or even, in extreme cases, days. One major result of storage tube technology is that the electron beam can continue writing a complex image long past the time at which, in a normal CRT, the beam would have to begin refreshing the display.

There are several versions of storage tubes. In one method, the image is actually written on a fine-wire grid that maintains a pattern of positive charges for a length of time. Another cathode, or set of cathodes, continually emits a broad but slow-moving electron stream that floods the entire storage grid; when these electrons reach the positively charged areas of the storage grid, they pass through to the phosphor surface, maintaining the visible image. In another similar method, the image-writing cathode has a negative potential, and when this beam hits a spot on the phosphor surface, the immediately surrounding phosphors develop a positive charge that then attracts the electrons from the flood cathodes.

One of the advantages of the storage tube technique is that extremely detailed, high-resolution displays can be built up beyond the capability of conventional CRTs because there is no need to rewrite the image continually, say, sixty times a second. A major disadvantage is that to change the image, the entire stored image is erased by increasing the positive charge to the storage grid or anode. This causes the flood electrons to affect the entire phosphor surface, creating somewhat of a flash that might last half a second. With some exceptions, a storage tube image, therefore, cannot be changed quickly and cannot be changed partially. Also, in some storage tubes, an effect of the flood electrons is a gradually increasing background glow that eventually overpowers the image.

NON-CRT DISPLAYS

The CRT is the dominant display device now, largely due to the previously mentioned decline in memory chip prices as well as the investment in the technology engendered by the television industry. Other means also are available for creating visible displays suitable for information systems, although these methods generally do not yet approach the resolution of CRTs. Some of these technologies are liquid crystal, electroluminescence, light-emitting diodes, gas-discharge plasma panels, and electrophoretic displays.

Liquid Crystals   One of the more common methods of producing a liquid crystal display (LCD) is known as the twisted-nematic, or twisted liquid crystal technique. The display is formed by a layer of liquid crystals between two polarizing layers. Light is filtered by the first polarized layer, then twisted ninety degrees by the liquid crystal molecules, passed through the second polarized layer that is polarized at ninety degrees to the first, and finally reflected back in the same manner. When an electrical charge is applied to a portion of the display, the liquid crystals reorient themselves, thus not twisting the light, which then is not able to pass through, producing a dark spot or dark section of a character display. For LCDs that are designed to use pixels rather than to display segments of a limited number of digits or characters, current pixel resolutions range up to 200 × 640. Several companies have also developed color versions of a twisted-nematic display using filters to pass red, green, and blue wavelengths.[14]

Other types of LCD techniques are dynamic scattering and phase. In the dynamic scattering method, the application of an electric field to the liquid crystals causes them to block light, and no polarization is involved. In the phase method, light is controlled by using heat to change the phase of liquid crystals between two glass plates. Heat is generated at specific points by a combination of horizontal heating elements on one glass plate and vertical electrodes on the opposite glass plate.

Generally, liquid crystal displays are still difficult to view under certain lighting conditions and from certain angles, and do not have the resolution of CRTs. In addition, the time required to rotate physically the twisted liquid crystal molecules is greater than that to affect a phosphor glow. On the other hand, LCD technology continues to improve. To enhance the readability of the screens, back-lighting has been added instead of relying solely on reflected light, and supertwist crystals have been developed that improve the contrast by twisting the light two or three times as much. Full-color LCDs are used in a number of miniature portable televisions with screen diagonals from 1.5 to 4 inches, and resolution of about 200 × 200 pixels. The largest color LCD display, so far, using a technique known as thin film-active matrix technology, is a six-inch Hitachi screen with a resolution of 640 × 200 (640 × 600 in monochrome).

Electroluminescence   Electroluminescent displays are created by a layer of phosphors between layers of material providing horizontal and vertical addressing. In one version, a layer of zinc sulfide is contained between a transparent insulating layer and a layer of aluminum vertical electrodes on one side, and a transparent insulating layer, a layer of transparent horizontal electrodes, and glass on the other side. Multicolored electroluminescent displays are not yet possible, but the major disadvantages of electroluminescent computer screens are the need for high write and refresh voltages and stringent manufacturing requirements. The resolution capabilities are in the range of 640 × 200 pixels.

LEDs   Light-emitting diodes (LEDs) are electroluminescent devices made up of a semiconductor layer, a junction layer, and a transparent semiconductor layer. Charges at the junction prevent electrons from flowing from the transparent semiconductor to the solid layer. When a battery is connected, electrons are driven across the junction to the solid semiconductor where they lose energy in the form of photons that radiate back through the transparent layer. The visual characteristics and uses of LEDs are similar to those of LCDs.

Gas Plasma   Gas plasma panels are formed by trapping a gas such as neon between two layers of glass, one with invisibly thin vertical electrodes and one with horizontal electrodes. When voltage is applied to the horizontal and vertical electrodes, a sustaining signal is created. If the voltage at a given point is increased quickly and momentarily, the gas at the area of intersection begins to discharge and a glow develops, which is maintained by the sustaining signal until a slight drop in voltage occurs at that point. Gas plasma panels have been used for over twenty years, and some now have pixel resolutions of 960 × 768 at fifty frames per second. The panels have remained monochromatic, however, with neon producing an orange display; other gases have been tested to produce green and blue-green displays. Gas plasma panels also have high voltage requirements, and are not economical for small screens.

EPIDs   Electrophoretic imaging displays (EPIDs) are composed of glass panels enclosing particles of one color suspended within a solution of the opposing color. Charges applied to electrodes inside the glass plates can cause either the particle or the solution to be visible at the front plate, or even a rapidly alternating mixture. When the charge is removed the positions of the particles are not lost, and thus the screen can retain an image without being constantly refreshed. Some observers believe that EPIDs may become the dominant type of flat panel display due to lower power consumption, high resolution, color combinations, and good contrast and readability.[15]

3D CRTS

Without getting into holographic displays, which are mentioned in the final chapter, attempts have been made to develop three-dimensional (3D) displays using CRTs that do not rely on perspective, shading, color, or special glasses to indicate the third demention. One system uses a "plastic-mirror" disk in front of the CRT that actually vibrates in and out. The vibrations, with a physical movement of up to 4 millimeters, are timed to successive images created as if the image had moved an inch forward or backward. With twelve successive images, the viewer sees an image with an apprarent depth of twelve inches.

Other systems that require the use of special glasses continue to be examined. The more promising are those in which the glasses do not have to be cabled physically to the display system.

A 3D CRT developed by Tektronix combines both CRT technology and liquid crystals. A liquid crystal shutter panel is placed over the front of the CRT to control the rapid shift between two images, one a slightly displaced version of the other. When viewed with polarized glasses, a stereoscopic image results, since each eye sees only one of the images. A version of this liquid crystal shutter CRT has also been used to increase the resolution of color CRTs while using the phosphor arrangement of a monochrome CRT. Under control of a liquid crystal polarizing shutter, red, green, and blue images are displayed sequentially, within one-sixtieth of second, and the human eye combines the three colors to see a multicolored image.

Light Versus Sight

Given all of the variables of the creation or reflection of light by visual display devices, we can now return to a summary of the more subtle effects of viewing a video display and of light perception in general, starting with effects that take place within the eye itself.[16] In some cases, what we see is not an exact response to specific waves or energy levels of photons emitted from a CRT's phosphors, but a counter-response caused by the reactions of rods and cones to an influx of photons.

INTENSITY

Intensity is one aspect of lightwaves/particles that can cause us to see differently even if the wavelength and frequency of a light remain the same. Intensity is a measurement of the magnitude of energy, and more commonly is known as the brightness of a light. In wave theory, intensity is directly related to the amplitude of a signal—the height of the crest of the wave— in that it is proportional to the square of the amplitude. In quantum theory, intensity depends on the number of photons, or quanta of energy, present; the higher the intensity, the more photons are present.

Intensity affects rods and cones somewhat differently. Rods, which do not contribute to color perception, are sensitive to low-intensity, or low-energy, light. They also respond best to a wavelength of about 505 nanometers (green is approximately 500 nanometers), so that a light wave of 505 nanometers can seem brighter than a similarly intense light of another wavelength. As for the effect on cones, the intensity of the light can affect color perception. The perceived color of yellowish or bluish objects can change if the intensity of the light is altered even though the wavelength remains the same.

LATERAL INHIBITION

In relative terms, intensity is also perceived in relation to surrounding light, or background, and this can be demonstrated dramatically in studies of contrast. One familiar example shows a relatively small grayish object on a light background compared to an identical grayish object on a dark background. The two objects do not look identical in brightness or intensity even though they are. The object on the bright background looks darker than the one on the dark background. The explanation for this effect is referred to as lateral inhibition, based on the reaction of the photoreceptors in the retina. When light is absorbed at a given point in the retina, there is a ringlike area outside the immediate area where light absorbtion is actually inhibited. Because many rods feed into a smaller number of ganglion cells, the response for a given ganglion cell is the combination of the inhibitory ring and the responsive central area of rods. For the object on the dark background, less light affects the inhibitory ring and therefore the response is less inhibited, and so the object looks brighter than the same object on a light background.

CHROMATIC LATERAL INHIBITION

Lateral inhibition similarly affects color perception. When areas of different colors are adjacent, the response of a ganglion cell is composite based in part on the inhibitory reaction in the area surrounding the central area of response. The inhibitory reaction is actually a stimulation of the opponent color of the central area, such as red in the central area and green in the surrounding area. When we look at two large adjacent color areas, the color of the first will cause us to see some of the opponent color in the second area. For instance, a red area around a green area tends to make the green greener, as the red portion causes us to see some of red's opponent color, green, in the green itself.

The color opponent theory also includes the blue-sensitive photoreceptors, but it is a little more complicated than the red-green explanation. The opponent color to blue is yellow, but no class of cones is primarily sensitive to yellow. Instead, the inhibitory reaction, or stimulus of an opponent color, is provided by a combination of red and green cones.

COMPOSITE COLOR

As mentioned earlier, cones absorb some wavelengths more easily than others, and there are three areas of sensitivity— red, green, and blue. But these are only designations of the primary sensitivity for a cone, not an indication that this is the only wavelength a cone can absorb to instigate the enzyme cascade that becomes vision. When we see a color, it is a mixture of all the wavelengths absorbed by the relevant cones, and in fact a specific color can be achieved by a multitude of different combinations of light waves. White light is, of course, a combination of light waves throughout the visible spectrum, but if we view a wavelength of 580 nanometers (yellow) with a wavelength of 480 nanometers (blue) we will still see white even though only two wavelengths are present. This occurs because the 580-nanometer wave affects red- and green-sensitive cones roughly equally and blue sensitive cones hardly at all, while the 480-nanometer wave affects the blue-sensitive cones much more than either of the other two classes of cones. The result is that all the cones are affected in an equivalent manner, and white becomes the perceived color.

SPATIAL FREQUENCY

Another topic that crosses the boundary between a discussion of the eye and a discussion of the nature of light is that of spatial frequency. The eye does not react uniformly to variations in both the intensity of light source and the frequency of alternations between light and dark. Test patterns, called sine-wave gratings, have been devised for CRTs that present alternating bands of light and dark, sometimes varying the intensity, or contrast, as well, in order to study spatial frequency.

The frequency of alternation is in terms of the number of changes, or cycles, per degree of angle of vision. Measuring the degrees of angle of vision is dependent on the distance between the eye and the object(s) comprising the field of view, because the closer the object, the wider the angle, if the size of the object remains the same. Because the measurement of the field of view could be expressed horizontally or vertically, the one commonly used is the diagonal.

There have been several results of these tests of spatial frequency. For example, we are not particularly sensitive to either the very low or the very high spatial frequencies. As the contrast decreases, this insensitivity at either end narrows toward the middle, producing a rather hump-shaped pattern as shown in Figure 2.2. Based on spatial frequency patterns, researchers have come up with a unit of measurement called the "just noticeable difference" (JND) to determine when, on average, people can perceive the gratings. Studies of spatial frequencies are used to determine how to manipulate the creation of video screen displays so that noticeable differences are accommodated, but unnoticeable differences are not.

The studies of reactions to spatial frequencies also indicate that, unlike the effects mentioned previously, spatial

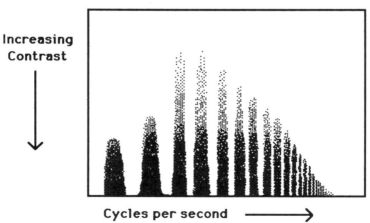

Figure 2.2. Contrast effects on spatial frequency. The ability to distinguish spatial frequency drops off as contrast decreases and as the frequency becomes either very low or very high.

frequency effects are produced in the cerebral cortex rather than in the retina or the immediate vicinity of the eye, which brings us finally to a consideration of how the brain processes the visual information that has been generated by the eye.

Assimilation in the Brain

The preceding sections outlined the creation of light in video displays and the reception of light by the retina, but this does not yet fully cover the process of vision. Although a substantial amount of visual information processing takes place in the eye, an even greater amount takes place after the neural signals leave the vicinity of the eye. It is in the brain that the visual stimuli are assimilated into the associations and structures that underly basic mental functioning.

One of the most important results of the continuing investigation of how the brain functions, especially with regard to visual input, is an appreciation of the extensiveness of any instance of visual input and the multiplicity of results. The visual sense provides much information, and our brains seem to make the most of it.

VISUAL PATHWAYS

The movement of visual signals to parts of the brain follows what is known as the visual pathways. Ganglion cells in the retina collect the signals from the much larger number of rods and cones, and the approximately one million axons of the ganglion cells then converge at a point called the optic disk and pass out of the eye, collectively forming the optic nerve. The optic disk is about 1.5 millimeters in diameter and is a blind spot, which we are normally unaware of, where no rods or cones exist just to the inside (the nose side) of the center of focus for each eye.

The optic nerves, one from each eye, come together at a point called the optic chiasma where some of the nerve fibers cross over to the other side of the brain. From the optic chiasma, nerve bundles on both sides of the brain, composed now of nerve fibers from both eyes, lead to two areas, one for each side of the brain, in the thalamus. Here neurochemical connections are made to two or more sets of neurons whose axons connect to the vision centers in the occipital lobes at the lower back of the brain and just above the thalamus in the region known as the visual cortex. The visual cortex itself is divided by function into both horizontal layers and vertical columns, with the columns in each visual cortex responding selectively to one eye or the other. The size of these ocular dominance columns, as well as the relative selective nature of their response, has been related to very early visual experience, such that lack of sight in one eye soon after birth can affect how the visual cortex grows and develops structurally.[17]

The entire process involving the relay and reforming of signals constituting vision, from the eye to the perception of sight in the brain, is still not fully understood. What is known is that the process is substantially more complex, and complex in subtle ways, than is indicated by our knowledge of what connects to what. For example, as half of the nerve fibers from each eye cross over to the other side in the optic chiasma, visual input to half the eye goes in one direction and visual input to the other half goes in the other direction. The result is that neurochemical reactions from the left side of each eye, which are caused by photons coming from the right, stay on the left side of the brain and reactions from the right side of each eye stay to the right. If the nerve fibers are damaged on one side, for instance, at any point between a person's optic chiasma and one occipital lobe, that person would still be able to see through both eyes and yet be blind in half of each, either the right side or the left side of each eye. In normal vision, we steadily see and process images even though the light conveying them may shift back and forth from one side of the retina to the other, and thus from one visual pathway to another, as the eyes and head move.

The broad locations of brain activity related to vision and other activities have been confirmed by direct "photographs" of mental functions. One way that this can be done is to use positron-emission tomography (PET), in which radiation detectors record gamma rays given off by radioisotopes of natural elements of the brain after a person has been given either a gas with a positron-emitting isotope or an injection with a positron-labeled compound. The detecting device can then locate concentrations of positron-labeled molecules, and brain activity can be mapped as areas of high glucose use.

In one collection of PET scans, an obvious difference can be seen between subjects with their eyes closed and those with their eyes opened.[18] In another set of PET scans, visual activity can be seen clearly in the lower back of the brain as test subjects were presented with large checkerboard patterns.[19] Patterns also showed up in roughly the same area for tests of auditory stimuli, cognitive tasks, and verbal auditory memory tests, even though the PET scan shows the primary activity elsewhere in the brain during those tests. This suggests that our ability to visualize mentally is also instrumental in auditory and cognitive activities. The PET pictures have also confirmed that activity in the visual cortex is related to both the complexity and the rate of visual stimuli, and that half of the input from each eye goes to each visual cortex.

Recent experimentation and studies concerning the visual pathways and visual signal processing in the cortex seem to indicate that vision is the result of a number of different sets of selective responses that are "tuned" to specific aspects such as wavelength, motion, speed, size, orientation, and the like. These sets of responses may occur along the visual pathways and not just in the visual centers in the cortex. At the thalamus, for example, the transfer of color information is affected by the sensitivities of the neurons leading to the cortex, and this pattern of sensitivity is unlike that of the rods or cones. Another example of an effect similar to a retinal response yet occurring outside the retina is that of spatial frequency, which can be tested by staring at various patterns of light and dark bars. If only one eye adapts to a particular pattern (and does it by continually moving so that an afterimage is not formed in the retina), both eyes will be less sensitive for a time to patterns that are very close in spatial frequency. Because the effect is not confined to the eye that saw the test pattern, some processing of the visual input is taking place outside the retina of the active eye. On the other hand, the eye that did the adapting will see more of an effect than the other eye. Several similar effects are produced outside the retina, such as looking at a waterfall for awhile, then turning away and seeing things drifting upward, because the visual process recognizing downward motion has become desensitized and needs time to readjust to normal.

Many of these effects are similar to the afterimage phenomenon, where the chemicals in the rods and cones in the retina become less likely to respond as the steadiness of the input to a given spot is maintained. The effects just mentioned are the result of reactions not in the retina but elsewhere in the visual pathways or vision centers.

VISION AND MEMORY

Humans have various types of memory. Evidence exists that these are sometimes located in different parts of the brain and provide both redundant and unique functions, and that there is no one location or procedure for the memory of visual images.

At a gross level, memory has been divided into short-term (or immediate) and long-term memory. Damage to a certain part of the brain may affect long-term memory but have no effect on immediate memory. One theory is that immediate memory can occur in both halves of the brain, and can occur in the same area that long-term memory can occupy. Damage can affect the capability for the formation of long-term memory even though the physical location might coincide with immediate memory.

For long-term memory itself, two further categories have been identified, declarative and procedural, and each of these has subcategories. Declarative memory is related to names, places, dates, and the like, while procedural memory is related to skills and things learned through practice. As Table 2.4 indicates, declarative memory can be subdivided into memory for specific events (episodes) and memory for facts (references). Procedural memory can be subdivided into skills, recall based on cues (priming), conditioning, and others. These categories and subcategories are used to demonstrate that, based on current evidence, the brain seems to contain a series of "fundamentally different information storage systems."[20]

The location of declarative memory has been isolated to the hippocampus and the amygdala, the most important areas for visual memory, while procedural memory is identified with

Table 2.4: Types of Long-Term Memory

Declarative (retrieved verbally or or as an image)	Procedural (accessible through performance)
Episodic (specific time, place events)	Skills Priming Classical Conditioning Habituation
Semantic (facts and general information)	Sensitization Perceptual Aftereffects

Adapted from: Larry R. Squire, "Mechanisms of Memory," *Science*, vol. 232 (27 June 1986), pp. 1612–1616.

sections of the cerebellum. Even within the hippocampus and the amygdala there are different types of memory. Studies with monkeys have shown that removal of the hippocampus erases memory of spatial relationships, but not of physical appearance, while removal of the amygdala apparently affects the memory of emotions and social relationships but not of spatial relationships.[21] Support is strong from a variety of disciplines for the notion that emotions affect memory, helping us to remember some things quite well and to forget others.

Even before visual input reaches the hippocampus and the amygdala and the other areas associated with memory, it seems that it may have split into two simultaneous paths, one involving size, shape, and color, and the other involving spatial arrangements.

There also may be a relationship between the physical location of certain types of memory and the logical relationship of the items. In one publicized case, a stroke victim lost the ability to name a fruit or vegetable when presented with one, yet he could name all other types of familiar items.[22] When shown a group of items and told to pick the apple, for instance, he could easily do so. He just could not arbitrarily name fruits and vegetables.

RIGHT/LEFT PROCESSING

Although both sides of the brain are involved in mental functions, it has become well known that one side or the other can apparently predominant in certain activities. Oversimplifying to some degree, the left side is said to be more concerned with logical thinking and speech, while the right side is more involved with spatial relationships, unified views, and artistic responses.

This suggests that we actually have two generally separate ways of processing visual input at the same time, and each procedure contributes to the sum of our perception. Studies of medical patients with disorders that necessitated surgical separation of the two brain hemispheres showed how each side of the brain can "see" something different.[23] In one test, a picture of a spoon was flashed in front of one eye while a picture of a knife was flashed in front of the other eye. When asked to name the picture, the patient would say "knife," but when asked to retrieve the object from under a cover concealing a knife and a spoon, the patient would pull out the spoon.

Betty Edwards popularized the idea that artistic endeavors, such as drawing a perceived form, should be more a function of the right side of the brain than the left, and that we can learn to let the right brain take the lead even if we are not usually inclined to do so (and this has nothing to do with being right- or left-handed). Researchers now believe that hemispheric differences have been exaggerated, although evidence still supports the basic underlying notion, albeit the relationships are somewhat more complex.

Visual displays in information systems can take advantage of the numerous modes of processing suggested by the left/right studies, and of the many ways of affecting or creating memories. Reading text, for example, is one mode of processing that might be characterized as a left-brain function, but viewing text areas in relation to a spatial arrangement or graphic designs involves other modes of processing as well. Therefore, even though several modes of processing may be active in normal reading and contribute to the resulting perception, display techniques that capitalize on the known functions of the less verbal mode can trigger additional simultaneous processes that are in addition to, and do not in any way hinder, the verbal and logical processing functions.

Much of the power of graphs, for example, as a means for conveying information is attributed to our right-brained ability to perceive relationships. Researchers have not only recognized the value of this "preattentive vision" but have also begun studying the aspects of graphs that best use this capability. One study of how persons look at graphs of scientific data suggested that some aspects of the visual display have more effect than others.[24] The researchers first identified ten visual aspects of looking at a graph or chart: angle, area, hue, saturation, amount of black, distance, position along a common scale, positions on identical but nonaligned scales, slope, and volume. Based on the results of various measurements of reactions to these aspects, it seems that position along a scale is the most accurately perceived aspect, followed by position along nonaligned scales, and distance or length. The less accurately perceived aspects of charts of scientific data are volume, amount of black, and color (both saturation and hue). The latter conclusion matches the generally held belief that, while color does have a role in video displays, different individuals do not see small changes in saturation and hue in the same way.

ASSOCIATIONS

The process of visual comprehension has been traced from photons being absorbed by the photoreceptors in the retina to the labyrinthian nature of visual pathways and the visual centers. One more aspect of visual perception should be mentioned, and that is the role of mental associations.

When we see, perception is not based merely on the visual input at any given time, but also on the relationship of that image with a lifetime of previous images, beginning with the immediately previous moment. It is possible that as we experience something, the brain is actually building physical structures to record the perceptions, changing the shape of nerve spines, and building new synapses. Beyond the neurophysiological level are broader attempts to understand how a particular sight triggers the retrieval, if that is what it is, of the related stored experiences that give the current image contextual meaning. One possibility is that a given image is in some way matched by the brain against a generalized image, permitting us to recognize a specific object as an example of a group. In the near future, more emphasis probably will be placed on such topics as metaphor comprehension and spatial maps.[25] Just as the discussions of activity attributed to the right brain led to an appreciation of the extent of information-processing capability that was being overlooked, recognition of the role of associative mechanisms in the brain also opens up a new dimension to consider in designing information systems.

Although this section has perhaps oversimplified the visual processes in the brain, the point is that such activities in the brain involve many areas in complex ways. Support is increasing at the molecular and neurophysiological levels for the fact that visual imagery provides a wealth of information—beyond the recognition of words—useful in apprehending, remembering, learning, understanding, and imagining. As we become more fully aware of these functions, and especially of the nature of the brain's image matching and associative activities, we can create information system displays that incorporate these strengths.

Summary

At the basic level of trying to understand visual perception, the nature of the eye, the nature of light, and the nature of the display devices that create (or reflect) light can be delineated. Knowledge of the known facts is helpful in understanding the relationship between video displays and the human visual system, explaining why we are able to see a continuous image that is actually only a fast sequence of very concentrated emissions of photons, and why sometimes the illusion does not work and we do see the imperfections in the image, or at other times we see effects that are more the result of internal processing than the external flood of photons. The major message in the mechanical view of the entire process is the multiplicity of responses in the brain itself. The visual, nonverbal aspects provide reinforcement, alternative processing, and different associations than available through strictly verbal input, and may do it faster, such as in the cases where a visual representation gives us an immediate grasp of a situation that would take paragraphs to explain.

3

Graphics Applications and Limitations

Within the past half-dozen years the forms of graphics and video have converged in a variety of ways. It is a routine matter now to convert live video to bit-mapped displays in real time, or to generate, by computer, graphic effects that become part of, and sometimes indistinguishable from, a camera-captured image. This intertwining of graphics and video is indicative of the current activity in display development, yet it is only part of the picture. In many cases, a division remains between the common meaning of graphics and the common meaning of video, while the discipline of computer graphics alone is covering an expanding number of techniques and applications.

This chapter and the next take a closer look at the ways in which computer graphics and computer video, alone or together, are providing the basis for a range of visual information systems. Accepting the sometimes fuzzy boundary between graphics and video in practice, the present chapter surveys the primary computer graphics applications, while the following chapter concentrates on video and image systems.

As a preface to both chapters, graphics and video systems are exhibiting a strong tendency to incorporate the functionality of other types of systems. In virtually all areas, computer systems that in the past were dedicated to the production of graphics are now expanding to include information management functions and are using the graphics capability to enhance these secondary activities. From computer-aided design to image processing, the graphics capability that supports the end product is being pressed into service to support the production procedure as well. At the same time, systems that previously supported one type of graphics work are now used for several types of work; for example, CAD systems are also used for business graphics, and electronic paint systems are used to enhance CAD drawings. More important, graphics systems of all kinds are adding or developing techniques for providing access to data bases of relevant information.

A major aspect that tends to cut across all applications is that users soon become aware of the technical constraints of digital graphics that affect display functions and quality. To aid in an appreciation of these technical boundaries, the latter part of this chapter discusses two of the dominant factors—other than the CRT—that affect applications' capabilities, especially at the personal computer level: display memory and graphics controllers, and standards.

Types and Techniques

Although this chapter organizes computer graphics into the major application areas, there are admittedly other ways to categorize the topic. A summary of these may help to establish the breadth of graphics activity.

At one level, graphics can be divided by the class of computer used to generate the display. A number of years ago, such a classification would have produced two major groups, mainframe and workstation graphics. To some extent, this would also imply what the graphic applications were. Workstations, for example, have been largely used for design work, such as computer-aided design, computer-aided manufacturing, or computer-aided engineering (CAD/CAM/CAE). Now, the largest graphics equipment class, in number of units, is the microcomputer or personal computer. Microcomputers are used for almost any application, thus helping to obliterate application distinctions based on the class of equipment used. Because microcomputers do share characteristics of the class, however, it is still quite reasonable to talk about microcomputer graphics as a distinct subject, with implications about the graphics capabilities under discussion.

It is also possible to categorize graphics and digitized video by the techniques used to hold and manipulate the display. As mentioned in the previous chapter, one distinction is based on the difference between raster and vector displays. The data comprising each type are different, and this can affect the entire process of display creation. Within the category of raster displays is a considerable range of graphics techniques for maintaining and changing colors and objects for either the whole screen or for only parts of the screen. For personal computers, which use raster display monitors, the graphics capability is essentially determined by the graphics board, or "card," which contains the chips that provide and regulate graphics functionality, although graphics software is also a powerful determining factor given the basic capability of the chips. These topics are included later in this chapter in the sections on display processing and memory, and graphics standards.

The National Computer Graphics Association recognizes at least fifteen categories of graphics in a mixture of industry, application, and equipment-related categories. Examples of the last are video technology and micrographics, while applications-oriented groupings include image processing/pattern recognition, business graphics, and artificial intelligence. Industry segments include architecture, biomedical, education, printing and publishing, and mapping and cartography. The association also recognizes distinctions among CADD (computer-aided design and drafting) systems for electrical engineering, for mechanical engineering or MCAE (mechanical computer-aided engineering), for software development or CASE (computer-aided software engineering), and for computer-integrated manufacturing (CIM), as well as a distinction between statistical and business graphics. A less detailed arrangement of computer graphics was used at a recent conference with two major categories, business/management and manufacturing/CAD/CAM; all other applications were split among design and visual arts, presentation graphics, and publishing graphics.

One more major way to look at graphics is as either ancillary to the use of a computer system, or as one of the primary purposes of the computer system. In the former case, graphics are used as tools to help the user do something else. This use of graphics in information systems is one of the major themes of this book and is treated at greater length in Chapters 5 and 6.

Graphics by Application

Within the variety of graphics categories is a handful of major application areas, and these are the subject of this section. The applications are business graphics; design, engineering, and manufacturing graphics; image processing; paintboxes and special effects; and games.

BUSINESS GRAPHICS

Despite the fact that business graphics do not generally involve the most sophisticated techniques, this is probably the most widespread application area. According to one estimate, among all commercial graphics systems, business graphics will rise from 25 percent to 40 percent of the market between 1986 and 1991.[1] During the same time, the previous leader, CAD/CAM/CAE, will drop from 59 percent to 48 percent in terms of the market value.

Phenomenon of the 80s   The dramatic growth in business graphics began in the early 1980s. A 1984 survey by researchers at the University of Minnesota revealed that 90 percent of the surveyed companies used computer-created business graphics of one sort or another, although less than one-half had such facilities before 1981, and about one-third had just invested in such capability within the past year.[2]

In fact, it is the proliferation of personal computers in business applications that has provided the means for the expanded use of computer graphics. Originally, the personal and desktop computers in business were used primarily for looking at numbers in electronic spread sheets. The second major application, occurring some time later, was the use of microcomputers for word processing, and a more distant third application has been data base management. Now the shift is to graphics both as enhancement of the previous applications and as an application in their own right. A 1986 survey of microcomputers in 13,000 business locations showed that nearly 90 percent used spread sheet software, 60 percent word processing software, and 40 percent data base software; but looking ahead, more sites were planning to obtain graphics software than any of the other categories of software.[3] Nearly 50 percent were planning to purchase graphics software, while 30 percent were intending to buy CAD/CAM software, and less than 30 percent were intending to add either spread sheet or word-processing capabilities.

Another way to judge the growth of business graphics for personal computers is by the size of the market for the relevant software and hardware. According to one account, that market was $15 million in 1983, which more than doubled to $40 million in 1984, and doubled again to $80 million in 1985.[4] While the totals are large, the cost of an individual business graphics package available for the personal computer can be relatively minor. A mid-1986 survey of business graphics packages for personal computers compatible with the IBM PC listed over 85 entries, with prices ranging from $30 to $995.[5]

Presentation Graphics One of the primary purposes of business graphics is to create charts and graphs from files of numbers for presentations. The packages that are designed specifically for formal presentations place emphasis on presentation quality in terms of colors, fonts, design flexibility, some forms of animation, and, where the hardware is part of the package, display resolution. One aspect of presentation graphics is the inclusion of traditional formats, designs, and illustrations that are available in libraries of images on diskettes, so that the appropriate elements can be assembled into a finished slide that will look like the work of a professional artist. One set of software for the IBM PC and compatibles is Execuvision, said to be the granddaddy of presentation graphics, which contains at least nineteen different libraries or collections of signs, symbols, and illustrations.[6] Between 1984 and 1986 over 30,000 copies of the basic Execuvision were sold to business users of presentation graphics. One of the major advantages of this and similar packages for most business applications is that users do not have to worry too much about the look of the chart or graph, as the program takes care of most details once a design type is selected.

The acceptance of presentation graphics generated by a computer of any size has led to the development of equipment designed for showing business graphics in a group environment. These electronic "slide show" devices offer several advantages over a real slide show. First, the slides or frames can be taken directly from a microcomputer, where they were probably created, and because the frames are always in digital format they can be easily updated. Second, the nature of the frames permits the use of certain forms of animation or sequential display of portions of a frame to overwrite and alter the previous image. Finally, as the piece of equipment is essentially a special-purpose microcomputer, the operator can use the capability of the device to select any frame at will, without being forced through a fixed arrangement. Videoshow, from General Parametrics Corporation, is one example of such specialized equipment, and has been designed to display a wide range of colors with equal emphasis on a range of high-resolution text fonts. The attention to text fonts gives Videoshow an advantage over most microcomputer-generated business graphics with a limited range of text styles and resolutions.

Data Analysis   Business graphics are also used to summarize and compare volumes of data for a wide variety of purposes that do not necessarily involve presentations. For example, they give the user a quick grasp of a situation or help to explore the relationships among numbers. Usually, the plots and graphs are in two dimensions, the familiar x and y axes, although more recent analysis packages provide three dimensions. MacSpin for the Apple Macintosh allows users to plot data in a three-dimensional representation and to rotate the image along any of the axes to look for patterns in the data. Graphics have become increasingly popular for exploratory data analysis as capabilities have become more common. Graphics are recognized as a major tool in both business and research, even though they are not often singled out as such in discussions of business applications.

Spread Sheet Support   One dominant characteristic of business graphics at the desktop level, whether for presentation purposes or data analysis, is the ability automatically to use data files generated by spread sheet programs as the input to graph or chart drawing programs. It is quite likely that if it were not for this capability, based on the earlier success of spread sheets, there would not be nearly as much interest in business graphics. The companies that have been leaders in the development of spread sheet- and data base-management programs have acknowledged the close link to graphics, especially for future development, by buying graphics companies. In 1986 business software leaders Lotus Development Corporation and Ashton-Tate both bought companies specializing in business graphics. Lotus acquired Graphics Communications, Inc., and Ashton-Tate took over Decision Resources, Inc.

Problem Areas   The nature of the growth of business graphics may be instructive for designers of general visual information systems in that, despite the statistics given above, the field has experienced problems as well as successes. In some cases, business graphics have been unable to penetrate the executive level. In other situations, their acceptance generally for routine portrayal of data has been slow. For one thing, objections on the basis of cost have been valid, but have become less so as prices for graphics hardware and software started dropping substantially during the last several years. More important, the sheer weight of familiarity with nongraphic procedures in the business environment has meant that the expanded utility of graphic representations has been accepted only slowly in some cases.

Another reason for the sometimes luke-warm reception may be the fact that some business graphics are not done very well. Edward Tufte, author of a book on computerized displays of data, argues that graphics packages have often ignored hundreds of years of publishing experience with the design and layout of charts and graphs.[7] He believes that the wide availability of graphics packages and the ease with which they can be used has led to excessive application and crude results. He also notes that the technology of computer displays, at least for the equipment usually available to the business user, is not yet as good as print technology. Especially in the area of display resolution, the gap is still wide. As mentioned in the previous chapter, the resolution of a CRT in noninterlaced mode could be as low as 200 horizontal lines from the top edge of the CRT to the bottom, while the resolution required for fine graphics is 500 to 1000 lines to the inch, which could mean 10,000 lines on a CRT measuring 10 inches vertically.

In the near future, as graphics become an integral part

of information systems, we may see a similar range of presentation quality, with similar judgments about the value and utility of the graphics themselves.

DESIGN, ENGINEERING, AND MANUFACTURING

Historically, the application area of design and engineering has led in the development of graphics technology, in particular with regard to the interactive manipulation of on-screen graphics. These systems pioneered the use of CRTs and interactive devices to create and amend screen images, and to be able to do so in real time.

One of the earliest known applications of computer graphics on a CRT was the display of charts and graphs of engineering data at the Massachusetts Institute of Technology (MIT) in 1958.[8] Although the MIT system was not interactive, by the early 1960s a rudimentary interactive CAD system was in place at General Motors to sketch automobile designs, and other early systems were used for similar work. The CAD applications have continued to lead the technical advances in interactive graphics ever since.

Originally—in the 1960s and 1970s—CAD/CAM systems that could provide interactive complex image-generation and analysis functions required mainframe computer resources, or at the least a high-level minicomputer. One of the most extensive systems was Computervision's CADD 4X, a set of programs that together totaled nearly ten million lines of code and when stored on magnetic tape required twenty-seven reels. Computervision, founded in 1969, was in fact the industry leader for about a decade. But in 1981, International Business Machines Corporation (IBM) began marketing third-party CAD software to run on an IBM mainframe, such as the CADAM software from a subsidiary of Lockheed Corporation, and Digital Equipment Corporation (DEC) began selling its super minicomputer to CAD software suppliers such as McDonnell Douglas for resale to general designers. By 1984 IBM had taken the lead in what is known as the mechanical CAD market, and CAD capability had migrated to stand-alone minicomputers or workstations that rivaled the earlier mainframe systems. Computervision adapted its software to a workstation called the CADDStation, with a liberal use of graphically expressed functions such as icons and windows (Fig. 3.1).

Workstations to Micros On the hardware side, the workstation market for general technical and engineering applications is dominated by general-purpose manufacturers, such as DEC, IBM, and Hewlett-Packard, and by two companies targeting the CAD workstation market specifically—Apollo Computer and Sun Microsystems. (In the manufacturing sector, the leading suppliers of complete CAD/CAM systems are currently IBM, Intergraph, and Computervision, but the last two incorporate hardware from Sun or DEC.) The presence of IBM and DEC hardware in computer-aided design systems is indicative of a shift that took place in the early 1980s, from workstations produced by specialist companies to workstation hardware provided by the dominant general-purpose computer manufacturers, although the specialist companies continue to rank among the market leaders. The fact that two relatively new compa-

Figure 3.1. Computervision's CADDStation system. The CADDStation is a UNIX-based system with highly functional CAE/CAD/CAM software and a screen-oriented user interface. (Courtesy of Computervision Corp.)

nies—Sun was founded in 1982 and Apollo in 1979—could rival established corporations is not uncommon in specialized areas where a smaller company can capitalize on its expertise.

The biggest change in the computerized design market in recent years has been the impact of the microcomputer and the proliferation of CAD software for the desktop machines, which once again could provide a large percentage of the capability of previous systems requiring larger computers. For example, one of the more popular CAD products for personal computers, AutoCAD from Autodesk, Inc., was first introduced in 1982 and by 1987 had sold over 100,000 copies, mostly for microcomputers but also for some workstations from Sun, Apollo, DEC, and IBM. By the mid 1980s microcomputer CAD software could be purchased for a few hundred dollars that could do some of the same things that a decade earlier would have required software costing a few hundred thousand dollars.

In addition to software designed originally for microcomputers, the mainframe and workstation software that built the CAD market has now been reworked for the microcomputer market. The CADAM software, for instance, that helped IBM become the leader in the design systems market was made available for the IBM PC/AT in 1986.

Integrating Functions   A second trend in the CAD/CAM/CAE area is the integration of a variety of related functions from analyzing the performance of parts under design to searching data bases of reference material to driving manufacturing systems that will actually produce the part.

One of the long-time advantages of CAD systems has been the ability to analyze models in addition to creating images of them, whether the images are line drawings, three-dimensional wire-frame drawings, or solid objects with texture, shading, and reflective surfaces. Beginning about 1985, such systems began to integrate even more of the complete process, from conceptualization to finished product. One of the founders of former industry leader Computervision, Phillipe Villers, helped establish Cognition Inc. in 1985 to produce a system that he believes will be so far beyond current mechanical computer-aided engineering systems (MCAE) that it will be considered a different thing entirely.[9] The system is intended for conceptual engineering work that typically precedes the CAD stage. It will tie together hand-drawn sketches (Fig. 3.2), conversion to mathematically correct renderings, matching of the drawings with analytical models and performance calculations, links to manufacturing tools, reference to standard measurement data, access to libraries of handbook data and related materials, maintenance of notes and notebook entries, project management, and, eventually, an expert tutorial to assist engineers when they either want some advice or seem to need it.

As might be expected, the CAD/CAM/CAE systems of all sizes in recent years have begun to use graphics as tools as well as objects, that is, to use icons, windows, and other representations of actions and work areas. Although in the past, design and drafting systems may have been no more advanced in capitalizing on the visual element for assisting designers in nondrawing functions than systems in other application areas, the design and engineering workstations are now leaders in the use of graphics as tools. In 1985, for example, Apollo announced the Domain/Dialogue package so that applications developers could create customized displays of icons, pop-up

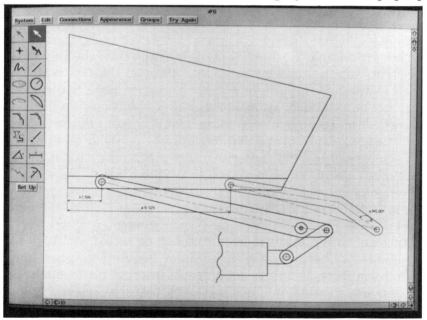

Figure 3.2. Cognition's MCAE system. Cognition's Mechanical Advantage 1000™ is an integrated mechanical computer-aided engineering workstation that allows mechanical engineers to link geometric entities (like the sketch shown above) with engineering equations and tools to create an integrated engineering model. (Courtesy of Cognition Inc.)

and pull-down menus, text input areas, and scroll bars. The use of graphics as tools in the workstation environment is so common now that it is almost a part of the definition of a workstation.

Another outgrowth of the overall CAD/CAM/CAE market is that some of the systems have expanded from strictly design and analysis for construction or engineering purposes to other graphic-related activities such as electronic publishing, where text and graphics are intimately associated. Apollo has added both data base-management software as well as publishing software to the workstation's repertoire. This integration of text and graphics for publishing purposes, referred to again in Chapter 4, is yet another manifestation of the expanding capabilities of design and engineering systems.

As indicated in the preceding paragraphs, the various types of CAD systems, while perhaps behind business graphics in numbers of installations, are in the forefront of exploiting graphics technology for procedural and informational purposes.

IMAGE PROCESSING

Image processing requires more explanation than the previous two application areas because, as a phrase, the term can be used in a number of different contexts. Many of these contexts may not be as familiar as business graphics and computer-aided design, although image processing is currently one of the fastest growing segments of computer graphics. A major distinction also has usually existed between image processing and business graphics or computer-aided design on the basis of technique. The distinction is that the images in image processing systems are internally composed entirely of pixel data. That is, the picture is a multitude of points, or picture elements, where each point can be represented by a number or set of numbers to designate color or intensity. In contrast, business graphics and design graphics are largely represented internally by sequences of drawing instructions, such as commands to select a color and draw a solid circle of that color centered at point A, and only subsequently converted (sometimes) to pixel data for display. This is not a clean distinction, however, as some systems such as electronic paintboxes, described later in this chapter, can be entirely pixel based throughout the process and yet be used solely for design purposes. In still other situations, a digital image can be converted to the drawing instructions of computer graphics, and unconverted digital images can be mixed with graphics drawing instructions to present single, unified displays.

Image processing is also one of the areas with increasing crossover between computer graphics and video. In some cases, image processing encompasses digital video as a prerequisite—it is digitized video that is being processed. In other cases, the image being processed is created by laser scanners and other types of scanning and sensing equipment.

Sample Applications   One of the earliest applications for image processing goes back at least twenty-five years, image enhancement in astronomy. Basically, computers are used to evaluate each pixel of an image in relation to neighboring pixels to eliminate "noise" caused during the transmission of data through space. In general, image-processing software has been used to compensate for a variety of atmospheric and transmission conditions, sometimes interactively with the astronomer, so that the astronomer can judge a result and determine what the computer should do next. Over the years, satellite image processsing and remote sensing and image capture from distant spacecraft have continued to lead image-processing development, and have changed considerably in that time. It may sound surprising now, but in 1965 when the Mariner IV spacecraft sent back a digitized photograph of Mars, even a large computer was not up to creating a color display; instead, the gray-scale values for each pixel were printed as numbers, and then each number was color coded by hand, in crayon.[10] Now, satellite image processing can be done on a personal computer.

Generally speaking, image processing for satellite images and similar forms of image capture can involve a variety of operations on the value of each pixel in the image. The Landsat earth resources satellite, for example, records images in four spectral bands, three of which are in the visible spectrum and the fourth is near infrared.[11] Each pixel can be displayed according to preset levels or mixtures of one or more of the bands, depending upon the type of analysis being done. Parts of an image can be emphasized by subtracting a minimum gray-scale value from each pixel and then multiplying the result by a constant. In another enhancement technique, the color assigned to a pixel can be a ratio between values derived from two of the spectral bands used for image capture. Perhaps some of the most involved satellite image processing is done at the Jet Propulsion Laboratory to monitor earth resources, where data from Landsat, orbital radar, U2 infrared photography, geologic maps, and geophysical data are all digitized and coordinated pixel by pixel in a massive Geographic Information System.

Another major application of image processing is for biological and medical purposes. In medical imaging, one of the more recent developments is volumetric rendering, where a 3D image is built up from CAT scans (computed axial tomography) or thermography such that the resulting image is conceptually retained as a solid.[12] In other words, layers of the 3D image can be peeled away electronically, revealing successive underlying surfaces. A substantial amount of processing power is required to do this type of work, which merges computer graphics modeling with image processing in real time. One of the special computers used for volumetric rendering is the Pixar, with four parallel processors and a large high-resolution memory. At the other end of the scale, some medical image processing is also being done on personal computers. Figure 3.3 shows a screen image from an Imaging Technology system, where a digitized x-ray of a bone has been enlarged and then subjected to a filtering technique to highlight certain lines. In biological research, video cameras, fiberoptics, and write-once optical disks are being used in conjunction with polarizing microscopes and pixel processing to produce stereo images from a sequence of images, and to add the fourth dimension of time to microscopic matter.[13]

A rather different application area of image processing is document storage and retrieval. The purpose of document image processing is to covert paper files and microfilm images to digitally stored data bases, and therefore this topic comes up again in more detail in Chapter 4 as an example of image data bases. The amount of processing of the image, other than converting an analog image to pixel data, can be minimal, or it can be considerable if the objects in the image are to be recognized and stored as something other than pixel data. For

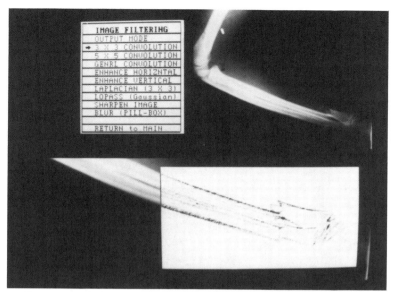

Figure 3.3. Medical image processing on a personal computer. Imaging Technology's Image Action is a high-performance interactive image processing system for IBM personal computers. Users can select functions from menus that appear on the screen, and can designate "areas of interest" for selective image processing. A section of the bone x-ray has been enlarged, and then a section of that has been subjected to convolution filtering. (Courtesy of Imaging Technology, Inc.)

example, in document image processing devoted to engineering drawings, the scanned image might be converted to CAD drawing commands in order to allow the digitized drawing to be reworked on a CAD system. Another large part of document image processing is the automatic recognition of alphanumeric characters, or OCR (optical character recognition), and the subsequent storage of the information not as pixel data but as character codes.

Image processing of documents at the microcomputer level began about 1983, when Datacopy Corporation began selling a camera-based system for microcomputers compatible with the IBM PC, and Wang introduced the Professional Image Computer system for its own office computers. Within a short time, other products appeared that emphasized the integration of digitized images with text and database management systems, such as PC-Eye from Chorus Data Systems (Fig. 3.4) and MacVision from Koala Technologies. Since then, desktop systems have included scanners in addition to video cameras to read the original documents and to provide OCR capabilities.

Image processing can also refer to simpler procedures

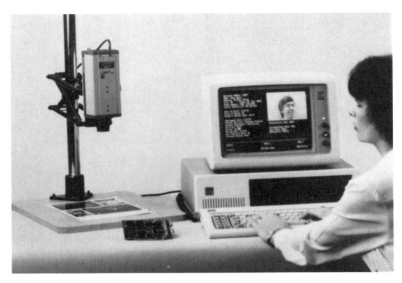

Figure 3.4. Integrating video images with text. Using a video camera, images of people, products, diagrams, maps, etc., can be captured and integrated with database management systems such as dBase II and III, R:Base 4000 and 5000, and the IBM Filing Assistant. (Courtesy of Chorus Data Systems.)

for capturing, digitizing, and transmitting scenes in real time, such as picture-telephones, or at slower speeds, such as facsimile, or to more complicated analysis of real-time images, such as machines or robotic vision systems.

Functional Categories To provide a framework for this range of applications, most forms of image processing can be grouped into one of the following functions: restoration and enhancement; regionalization (or segmentation); reconstruction; and recognition and understanding.[14] These groups are not mutually exclusive, and one may lead into another with some degree of overlap.

Restoration and enhancement encompasses the basic processing of satellite images, astronomical photography, and similar capturing of electromagnetic radiation (including the visible range) from remote objects. Restoration techniques are used to compensate for loss of data during transmission, while enhancement techniques are used to improve the final image based on an analysis of factors that could have affected it negatively. In some cases, the restoration and enhancement process requires so much data processing per pixel that images cannot—yet—be digitally generated in real time. In satellite and airborne image systems, for instance, a technique known as synthetic aperture radar (SAR) can accumulate data without regard to time of day or weather or cloud conditions, but the determination of each pixel is the result of not only receiving a constant stream of radar reflections but also of adjusting for a Doppler effect, the shift in frequency caused by motion. Consequently, the processing has traditionally not been done in real time. In addition, as SAR is increasingly used for radar mapping, and when specifically used to produce 3D displays, processing requires even more time.

Segmentation, or regionalization, refers to the various procedures for deducing segments, or subsets, of an image, such as lines, edges, curves, and shapes, and is at the heart of pattern classification and matching. Segmentation might be considered a simpler form of recognition and understanding, where segments are interpreted as well as isolated and identified.

Reconstruction involves the creation of two- and three-dimensional representations from essentially one-dimensional data streams. The primary example is in medical imaging as mentioned previously, such as CAT scans, positron-emission tomography (PET), and magnetic resonance imaging (MRI). In general, the scanning device moves through a range of positions in order to build up enough information to derive the two-dimensional coordinates of the points under study. The CAT scans use photon beams in the x-ray spectrum, PET relies on gamma rays, and MRI results from the effects of a magnetic field on the nuclei of hydrogen and other elements. (In MRI, a radio frequency pulse excites the spinning nuclei, which, under the influence of an external magnetic field, exhibit a specific gyroscopic effect and release a "free induction decay" signal as the nuclei return to equilibrium.) Other imaging processes have been developed for medical purposes that are either along these same lines or are variations of more traditional approaches, such as digital radiography, which is an outgrowth of x-ray systems.

Medical imaging systems often use restoration and enhancement techniques to improve the image, such as edge detection, contrast enhancement, and compensation for movement. In the case of digital radiography, the enhancement techniques can be used to permit lower x-radiation levels and to provide capabilities not possible with traditional x-rays, such as digitally subtracting "before" and "after" images, as in digital subtraction angiography.

Aside from the incredible capabilities of medical imaging systems, the most notable characteristic is the amount of data generated and the subsequent storage and retrieval requirements. One estimate is that the average radiology department can generate 2000 images per day, and hospital personnel will consult 10,000 images per day. Just to retain the images in digital format would consume sixteen gigabits per day of storage media, and the processs of consulting the images would involve access to, and transmission of, eighty-five gigabits per day. The design and creation of large-scale systems to handle the data requirements of medical imaging and to integrate the graphics and images with the entire information-processing load of a medical center is a formidable task that has attracted the largest computer companies, and will likely require such resources before solutions are ready. One attempt is a joint venture between IBM and General Electric, formed in late 1985, to produce a system called Integrated Diagnostics, which is to tie together the various manifestations of patient-related information. Another similar joint venture brings together AT&T and a subsidiary of Johnson & Johnson, and at least twenty other firms are in the same market. An acronym for this market summarizes the combination of imaging and information systems—PACS, or pictorial analysis, communication, and storage systems.

The final functional category, recognition with some level of understanding, covers a range from character recognition to probably the ultimate in computer video—machine vision coupled with machine comprehension. Such an outcome is one part of the realm of artificial intelligence, and includes all the problems associated with creating systems that can understand, in addition to trying to capture some of the still unfathomed complexity of the human visual system. At present, machine vision has more prosaic uses. Nearly half of all current systems are used for limited inspection purposes such as in manufacturing; other prominent uses are guidance and control, and part identification.

In practice, machine vision starts with the matrix of points provided by the camera or other input device. Each point has a value representing intensity and, in more complex systems, color. The image processing that then takes place includes the techniques of segmentation. Edges can be detected and surfaces might be identified, and the resulting identification of a set of edges and surfaces can be matched against the definitions of a series of known objects, or object parts, in order to proceed to an identification of an object in view. This can be a relatively simple task if the system is required to recognize only the difference between a dark flat square and a dark flat circle on a light background, viewed head on by the camera. As soon as objects have depth, irregularities, an infinite variety of orientations, and can appear in a similar number of lighting conditions surrounded by numerous other things, and might even move, the problems multiply. Moreover, the system must take the essentially two-dimensional matrix of pixels and determine from that the three-dimensional reality.

The human vision system is a general model for machine vision, but when it comes to the details, the human model is not always appropriate; however, some of the characteristics of biological vision are adapted fairly closely. Basic edge detection, for example, can be done using a number of algorithms, but a particularly good procedure duplicates the phenomenon in human vision known as lateral inhibition (described in the preceding chapter), where the photoreceptors around a target area of photoreceptors actually act opposite to the central reaction, inhibiting the response that is being stimulated in the central area. Pixels surrounding a target pixel can be adjusted similarly with the result that edges become sharper.

Somewhere in the middle between machine vision and simpler forms of image processing for recognition are systems that combine camera input with a restricted amount of information extraction. A particularly clever procedure involving videophones is being tested to aid people who use sign language. Because normal telephone lines do not have the bandwidth to accommodate real-time video transmission unless the picture information is drastically reduced or the transmission time expanded, researchers at the New England Medical Center in Boston are trying to develop a video system that would take camera input of a person using sign language and reduce the data enough to convey just a stick figure of the actions. The person with a videophone at the receiving end would presumably be able to read the sign language of the stick figure.

For the most part, image processing as a component of information systems is a combination of document image processing as a means for storing documents and object recognition, including optical character recognition. Conversely, information systems are a component of image-processing activity when the imaging system is trying to make sense of visual input by referring to a store of knowledge about shapes, colors, textures, lighting, and so on. In the future, automatic vision systems may provide the input to information storage and retrieval systems as we develop devices that can accumulate knowledge by looking around the world as we do.

PAINTBOXES AND SPECIAL EFFECTS

Digital paint systems generally allow an artist to use a stylus or a mouse to create freehand drawings, sometimes with the ability to mimic the techniques of water colors, oils, or pen and ink. Added benefits include computer control to generate perfect lines and circles if desired, and to remove, reshape, recolor, or alter sections of a frame or the whole frame in any number of ways (Fig. 3.5). The internal representation of the on-screen display of paint systems can be a matrix of pixel data, a set of drawing commands, or a combination.

In the past, the systems known primarily as paint systems were built around the manipulation of pixel data, rather than vectors of computer graphics-generation systems. One of the first of these, which pioneered the ability to drag a stylus representing a brush across a tablet or screen in order to change pixels to the brush color, was the Superpaint system developed at the Xerox Palo Alto Research Center in the early 1970s. The frame-buffer-copying algorithm behind this system is credited with spawning the whole area of computer graphics now known as paint systems.[15]

As in the history of computer-aided design, paint systems were likely to be based on workstations or minicomputers until the arrival of the microcomputer and the migration from larger to smaller machines. Unlike the situation in CAD, how-

Figure 3.5. The Quantel Paintbox™. Everything that can be done in a graphics studio, and a few things that cannot, can be performed using the Paintbox. High quality output can be recorded on videotape, film, and magnetic disk and tape. (Courtesy of Quantel, Ltd.)

ever, there has long been a direct connection between paint systems and video, as some of the earlier models of the better paint systems were developed specifically for the creation of broadcast-quality images for television. By the mid-1980s, microcomputer paint systems became available that combined digital creation capabilities with color-camera input that was itself digitized in real time. A highly regarded system that does just that is being promoted by a division of AT&T, the Electronic Photography and Imaging Center. The system includes a series of boards and accompanying software for microcomputers that are compatible with the IBM PC. For all functions, users are presented with menus of icons that can be erased and recalled, and placed anywhere on the screen at the touch of the stylus. The selection of some icons leads to other sets of icons to appear, and the original set is dynamically altered to contain a handful of the most recently used icons from the subsets. Thus the subset does not have to be called up until a function is required that has not been used recently.

The use of icons and other graphic devices, especially at the microcomputer level, is often attributed directly to the influence of the Apple Macintosh (Fig. 3.6). Paint systems for personal computers, particularly the IBM PC and compatibles, have been judged by whether or not they can measure up to the way MacPaint does things. Although the Macintosh did not originate these concepts, it did popularize them, and it is possible that the entire selection of paint programs for personal computers benefited more from the Macintosh's use of graphics than from any other single influence.

Some microcomputer paint systems are also marked by the ability to incorporate text and data files from popular spread sheet and word-processing programs. For example, one paint system, PC Paint from Mouse Systems Corp., sold over 40,000 copies between 1983 and 1985 on the ability not only to paint but also to integrate graphics with text and data from packages like Lotus 1-2-3 and Wordstar.

Digital Effects and Character Generators Concurrent with the development of extensive digital paint systems was the development within the television industry of special-effects machines that can take a video image such as the analog input

Figure 3.6. MacPaint. Functions are listed as icons along the left edge, and patterns are displayed along the bottom edge. Other functions are selectable from the strip menu along the top. (Courtesy of Apple Computer, Inc.)

from a camera, digitize it, and then digitally create the effects of spins, flips, rotations, zooms, rolls, twists, contortions, and apparent movement through three-dimensional space, to name some of the more common effects. The Mirage system from MCI/Quantel is reputedly the most adept of the effects machines, and can create cylinders and spheres from flat images, in addition to performing all the previously mentioned tricks.

A third class of graphics machine, which also evolved from the television environment and is now part of computer graphics, is the electronic character generator. Originally introduced in broadcasting around 1969, character generators are standard in television studios and have now assumed some of the capabilities of paint systems and special effects generators, while the latter two have incorporated high-quality character fonts. The Chyron character generator was one of the first used in broadcast television, and now the Chyron Corporation has added to the line the Chameleon Paint System and the Digifex special-effects generator. One of the earliest extensions of simple character-generation capability was the Dubner CBG (Character Background Generator). Harvey Dubner created his first character-generation machines in 1970 in nonbroadcast applications, but was asked by the American Broadcasting Company (ABC) in 1972 to devise a way to handle the display of election-night returns under computer control. By 1977 the capability for background graphics was added, again in response to a request from ABC, and the CBG began to be sold as a product. In 1985 an estimated eighteen Dubner CBGs (worth about $100,000 each) were in use at the ABC television network, four at the National Broadcasting Company (NBC), and three at the Columbia Broadcasting System (CBS).

The paint systems in broadcasting also arrived in the latter half of the 1970s, but after the original character-generation systems. One of the first, the Ampex AVA (Ampex Video Art), using techniques similar to those developed by Xerox for Superpaint, was employed by CBS in 1978, and in fact CBS contributed to the development of the AVA. The paint systems, which usually cost at least $100,000, did not really begin to infiltrate broadcast television in the United States until the mid-1980s. At that time, according to one count, television stations across the country had collectively purchased over 75 Paintboxes from MCI/Quantel, 50 high-end paint systems and 30 microcomputer paint systems from Aurora, and 10 high-end ArtStars and 340 midrange LiveLines from ColorGraphics, among others.[16]

Art and Animation　Although the work of electronic paint-boxes, special-effects machines, and character generators can all be done to some degree by microcomputers, in some areas the larger minicomputer-based workstations, and even large mainframes, are required for the more difficult maneuvers. The best job of computer animation, or special effects such as mapping any texture to any surface, can take a large computer a long time. Animation and special effects in television and movies, such as those by the New York Institute of Technology's Computer Graphics Laboratory, have been known to take years to assemble by computer, and other productions have used even the largest of supercomputers. Yet despite the fact that complex computer-generated pictures have become almost commonplace in the movie industry, the entertainment industry is not necessarily the primary user of the best in computer graphics technology. Systems experts at Pixar, a company originally formed as part of Lucasfilm Ltd. and later sold to employees and to Apple Computer's cofounder Steven Jobs, developed a graphics supercomputer for movie effects, but found more of a market for the system in medical (as mentioned earlier), military, and geological applications.

In general, the electronic paintboxes and related systems are often referred to as art systems, whether used for broadcasting, the movie industry, business graphics, advertising layouts, or the like. As in CAD/CAM, the systems use graphic representations as tools in the process of creating graphic products.

One distinction, though, of the whole area of computer graphics for art and entertainment is the presence of a high degree of creativity, a blend of technologies, and startling effects. If a common thread runs through the creation of computer-generated film and video entertainment, it is the mixture of real action with simulation, so that ultimately it is impossible to tell the difference. Many times we can still tell the two apart, but as computer techniques continue to improve, that will no longer be the case. The use of convincing simulations in entertainment is to be expected, as entertainment has always been based on the willing suspension of disbelief, bringing the audience into its own world. The possibilities in other areas, especially information systems, for creating a believable artificial environment are just now being explored, with a variety of ways that we might use realistic computer-generated images to provide a setting for computer-stored information.

GAMES

One more application area for computer graphics and computer video deserves to be mentioned, and that is games. Ever since the beginning of the phenomenon in the early 1970s, graphics have been essential for a host of computer games, especially for personal computers and for micro-level game machines.

The value of looking at computer games is that the graphic procedures may presage visual options for other applications, including information retrieval, where previously nongraphic procedures can be expressed in pictures. Adventure, as indicated previously, involves the idea of motion where locations are described and a player uses command words to move in directions such as north, west, up, and down. Everything is accomplished in words, and the visuals are in the player's imagination.

With computer graphics, the same sort of motion through a sequence of locations can be provided with graphic reinforcement at even a very simple level, with the list of commands and weapons always available in pull-down menus (Fig. 3.7). Borrowed Time is another game available on several microcomputers whose procedural aspect is very similar to that of Adventure. In the Macintosh version, you can still move north, south, east, or west, but as a reminder of the options, a compass symbol is drawn and the player "clicks" on one of the points. There is also still a verbal description of the location, but in addition, a picture is provided of the scene, and sometimes animation.

Like Adventure, a set of verbs can be used (get, drop, kill, etc.), but the possible verbs are always in view in a delimited area of the screen. This aspect is one of the least dramatic changes, and yet an important one in appreciating the added

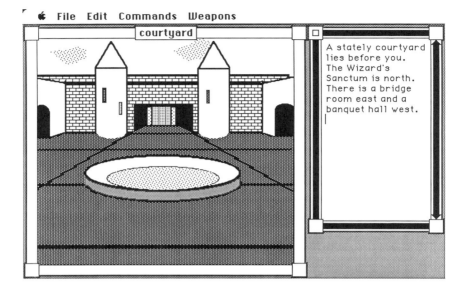

courtyard

A stately courtyard
lies before you.
The Wizard's
Sanctum is north.
There is a bridge
room east and a
banquet hall west.

Figure 3.7. The Game of Enchanted Scepters. A simple description appears in the window on the right. Commands and weapons are available from pull-down menus listed at the top. (Courtesy of Silicon Beach Software.)

value of the full-screen implementation. Players no longer have to keep track of the possible verbs; the list is always present, just off to the side of the action, or only a touch away in a pull-down list. Thus the full screen, with locations for different purposes, can keep the action visuals in one location, the verbs and nouns in other locations, and movement options in still another.

In this example, graphics are indeed only an enhancement for a type of game that preexisted in nongraphic form, but their addition provides both obvious and subtle enhancements. In the same manner, as graphics are added to more serious information systems, the results will range from simplistic add-ons to profound differences.

Bit Maps and Display Memory

The various types of computer graphics and digital video discussed above share one thing in common, namely, that the display is dependent on the sum of the graphics hardware and software capabilities. Chapter 2 presented the constraints of the components of the display monitor as limitations on resolution, but more factors affect both the manipulation of display data and the final resolution. These include such topics as bit maps, bit planes, color look-up tables, frame buffers, graphics controllers, DRAM and video RAM, device-dependent and device-independent graphics processing, and the effect of graphics standards.

Another look at the technical features of computer graphics may help balance the view of their applications. Because of the now pervasive influence of the personal computer, particular attention is given to graphics hardware at the microcomputer level and to raster graphics as the output.

DISPLAY MEMORY

In raster graphics, as described previously, the visual display on a screen is composed of horizontal lines, and each line is composed of a discrete number of pixels, or picture elements. The number of pixels vertically is based on the number of visible scan lines, while the number of pixels horizontally is somewhat more arbitrary. Some systems have the same number of pixels in each direction, such as 256 × 256 or even 1024 × 1024, but it is more common to see combinations like 256 (horizontal) × 200 (vertical), 640 × 480, or 1024 × 768. As the display needs to be refreshed repeatedly on the order of 60 frames per second, there must be a table of data that contains values for each pixel to denote light or darkness, or color in such a fashion that the data can be read by the screen-generation subsystem as fast as necesssary. Thus the capabilities of the system are defined by the amount of memory that can be dedicated to holding pixel data and the techniques used to take advantage of that memory.

For pixel data, the amount of display memory required can escalate rapidly to accommodate higher resolution or more color. If only 1 bit is used per pixel, which creates a monochrome display (the bit is either on or off), a display of 256 × 240 needs a table of 61,440 bits, or one 64-kilobit chip. For resolution of 1000 × 1000, a table of one million bits is required. If color is to be used, the memory demands multiply. In systems where a color is designated by a numeric value for each pixel, two bits per pixel would provide four colors with double the memory requirements. Eight bits per pixel yields 256 colors, 16 bits gives over 65,000 colors, and 24 bits provides over 16 million. In fact, it was not until prices for computer memory began to drop at the beginning of the 1980s that raster graphics with high resolution and extensive capabilities became feasible on a wide scale. The 1984 price for a sixty-four-kilobit chip was approximately $1.00, but if current trends hold, the 1990 price for a one-megabit chip will be only $2.50.[17]

The number of bits per pixel is sometimes referred to in terms of the number of bit planes. Physical storage for the display memory is described conceptually as a set of two-dimensional surfaces, or planes, holding one bit per pixel. As bit planes are stacked together, the bits representing each pixel are located, one by one, in the same position on successive planes. Two bit planes would mean two bits per pixel, or four possible intensities for each pixel. If two bit planes are used for each color gun, the total number of bit planes is six, providing up to sixty-four colors, and so on, as bit planes are added.

Bit planes used for display memory do not have to be used in the same way all the time. The same number of bits can be used to provide several different combinations of resolution and color intensity. Personal computers with color graphics capability often have one mode with a higher resolution but fewer possible colors than a second mode. This is a result of the fact that the total number of bits available for display memory is fixed. Therefore in the high-resolution mode there might be as many pixels as bits, while in a lower-resolution mode there are two or more bits per pixel to designate four or more colors or intensities.

The color possibilities can be greatly expanded, without a large number of bit planes to hold the color values, by using changeable color look-up tables or color maps. The bits for each pixel are used as an index number into a table of color values, where the color value itself requires more bits than used in the index number, and the color table can be readily altered to include any of the possible colors. For example, eight bits per pixel can reference 256 colors in a color table, but each of the colors in the table could be specified by sixteen bits representing over 65,000 colors.

Display memory and bit planes can be configured in a number of ways to produce specific effects or to provide certain capabilities, usually in a way that will minimize the amount of display memory required, which means lower cost for the hardware. The relationship between the size of the display memory in bits and the number of viewable pixels is not necessarily direct. There may be more display memory than can be represented on a full screen, or there might be less, or there can be a combination of different display memories for subsets of the screen as well as for the full screen.

When there is more display memory than necessary for the visible display, the additional memory is used to hold images or even full screens that can be built up before actual display, and then displayed in one refresh cycle, creating the "instantaneous" appearance of complex images. When two sets of bit planes, for example, are used, one to hold the image being updated and the other to hold the image being displayed, this is called double buffering. The additional memory can also be used to provide other special effects and some forms of animation. Special effects such as fades can be accomplished by storing subsequent images on different memory planes and sequentially moving down through the memory planes to feed the visible image. Animation can be effected by using specially designated portions of display memory for objects or designs that are to move about the screen. In a similar fashion, panning and zooming can be effected by having the visible display refer to successive areas of the display memory.

CHARACTER MEMORY

Before computer memory began dropping in price and bit-mapped displays became common, alphanumeric CRTs required only enough display memory for individual character patterns, rather than for a full screen. Because the number of characters that a given system would be expected to display is limited, the patterns or bit masks for each one can be maintained in software or in hardware in what is known as a character generator (not to be confused with the character generators used in the television industry). Thus the alphanumeric displays of traditional computer screens are possible without needing a large amount of display memory, but the presentation range is limited to the stored character set. Usually, the stored character set is in read-only memory (ROM), but in some systems, different character sets can be loaded from disk into random-access memory (RAM) and are known as RAMfonts.

Character generators can also be used to manipulate character shapes. The pixels of a character mask can be shifted or rewritten to produce such effects as slants, reverse direction, and the like. Characters are also sometimes stored as drawing commands, or vector lists, rather than pixels, and the vector lists can similarly be transformed to create new versions of a character.

The character mask approach can also be used for other than alphanumeric characters. Sets of pixel patterns can be defined, and graphic images can be composed by aligning the available patterns. The number of defined patterns is, however, usually far less than the total number of pixel patterns possible within a character cell or more than a few pixels in either direction.

BIT TRANSFERS

One of the keys to the success of bit-mapped displays with windows, icons, and pop-up menus is the ability rapidly to update the display memory. In many of the arrangements of display memories and frame buffers, this means moving sets of data to new locations at extremely high speeds. A procedure to do just that is the block transfer, or BLT. When the block transfer is related to a bit plane, it is a BitBLT (pronounced "bit-blit"). The BitBLT function, originally developed at Xerox during the early work on graphically manipulated systems, has made it possible to have visual displays in which graphic designs or formats can be quickly swapped in and out. This in turn makes it possible to have screen formats with overlapping windows, work areas that can be juggled around at will, and pop-up menus that all respond instantaneously to the click of a mouse.

GRAPHICS CONTROLLER

The display memory is only one of the basic parts of the larger category called the graphics controller, which includes additional hardware and software for taking data and producing a signal to drive a display device. In general usage, the graphics controller could be a stack of equipment within a large sophisticated imaging system, or it could be a single card to plug into a personal computer, or could even be just a chip or two on a given card. One of its main functions in any configuration is to provide a way for programs to affect the ultimate display.

A graphics controller card for microcomputers can contain, in addition to the display memory or DRAM (dynamic random-access memory), a microprocessor of its own, an instruction set, or firmware, to convert image coordinates to pixel data, and digital to analog converters (DACs) that provide the analog signals to the monitor's color guns. The firmware can be designed to accept commands from a programming language like BASIC, that might have a simple command like "Line x, y," where x and y are the end-point coordinates, and convert that to a set of intermediate instructions (a driver program) linking that higher level programming language to the controller's way of doing things, which in turn is determined by machine language statements in the controller's microprogram.

The fact that a graphics card for a personal computer contains the hardware and firmware to control both the display and the way a program or software package can create the display has meant that users of personal computer graphics have had to make sure that there is a match among the software package, the graphics card, the display monitor, and the quality of the desired display. Software packages may only work with specified graphics cards, and different cards may generate displays differing in number of colors, resolution, and other capabilities. The section on graphics standards later in this chapter may help to explain the attempts to achieve better coordination among all the elements of microcomputer graphics systems.

The microprocessor chip on a graphics card is the fundamental piece that supports the graphics subsystem structure. Improvements at this level provide system developers and software writers with additional capabilities that will eventually be incorporated into a range of applications. While there are hundreds, if not thousands, of graphics software packages and graphics system integrators, however, there is only a relatively small number of sources for the graphics processor chips. Some chips are proprietary designs and some are general-purpose used as graphics controllers, such as the popular Motorola 68020. The graphics capability of a wide variety of systems is tied to the characteristics of that particular chip. Other chips commonly used for graphics control are manufactured by NEC, Hitachi, Advanced Micro Devices, and NCR. Because of the relatively small number of manufacturers, developments at this level can have a very broad effect, especially in the case of graphics processor chips designed as such, for use with other manufacturers' hardware.

In 1986 two such chips were introduced that are specifically graphics processors with extensive capabilities: the 82786 graphics coprocessor produced by Intel, and Texas Instruments' TMS 34010 Graphics System Processor. Both of these chips, and a few others with similar properties, are expected to have a dramatic impact on the use of graphics as the procedure for interacting with a computer, and on the development of high-quality graphic products as the chips are incorporated into graphics boards used in personal computers. The possible graphic enhancements that can be built on both of these chips are such that graphics-dominated procedures, similar to and yet better than those now popular on the Apple Macintosh, will become more available across the entire spectrum of microcomputers and workstations.

At present, we are in a transitional phase between the capabilities of graphics workstations and graphics-oriented microcomputers such as the Apple Macintosh and the new IBM Personal System / 2, and the less-graphics-capable majority of personal computers. At the microcomputer level, the integration of graphics tools for accessing information has come about in complete systems designed with that in mind, and such systems may involve proprietary graphics chips. But the proliferation of bit-mapped graphics for the personal computer, and the exploitation of the graphics capability, is not likely to rest on proprietary graphics chips and cards, or necessarily on complete systems designed for just that purpose. Rather it will rely on more general acceptance of graphics as evidenced in graphics controller chips that can be used by many manufacturers because the procedures for using the chips are commonly known or are accepted standards.

Graphics Standards

In the past, the field of computer graphics was marked by an absence of standards. Designers and developers created their own way of implementing graphics capabilities, and the main use was in workstations that could contain proprietary graphics technology and procedures without detriment to the often dedicated use of the workstation.

At the same time, there was no lack of attempts to define industry standards, and a certain acceptance of ad hoc standards maintained by a given manufacturer's forceful presence in the marketplace. In the world of personal computers, for example, IBM's graphics cards are the acknowledged standard. Thus manufacturers of graphics boards and writers of graphics software will make sure that their products are compatible with the IBM system if they hope to sell to owners of IBM-compatible PCs. The dominance of IBM display cards begins with that company's monochrome display adaptor (MDA), still referred to as "the most common display standard in today's market."[18] For color, IBM introduced the Color Graphics Adaptor (CGA) in 1981 and this provided the starting point for all graphics products designed to work with, or to be equivalent to, the IBM PC. The CGA card did not provide the best in microcomputer graphics, but it did establish the norm, with a resolution of 320 × 200 when in the four-color mode.

In the next several years, other companies brought out graphics cards with enhanced capacity that to one degree or another maintained compatibility with the MDA and CGA cards. Hercules introduced in 1983 an improvement over the CGA card by bringing together graphics and high-resolution text, but at the expense of color. Paradise Systems brought out a card in 1984 that, while still compatible with CGA graphics, improved on color. At roughly the same time, in late 1983, Number Nine Computer Corporation began marketing a graphics card with twice the resolution of the CGA in both the horizontal and vertical dimensions and with 256 simultaneous colors drawn from a palette of over 16 million. The drive for more colors and higher resolution has continued, sometimes with a trade-off between the features if the display memory is held constant. Color cards with resolutions of 512×512 (262,000 simultaneous colors), 1024×1024 (256 simultaneous colors), and 2048×1024 (16 simultaneous colors) are available, and improvements are still coming.

In the more traditional world of graphics workstations, other manufacturers also more or less set the standard by achieving market dominance. The Tektronix protocol for the Tektronix 4010 graphics terminal became accepted as a procedure for others to be compatible with for nearly ten years before graphics standards as such gained wide attention. During a similar time span, the graphics software from Integrated Software Systems Corporation, known as DISSPLA, was also accepted as a de facto standard for certain applications.

With increased recognition by many users of the value of industry standards not dominated by one company, various graphics standards have now gained wider acceptance. Dating roughly from 1982 or 1983, adherence to standards has begun to be accepted across the range of hardware and software suppliers. Therefore, keeping track of the standards or proposed standards and the numerous revisions is both more pertinent and less of a worry. That is, at the heart of a given system, even at the chip level, the likelihood is increasing that procedures from an accepted or semiaccepted standard have been implemented, and thus the systems and applications programmers, and ultimately the users, need not worry about maintaining compatibility among chips, boards, and application programs.

On the other hand, an appreciation of how graphics capabilities are affected by standards must be based on the realization that many of the standards overlap, that it takes years for industry groups to agree formally on standards, that companies often implement a proposed standard to varying levels of completeness before the standard is formally published as such, that even formal standards evolve over time, and that some companies, alone or in groups, will establish and promote their own standards for some parts of the graphics process.

The most relevant basic standards, perhaps, are the Graphical Kernel System (GKS), the Computer Graphics Interface (CGI), the Computer Graphics Metafile (CGM), the Initial Graphics Exchange Specification (IGES), and the recently announced, privately developed Direct Graphics Interface Specification (DGIS) (Table 3.1). Other standards also directly affect the screen display, especially for windowed displays. Still others are available for text files, mixing text with graphics, composing printed pages, and transferring graphics, text, or a mixture of both to a variety of devices such as printers and plotters as well as CRTs.

GKS AND CORE

The early beginnings of GKS, and a related graphics standard known as the Core proposal, stem from work done in the mid-

Table 3.1: Graphics Standards and Proposed Standards

	name	comment
GKS	Graphical Kernel System	applications programming
GKS-3D		GKS with 3D
Core	Siggraph Core	similar to GKS
CGI	Computer Graphics Interface	for I/O devices
DGIS	Direct Graphics Interface Specification	for I/O devices
CG-VDI	CG-Virtual Device Interface	similar to CGI
CGM	Computer Graphics Metafile	file storage and transfer
GKSM	GKS Metafile	similar to CGM
IGES	Initial Graphics Exchange Specification	CAD file transfer
PHIGS	Programmer's Hierarchical Interactive Graphics System	highly dynamic applications
PMIGS	Programmer's Minimal Interface to Graphics	subset of GKS

1970s by the Graphics Standards Planning Committee of the Association for Computing Machinery's Special Interest Group on Computer Graphics. Core is an applications-level standard that defines the ways in which graphics are created and ways in which interaction with a graphic can take place. For example, Core defines a handful of "primitive" functions that can be used to create any object, such as Polyline to draw a sequence of connected lines and Polygon to define an object by a list of vertices. Over a hundred other functions are defined that build upon the primitives or affect interaction.

The GKS standard also began about the same time, or only slightly later. Much of the design methodology was developed at a 1976 meeting under the auspices of the International Federation for Information Processing, and the actual standard as such was created by the West German Standardization Institute, or Deutsche Institute für Normung (DIN), in 1978. Further work was done in the early 1980s by a committee within the International Standards Organization (ISO), and GKS was subsequently approved as a standard by both the ISO and ANSI (American National Standards Institute) in 1985. In the early 1980s, Core and GKS were seen as rival standards and heated debate arose regarding the benefits of one over the other, but the contention has subsided as GKS gained dominance. At the same time, the contributions of Core have been acknowledged. In fact, GKS was built directly upon the 1977 Core system proposal, and at the time, the German researchers translated the word "core" as "kern," which was later inexplicably retranslated back into English as the "kernel" of Graphical Kernal System.[19]

As GKS was heavily influenced by Core, they share many of the same elements, although GKS has been primarily concerned with 2D graphics. Like Core, GKS has a handful of graphic primitives but they are not identical to the Core primitives. In addition, GKS is organized around the concept of an abstract workstation, which is not a physical workstation but a combination of logical display surfaces and logical input devices. A physical workstation may have a number of these logical units, or may lack one entirely, for example in cases where there is no input device. Another concept introduced in Core and subsequently in GKS is the metafile, a prescribed way of listing sets of commands, which represent images, that can be transferred from one program or device to another. The GKS metafile (GKSM) is a sequential list of graphic information that can be stored or transmitted, where the information has been coded according to another standard such as VDM (see below).

The value of GKS and other similar efforts is that they are independent of the hardware and independent of individual programming languages. They are, in the words of the standard itself, "a language-independent nucleus of a graphics system."[20] As such, GKS provides the common ground between developers of graphics software and hardware. Each has only to conform to GKS as the middleman, and an entire process can be translated from applications program to resulting display. For applications programmers to use a standard such as GKS, the graphic functions have to be defined in terms of a given programming language, and these definitions are known as bindings. The bindings between GKS and various languages are now established, and a programmer using a graphics function may not even be aware that the GKS standard is being used.

On the hardware side, an equivalent binding procedure must take place to relate the GKS functions to the capabilities of specific pieces of equipment, including both vector and raster displays, storage tubes, and microfilm recorders. The VDI standard, for example, defined below, is such a "device driver" and therefore can be used in conjunction with GKS.

One of the difficulties with standards is that advances in technology can render them outdated. The development of GKS, for example, took place when graphic workstations were largely concerned with two-dimensional displays. Now the manipulation of three-dimensional displays must also be accommodated. For these applications, an enhancement of GKS, dubbed GKS-3D, is being developed.

CGI (VDI) AND CG-VDI

The Computer Graphics Interface (CGI) is a proposed ISO standard and is a renaming of the Virtual Device Interface (VDI). Within ANSI, the related standard is known as CG-VDI. The chief purpose is to correlate the coordinate system from the graphics-creation system with the demands of an output device, or even an input device. In some cases, however, a device driver is still needed to relate the CGI (or VDI) code with the capabilities of a particular device. Another way to describe CGI is as a standard for object code, in contrast to GKS, which provides a standard for source code. Object code is the compiled version of the source code of a program. To look at it another way, GKS operates at the applications level, while CGI operates at the hardware level. As in the case of GKS, bindings can also be made to programming languages such as C or FORTRAN at the CGI level.

Implementations of the CGI or VDI concept have preceded the formal acceptance of CGI as a standard. In 1983 Digital Research marketed its GSX (Graphic System Extension) as a VDI for microcomputers, and later Graphics Software Systems released GSS*CGI. The latter supports 20 different output devices including the IBM EGA card. An earlier version of a CGI implementation, GSS Drivers, has been marketed by IBM as the PC Graphics Development Tool Kit, thus becoming part of the de facto IBM standard for microcomputer graphics.

CGM (VDM), IGES, AND STEP

The Computer Graphics Metafile (CGM), originally called the Virtual Device Metafile (VDM), is one of the ways of constructing a metafile, as referenced in GKS, and was proposed as an American National Standard at the same time as GKS, in late 1983. Now CGM is both an ANSI and an ISO standard and is considered to be primarily a procedure for exchanging graphics information from one program to another. Current work centers around defining an extended metafile as a standard GKS metafile, expanding the work to include GKS-3D, and incorporating the remaining CGI functions that have not already been included.

The Initial Graphics Exchange Specification (IGES) evolved from the CAD/CAM industry, specifically from the aerospace segment in concert with the National Bureau of Standards, and is similar to the metafile standards in providing a way to transmit images and data from one system to another.

Aerospace designers found that they could not readily transfer CAD files from one machine to another for amendments on the second machine, and consequently IGES was conceived for just that purpose. The Standard for the Exchange of Product Data Models (STEP) is a proposed international standard to go beyond IGES in facilitating the transfer of CAD data to computer-aided manufacturing systems.

DGIS

The Direct Graphics Interface Specification (DGIS) is a recent move to improve on CGI and the transferring of graphics from device-independent languages to specific devices by providing an interface in ROM (read-only memory) that can communicate directly between a graphics processor chip and a microcomputer's central processing unit. One difference between CGI and DGIS is that CGI is a generalized standard, while DGIS is specifically designed to work with the DOS system of IBM PCs and compatibles. Although DGIS was developed by a private company, Graphic Software Systems, it has been released to the public domain and has been accepted by a number of the leading graphics development companies.

OTHER STANDARDS

The list of graphics standards also includes the Programmer's Hierarchical Interactive Graphics Standard (PHIGS), the Programmer's Minimal Interface to Graphics (PMIGS), and the North American Presentation Level Protocol Syntax (NAPLPS), among others. In addition, other standards do not relate specifically to graphics but are nonetheless concerned with the arrangement of text and graphics on a page or screen, and the mixture of graphics and images with text.

The Programmer's Hierarchical Interactive Graphics Standard (PHIGS) is a proposed standard that grew out of Core in that it is the result of more recent work to extend Core to cover the requirements of highly realistic computer modeling.

The impetus behind PHIGS is to provide a way for graphics subroutines to call other subroutines, that is, a hierarchical approach or nested segmentation. This is not posssible in the current versions of either Core or GKS. As PHIGS is still under development as a standard, one of the open questions is the relationship between it and GKS-3D. Most likely, programs written using GKS or GKS-3D would not run directly under a PHIGS system, but metafiles adhering to CGM produced by GKS or GKS-3D would be completely acceptable to PHIGS.

The Programmer's Minimal Interface to Graphics (PMIGS), on the other hand, is a subset of GKS and goes in a direction opposite to PHIGS by providing a standard for a beginners' system, a graphics language with restricted capabilities to be used by programmers without graphics experience.

The North American Presentation Level Protocol Syntax (NAPLPS) is like IGES in that it is the product of a specific industry segment, the so-called videotex industry. As a videotex standard, NAPLPS competes with other videotex standards, and particularly with the European composite known as the CEPT standard, from the initials for the international conference of European postal and telecommunications authorities. The CEPT standard is based on the early videotex systems in England, France, and West Germany, but has also been influenced by NAPLPS and by GKS. Conceptually, NAPLPS can be considered a mixture of a subset of GKS and CGM, in that a NAPLPS display is a sequence of graphic commands, but there are no bindings to programming languages.

Although GKS includes commands for inserting text, several other standards are much more centrally concerned with text and with the mixture of text and graphics on CRTs, printers, and other output devices. The Standard Generalized Markup Language (SGML) was developed for converting text files to typographic files for typeset output. Within the U.S. Department of Defense, SGML has been tied to IGES and another protocol, the Product Definition Exchange Specification (PDES), to provide a standard way of exchanging various combinations of text and graphics. Other standards activity involving text and graphics centers around the ISO standard for Office Document Interchange Format (ODIF), although this does not currently include graphics, the proposed Office Document Architecture (ODA) that includes CGM for handling graphics within text, an SGML Document Interchange Format (SDIF), and general page description languages (PDL). Another proposal, the Computer Graphics Content Architecture (CGCA), is a subset of ODA and would specifically include raster graphics with text. Various companies also have standards to incorporate text and graphics, such as IBM's Document Content Architecture (DCA), Microsoft's Rich Text Format (RTF), and Digital Equipment Corporation's Digital Document Interchange Format (DDIF). The last is based on ODIF and includes SGML, and has been made public to encourage its use as an industry standard.

A privately developed standard that is also designed for controlling the output of text and graphics is Postscript from Adobe Systems. Originally, Postscript was built to drive printers, and its strongest feature is its ability to store and manage typefonts. Postscript has been placed in the public domain and has been accepted as the standard interface for printers by various manufacturers. The Postscript language also can be used for interactive graphics manipulation on a CRT. For example, the Adobe Illustrator product from Adobe Systems has been endorsed by IBM for electronic publishing.

WINDOW SYSTEMS

One more set of standards that should be mentioned, although they are more system procedures than graphics standards, is concerned with screen displays specifically in a format that includes windows and icons, mixing text and graphics. This is the subject of Chapter 5, but briefly, Microsoft's Windows, the X Windows System developed at MIT for Unix applications, and the combination of Microsoft's Windows with IBM's new Operating System/2 for personal computers are all providing a basis for a standard way of implementing graphically enhanced operating systems. At one time, it was thought that Smalltalk, a combination of an operating system, high-level language, and a graphics interface would form the basis for a standard for the graphic interface concepts made popular by the Apple Macintosh.[21] Now, the Windows system, or something similar, may fill that role as the accepted graphic operating system in the same way that MS-DOS became widespread as the basic operating system for IBM-compatible personal computers.

Summary

There is evidence across a wide range of applications of the increasing capabilities of, and desire for, computer graphics of all kinds. More important, activities in which the graphic or the image is the end product are also increasingly areas in which graphics techniques are used as tools in finding or creating the end product and in accessing related information files. The demand for graphics techniques both feeds on and fuels the wider availability, at lower cost, of graphics hardware, especially chips and cards for microcomputers. Moreover, newer generations of graphics chips are expected to increase the graphics level of the general-purpose personal computer. Finally, the long involvement with a proliferation of graphics standards is beginning to consolidate into a few standards that are having considerable impact, although in the area of mixed text and graphics, particularly in office applications, the standards process is just beginning.

4

VIDEOBASES AND IMAGE BASES

Among the many mixes of computer graphics and video is the class of systems known as video data bases, picture data bases, image systems, image bases, or simply videobases. The combination of pictures and text, stored electronically and separately but viewed together, essentially materialized first in the form of interactive videodisks. Since then, other techniques including digitized images stored on magnetic disks and optical data stored on compact disks have expanded the ways in which videobases can be created and manipulated.

Videobases have made a singular contribution to information storage and retrieval systems by providing a new way to think about the mixture of text and pictures. They can be mixed and matched dynamically, the order of presentation can be entirely ad hoc, movement can be displayed, and concepts such as spatial orientation can be accommodated readily. While traditional media have contained both pictures and text, and videobases can duplicate those arrangements, the creative videobase can provide a truly different experience. This chapter describes some of the systems and techniques that exemplify the importance of this relatively recent expansion of information retrieval.

Media and Methods

In the long history of the written word, text and illustrations have been displayed together in myriad ways, all dependent on the limitations of the medium, such as paper. Within those contraints, of course, there is a considerable range of visual and intellectual effects, from illustrations accompanying text to text that is itself a graphic or illustration.

Perhaps one of the best classic examples of intertwined text and graphics is the *Book of Kells,* written in Latin on vellum in the early ninth century in County Meath, Ireland. Some 340 pages of the *Book of Kells* have survived, and most contain at least some color designs. The most intricate pages contain just a few words of text almost hidden by the graphic technique. In one example, the initial letter of the first word (In) reaches from the top to the bottom of the page and is composed of finely detailed designs, while the second letter is abstracted so that it looks like a cross. The next work (principio) is written in four stages, with the initial letter occupying the top right quadrant of the page, the next three letters in a different style at the bottom left of the P, the next two letters at the bottom right of the P, and the final three letters in a smaller size below that, joined to the third word with no intervening space. The entire page is covered with other illustrations and designs that fill the page with color. As the words themselves would have been well known to the readers of the *Book of Kells,* the visual effect could transcend readability in order to convey the awe and majesty associated with the words.

In the 1200 years since the writing and drawing of the *Book of Kells,* many other imaginative mixtures of text and graphics have been produced on paper, but in every case the nature of the materials has bounded the outcome. However intricate and imaginative, the final result exists as a fixed design on a static sheet of paper or other material.

Thus, for centuries text and illustrations were always created within the well-understood capabilities of the print medium, until the development of moving pictures and television changed the way we could work with recorded information. A half-century later, the possibilities expanded again with the introduction of computer-controlled graphics, computer-controlled video, and digital images.

Of course, the mixture of text and graphics in videobases has been determined largely by the technologies used. In some cases, the technology dictated that the pictures be stored separately from the text and graphics, with the happy result that the new systems could do things with pictures and text that were simply not possible with printed material and with text/graphic systems that mimicked the printed arrangement.

The rest of this section summarizes the working details of a few of the technologies that have given rise to videobases, but it is not the technology that is important. Rather, the key is to concentrate on what has been done, and what might be done, with the capabilities that the videodisk or the digital image-capture system provides. The exploitation of the capabilities, such as providing spatial orientation and spatial data management, can continue to be enhanced even as any single technology might be replaced by another procedure. Optical disks have appeared in a variety of forms for a changing number of purposes, while at the same time digitized video frames can be stored even easier on digital media such as diskettes or memory chips.

VIDEODISKS AND LASER DISKS

The leading candidate for the technology that has done the most to foster imaginative manipulations of electronically stored words and pictures is the interactive videodisk, even though some of the same things can be done with other storage media such as videotape. It is also probably accurate to say that the types of things that have been done with videodisks are only a prelude to what eventually will be possible.

Videodisks, at least in concept, date back almost to the beginning of video, or television, itself. The Scottish inventor John Logie Baird, who has been called the father of television, suggested in the 1920s that moving pictures could be stored on a spinning disk similar to a phonograph record. A 1932 article in *Modern Mechanics* explained that 100 feet of film could be stored on a 10-inch record and played back on a self-contained unit about the size of a current desktop monitor, with the screen at the front and the video record on a turntable on top.[1] It was not until the early 1970s that the modern videodisk began to appear, when a prototype system was demonstrated in 1972 by the N. V. Philips company.[2]

Two features of certain versions of the laser videodisk

gave rise to the interactive, computer-controlled applications. The primary feature is that the video can be stored on the disk in concentric circles, with a single frame of video per circle. This enables both frame-by-frame access as well as special effects such as freeze frames, slow motion, and fast forward. For individual frame access, the reading mechanism can move quickly across the disk to the desired circle. For freeze frames, the reading mechanism stays on the same circle, replaying the same frame. Slow motion is achieved by reading each circle/frame several times before moving to the next one, and accelerated motion is produced by skipping circles. In all cases, the actual angular speed of the spinning disk remains the same, so that disks that have been created in this way are known as CAV (constant angular velocity) disks. This distinguishing feature of CAV systems—frame-by-frame access—can also be achieved on non-CAV systems given the appropriate control mechanism, but CAV systems did lead the way into interactive video.

The second feature of certain laser videodisk systems that contributed to interactive uses, particularly in the early years, was the fact that a small computer program can also be recorded on a track on the videodisk, and this program can be executed by a player equipped with an internal microprocessor. Because a program might contain conditional branching instructions dependent on which keys a user presses on a keypad, interactive viewing of frames or sequences of frames is accomplished. In more recent years, external processors such as personal computers have been used increasingly to control videodisk players and the programs that can be run on an external computer can be very much larger than the handful of lines of code that are processed by the traditional internal microprocessor. Even though the original arrangement has been substantially superceded, however, the initial inclusion of some form of computer-controlled interactivity was the beginning step.

The method for currently recording and reading information on the videodisks just described is basically the same across the existing range of laser disk systems, and can be summarized fairly easily even though the mechanisms are quite sophisticated. A varying signal is used to drive a laser beam that etches billions of micropits to encode the signal. For videodisks, the etching might be done on a master disk, and the signal might also include two other superimposed channels used either for digital instructions to the internal microprocessor or for audio. The master is then plated with nickel and used to stamp any number of plastic copies with identical patterns of pits. For playback, another laser in the player focuses a beam on the micropits, and the resulting shifts in phase in the reflected beam can be processed to reproduce the video and audio signals. In addition, the light wave is also split and analyzed to determine and correct for minute variations in the speed and stability of the spinning disk, which would adversely affect the reflected light.

The capacity of a CAV disk, with one video frame per circle of micropits, is established by the manufacturing process and the size of the disk. The common 12-inch disks hold 54,000 frames, each frame occupying one circle. When played at the rate of thirty frames per second, the television standard in the United States, the result is thirty minutes of video per side. Of course, the disk can contain any combination of individual frames and sets of frames for motion sequences, up to the total of 54,000. A newer 8-inch disk can contain either 24,000 still frames or 13 minutes of video, or any combination.

Another type is the CLV (constant linear velocity) laser disk, on which the video information is not confined to only one video frame per circle or track. Instead, as the circles become larger toward the outer edge, many frames are recorded per circle. When played, the angular velocity of the disk adjusts to the number of frames per track in order to keep the number of frames per second at the standard rate, for example, thirty frames per second, yielding a constant linear velocity. The common twelve-inch CLV disk can contain sixty minutes of video per side, in contrast to the thirty minutes for the twelve-inch CAV disk. The disadvantage for CLV disks for interactive purposes has been that they preclude individual frame access and freeze-frame display.

During the mid-1980s laser disks and optical technology became available for the routine storing of computer data. The technology is essentially the same as for the analog videodisk except that the micropits represent binary digits, or bits, of information. Unlike the procedure that evolved for the manufacturing of most analog videodisks, requiring expensive specialized mastering facilities, devices to etch or "write" the digital optical disks have been developed suitable for use in a desktop environment. The digital optical disk systems, sometimes referred to as WORM (write once, read many), DRAW (direct read after write), or DRDW (direct read during write), have been around at least since the late 1970s; Philips demonstrated one in 1978. (Once again, newer systems can blur distinctions among categories; an eight-inch Panasonic analog videodisk system also includes a desktop WORM recorder.) The advantages of these disks over magnetic media include their durability under conditions of heavy use and their vastly greater information capacity relative to comparably sized magnetic disks. For data storage, the twelve-inch laser disks typically hold up to 1.3 gigabytes per side (1300 megabytes), and newer fourteen-inch disks hold over 3.4 gigabytes per side (these systems are described in more detail in the section "Document Processing and Storage" later in this chapter).

The whole matter of writing optical disks, whether for analog video or for digital purposes, is one of continuing concern, with the goal of producing rewritable, or erasable, disks. Before too many more years, erasable laser disk systems for common computer usage are expected to be available and affordable. The Minnesota Mining and Manufacturing Company (3M) is said to have invested over $100 million in developing optical disks, in 5.25-inch and 12-inch sizes and is leading the effort to create marketable optical disks that can be repeatedly erased and rewritten.[3] This subject comes up again in the section "Related Methods."

CAPACITANCE SYSTEMS

In the history of videodisk development, not all systems have been optical. Capacitance systems, for instance, have used a stylus to read the disk.

There are several types of capacitance systems depending on whether or not the stylus actually rides in a groove on the disk as on a phonograph record. More well known, despite the overall decline in popularity of these systems during the past several years, is the grooved CED (Capacitance Electronic

Device), manufactured from 1981 to 1984 by the Radio Corporation of America (RCA), now part of General Electric. The manufacturing process, or mastering, is similar to that for optical disks in that a series of "microslots" is created on a vinyl surface that is coated with a metal and then a layer of plastic. The slots as well as the distances between them are varied to convey the video signal. The metal-tipped stylus that reads the recorded data follows tiny grooves, about 10,000 grooves to the inch, and decodes the microslots by detecting the varying capacitance between the tip and the depth of the metal surface as it covers a slot or a space between slots.

Another capacitance system, developed by the Victor Company of Japan (JVC) in conjunction with General Electric in the United States and Thorn EMI in the United Kingdom, uses similar techniques but without the grooves. This Video High-Density (VHD) system uses additional micropits that serve as guides to keep the stylus in line with the correct track of data. The control signals are detectable because the micropits are at a different depth than the depressions that carry the video signal. The VHD system, which was specifically designed to yield the same capabilities for individual frame access as in the CAV laser systems, continues to be successful commercially in Japan.

FILM DISKS

A variation of the laser-read hard-disk system is the film disk developed by McDonnell Douglas and known as Laserfilm. Video and audio signals are recorded by laser on a master disk-shaped film that then can be used to make duplicates using a photographic process. The disks are circular pieces of photographic 0.007-inch film, as thin and pliable as any other piece of film, such as movie film or 35mm slides without the frame. You can see through the film disk, and when the film is held at an angle to the light, you can also see the reflected rainbow pattern associated with the common optical hard disk. The capacity of the McDonnell Douglas film disks is 30,000 video frames or forty hours of audio, or any combination, or eighty-four megabytes of digital data.

The key difference between the film disk and the other optical disks is in the disk production process, or mastering. The source material does not have to be sent to a special production facility where the master disk is created and the duplicates are stamped out. Instead, both the master and the duplicates can be relatively easily and quickly created using the photographic process after the original images or data have been transferred to a disk-image videotape.

Similar to other optical systems, the film disk system can be controlled by an external computer or can incorporate an optional microcomputer that is compatible with the IBM PC. All of the features associated with computer control of individual frames are therefore available, together with the ability to superimpose video over computer-generated graphics, and to play compressed audio to accompany single frames as well as frame sequences.

COMPACT DISKS

Compact disks (CDs) are also optical systems using laser beams, and generally speaking are merely a smaller version of the optical videodisks. Like videodisks, CDs emerged first as a consumer entertainment product. There are at least three differences between the two, however, and the third difference might account for both the greater consumer success of CDs for entertainment purposes and the greater likelihood of their being used for data storage.

The first two differences are obvious. First, CDs are smaller and were introduced as an audio system. The original videodisks were 12 inches in diameter (they now come in other sizes) and contained analog video signals with accompanying analog audio channels, while CDs, using essentially the same technology, had a 4.7-inch diameter and contained audio only. Second, the fact that CDs were an audio product also meant that, unlike videodisks, they were not a departure from existing consumer habits, namely, the purchasing of recorded audio programs. In contrast, videodisks were offered to consumers who were generally not in the habit of buying recorded video.

The third difference is the fact that the audio of CDs is recorded using digital techniques. This might seem like a subtle difference, but it had two major effects. First, the digital techniques do indeed provide a better quality reproduction of a broad range of sounds and thus offer something that was not available in any other medium. A videodisk system may use a laser to record and play the video, but the end result is a video display that is only slightly better than that of a videotape. A compact audio disk, on the other hand, produces a discernable difference. A reviewer wrote in 1979, after listening to one of the first experimental machines, "I can only say that the clarity and definition of every tonal detail—even in the massed chorus in the last movement—seemed almost uncannily real . . . [It] stirred an emotional response I had previously felt only at an actual performance . . . [It] lent the music an aura of sensual immediacy I had not before experienced from any phonograph."[4] It is not surprising, then, that CDs have managed to achieve substantial success in the consumer audio market and are likely eventually to replace vinyl phonograph records, sales of which are already declining in the face of audio cassettes.

The digital nature of CDs, together with physical size similar to floppy diskettes, seems also to have put CDs ahead of videodisks, at least temporarily, with respect to storing digital information of any kind. The CD-ROM, for example, is a compact disk used for digital storage. Because the laser techniques used to date have resulted almost exclusively in disks that cannot be changed once they are manufactured, the initials for read-only memory (ROM) were borrowed from existing computer systems and attached to the CD. The CD-ROM label has not only highlighted the permanent nature of laser disks, but has also differentiated the CDs used for high-quality audio from those used in computer systems for data storage.

Other sets of initials have also been introduced to refer to CD systems—and optical disks in general—when used for data storage that reinforce the archival nature of the disks, including DRAW and WORM, mentioned previously. The initials OROM mean optical read-only memory and can presumably refer to any optical device regardless of size or even shape. In the past, however, the initials meant specifically compact disks that were slightly larger than the usual CD-ROM—5.25

inches instead of 4.7 inches— and contained a data arrangement that permitted faster access than the CD-ROM but fewer data.

The letters CDI, for interactive compact disks, refer to CDs with interactive capabilities, such as the ability to provide random access to any segment of audio or video, rather than data. The functionality of a CDI system overlaps interactive videodisks considerably, with the only essential differences being size and the fact that for the moment the CDI systems do not provide real time video. A CD product that has been announced by Philips and by Sony and that combines music with video on a 4.7-inch CD is the CD-V, or compact disk with video. In the current CD-V product, the video is in the first five minutes of the disk and the remaining twenty minutes contains strictly audio; the video is analog and the audio is digital. Yet another variation is the digital video interactive (DVI) CD-ROM, announced by General Electric's RCA Laboratories, which contains 1.2 hours of full video digitally compressed on a five-inch disk.

The use of CD-ROMs for storing large amounts of textual data, up to 600 megabytes of data per disk, has been helped by a certain amount of agreement regarding standards for the format of the data. Although such standards did not win early and universal acceptance, it now appears that a substantial number of the companies involved in building the systems will jointly support a specific format for defining the logical file structure. In mid-1986 a group of over a dozen major companies known as the High Sierra Group announced their backing for the standard that will be submitted to various standards organizations. The High Sierra Group includes computer companies such as Digital Equipment Corporation and Apple, as well as others usually connected with consumer entertainment systems, such as Philips and Sony.

At present, compact disks in the computer world are being used to sell copies of large data bases, for example, those that have been available on line are now available for purchase on a CD-ROM. In fact, with the proliferating number of such data bases on a disk, the companies that publish directories of on-line data bases are now adding directories of CD data bases. To achieve the timeliness of an on-line service with the local storage of a CD, some vendors offer microcomputer software that reads a local CD for the bulk of the information, but for the most recent data automatically calls out to the related on-line service and down-loads the pertinent data to magnetic disk. Datext offers such an arrangement encompassing the equivalent of over ten million pages of corporate financial information issued on CDs every month, integrated with optional on-line access to the Dow Jones News/Retrieval service. In 1987, Lotus Development Corporation, with a similar service of compact disks mailed weekly and daily updates available on-line or transmitted by FM radio, agreed to acquire Datext from its parent, Cox Enterprises.

The companies that are publishing the CD textual data bases are well aware of what might be possible with combinations of text, audio, and video. One of these companies, Grolier Electronic Publishing, has provided on-line access to its data base containing the text of a full encyclopedia, and now publishes that encyclopedia on a CD for less than the cost of the printed version. In addition, it has been working on a videodisk version that does not replicate the printed arrangement.[5] Instead, the audiovisual version seeks to make the most of the different method of presentation.

DIGITIZED VIDEO

The technologies of laser videodisks, CEDs, CDs, CD-ROM, CDI, and CD-V have all been used, or proposed for use, for purposes that sought to capitalize on the technology itself. Concentration on the particular technology should not be allowed to obscure the ultimate result, however, and the fact that a given result may be producible in several ways. Video and computer-generated text and graphics may be combined using a laser disk system, but the same thing can also be done with digitized video stored on a magnetic medium such as a microcomputer's hard disk or a floppy disk.

As explained in earlier chapters, a frame of video can be divided into a matrix of pixels, or discrete picture elements, and numbers representing each point can be stored digitally. As the cost of chips declines and more microcomputer graphics cards are offered for digitizing video, it becomes increasingly easier to create videobases on personal computers without using videodisks or compact disks. In fact, several products are available for microcomputers that facilitate the creation and searching of photo or image data bases, or simply videobases, where everything is digitally stored on floppy disks or hard disks. Typically, the photographlike image appears in an area of the screen probably less than one-fourth of the total, with text or other graphics surrounding the image. The software to manage the videobase may be a proprietary product or may enable the data base to be structured and queried using more common software such as DBase II or III, R:Base 5000 or IBM's Filing Assistant. Similar videobase software for mainframes is also becoming available. The Computer Corporation of America's announcement in mid-1986 of the ability of its mainframe data base software, Model 204, to process images reportedly marked the first of such products. To view the images, a microcomputer is used as the receiving terminal. In between the micro and the mainframe, at the workstation level, systems combine three-dimensional modeling with photographic images, such as Genisco Computer Corporation's Gbase and various medical imaging and computer-assisted design systems.

The reasons for using one technology over the other can be summed up in digital capacity and available hardware, and the effect of those two elements on acceptable cost. There are limits on the amount of digital information a microcomputer or workstation can store on hard disks and effectively retrieve and process in order to produce rapidly changing screen displays. The requirements for storing and displaying a video frame, or a sequence of video frames in real time (e.g., at thirty frames per second in the U.S.) are more easily met at present by an analog videodisk than by a system of digitized video on magnetic media. Some of the videobase applications that have been suggested for interactive videodisks involving a limited number of still frames, however, can be accomplished equally well using some of the digitized video methods mentioned above, where the digitized video is stored on computer memory chips or magnetic disks.

RELATED METHODS

Some laser optical systems also employ shapes other than disks. Still others are not strictly optical or strictly electromagnetic, but a combination of the two techniques, such as magneto-optics or thermomagneto-optics.

One of the laser-read devices that is not disk shaped is a card produced by Drexler Technology called the LaserCard. Like the optical disk, the card is permanently written using a laser. About the size of a conventional credit card, the laser cards or "smart cards" are promoted as a way for people to carry conveniently a great deal of digitized information, perhaps for retail, banking, or medical applications.

Going a step further, magneto-optics is put forward as a technical way to produce erasable optical media. In a system being developed by the 3M Company, recording takes place when a relatively strong laser beam warms a tiny spot over a magnet below the spinning disk. Molecules in the metal coating on the disk change their orientation then to that of the magnet. Like normal videodisks, reflected low-power laser light is processed to reconstruct the signal or pattern that was written. The magneto-optic disks can be erased by applying an opposite current to the magnet at the same time that the writing laser again warms the surface. As this is being written, magneto-optics, and other methods, such as a Philips disk with ordered crystals that can be reheated, still have problems that make them less desirable for computer storage than existing alternatives. For example, the access time is slower, or the error rate is too high, or the material is not as durable as electromagnetic disks under continuous read/write conditions. Kodak, however, has demonstrated a prototype 3.5-inch erasable thermo-magneto-optic disk that, when available in a double-sided configuration, will store up to 50 megabytes with a reasonable access time; and Sony Corporation has developed a 5.12-inch erasable magneto-optic disk to hold 325 megabytes per side.

Finally, some videodisks use electromagnetic rather than optical technology, and thus have all the read/write capabilities of a magnetic disk but are smaller than compact disks yielding less storage space. The Still Video Floppy Disc from Sony is about the thickness of a 3.5-inch microfloppy, but is only about

2 inches in diameter. It is intended primarily as an electronic slide show system and can only hold twenty-five full video frames, or fifty frames of noninterlaced video. The still-video camera from Canon similarly records up to fifty color pictures on a disk; the resulting pictures can either be viewed on a video display or transmitted to a printer that will produce the usual photographic print. Other prototype still-video cameras have been shown by Nikon, Fuji, and Chinon. Kodak has also been working on a floppy disk camera, but suggested in 1985 that it would be ten years before the quality of Kodachrome would be duplicated on a floppy disk or videotape system for the consumer market.[6]

The rest of this chapter focuses on what has been done and what might be done using the interactive video capabilities occasioned by the technologies surveyed above.

Spatial Data Management

The ability to use video and graphics as a tool in information systems was outlined in the first chapter, and one of the most important uses is to provide a sense of spatial orientation. Although almost all computer data bases available contain no mechanism for suggesting a spatial orientation between the seeker and the location of information, the possibilities for providing the seeker with an idea of where to look in computerized data bases has been acknowledged for some time.

THE DATALAND CONCEPT

One of the longest-running endeavors to create a spatial data-management system (SDMS) using video and graphics displays has been that of the Massachusetts Institute of Technology's Architecture Machine Group, established within the School of Architecture and Planning in 1971. The spatial data management experiments, which have been detailed in several books and numerous articles, began in the mid-1970s first under a contract with the Office of Naval Research followed by a contract with the Defense Advanced Research Projects Agency, and continues within the Architecture Machine Group's successor organization, the Media Laboratory at MIT's Center for Arts and Media Technology.[7]

The researchers at MIT over the years have employed interactive videodisks, touchscreen monitors, a large screen rear-projection display, touch-sensitive pads, joysticks, an electronic stylus and tablet, and a microphone and stereo speakers to create a visual data base, or videobase, that not only incorporated motion, pictures, and text but also used the visual arrangement to convey a sense of space. The configuration consisted of a special room—the media room—where a person could sit in a control chair and, through visual and audio effects, "move" through Dataland (Fig. 4.1). The intent was that persons should be able to find information by going to it in a synthetic projected space, instead of interrogating a computerized data base by typed commands. Within the general conceptual framework, the media room was also originally created as a defense agency project to address the use of technology as an aid to military command and control.

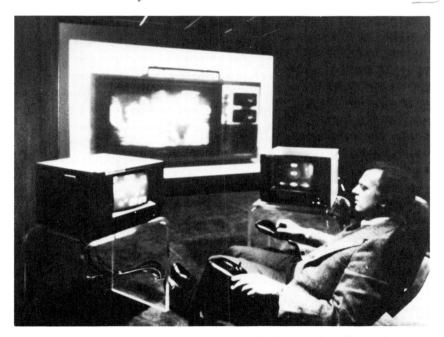

Figure 4.1. MIT's media room. A large screen is at the front, and smaller touch screens are on either side of the operator's chair. Joysticks are installed in the arms of the chair. (Courtesy of the Massachusetts Institute of Technology Media Laboratory.)

The physical apparatus provided a number of different ways to do things as well as a constant reference to the spatial arrangement of the world within the video screen—Dataland. The occupant of the chair (the voyager) viewed the spatial arrangement of the elements of Dataland, with graphics or icons indicating the contents of collections of items, and moved about or zoomed in and out by manipulating a joystick on the arm of the chair. A touchscreen to the user's right continually displayed an overview, or top view, of the entire Dataland, while a touchscreen on the left was used to interact with specified items such as "opening" a book, selecting a slide, or pressing the buttons on a calculator. The joystick on the right arm of the chair controlled movement across the plane of Dataland, and the joystick on the left controlled the zoom. The ten-foot screen in front of the chair displayed that portion of Dataland that the user was interested in at the time.

If, for example, the user wished to move across the Dataland plane to an icon of a book, the right joystick would be pressed until the book icon came into view on the front screen. Then the left joystick would be pressed to enlarge the icon until the book image was in focus and large enough to read the title. (Movement across the planes could also be effected with less elapsed time by touching the desired arrival spot on the right monitor instead of using the joystick.) On the right monitor, the user would see a rectangle indicating the location similarly moving across the overview screen. On the left touchscreen monitor, the user would see the full image of the book cover together with a table of contents or other index that could be touched to cause the relevant page to appear. To flip through pages individually, the user would make a diagonal finger motion on the touch-sensitive pad located on either arm of the chair near the joysticks. On the monitor on the left, a quick sequence of shadows would flicker across the screen, creating the distinct impresssion that pages were actually turning.

In addition to all the visual cues about spatial orientation and movement, sound effects from several speakers were used such that a sound associated with an object would become louder as the user drew nearer. The movement of the user past items could be reinforced by directing the sounds to speakers on one side and then on the other side of the front screen. The sounds were also used for identification purposes to the extent that those familiar with Dataland could move about and keep track of their relative location not by looking at the overview monitor on the right, but by listening to sounds.

The content of Dataland, for demonstration purposes, contained a mixture of things ranging from distinct collections of items to more general functions such as telephoning. There were, for instance, maps, books, letters and other documents, slides, photographs, logos, a calculator, a television, a telephone, and so on. Each type of item could be located and then examined in detail or otherwise used by virtue of the zooming joystick and the lefthand touchscreen. Maps lent themselves to a considerable amount of zooming, as Dataland contained a collection of images ranging from Landsat photos to slides of individual buildings. Starting with an image of northeastern United States, Dataland contained Landsat-generated displays showing the New England coast, the coast of Massachusetts, the greater Boston area and suburbs, and central Boston. This could then be followed by a graphic map of Boston, a map of a Boston neighborhood, and pictures or slides of buildings. The demonstration contained some 200 slides of Boston buildings, stored as still frames on a videodisk.

Books and other documents have already been mentioned, but it is worth noting that the technical capabilities of Dataland gave the researchers the chance to create new forms of books by mixing sound and video, including motion video, with the more traditional text. In fact, this is one of the more intriguing possibilities for videobases, or information systems with the capacity for video, graphics, and text. We are very familiar with the way that illustrations are included on pages of paper texts, and we know exactly what to expect when we read a book with illustrations. We are also just as familiar now with the visual displays of television, movies, slide shows, overheads, and the like. Therefore we can imagine a "book" on a screen where "reading" a particular section causes a short motion segment optionally to take over and explain something in more detail, reinforce a point, or give us the real image and voice of a historical figure. It is also possible that there are other, more subtle outcomes of the use of videobases that we are only beginning to glimpse.

An example of a mixture that was tried by Dataland and that involved juxtaposition of text and graphics (but not motion video) was business letters. These could be received as strings of standard text characters, but before display, the text would be superimposed on an image called up from a videodisk of a paper containing the appropriate organization's logo. The result was a letter that looked like a letter, but only because part of it came from the author and the other part, which could have required much more transmission capacity or time than the message, came from a locally stored collection of backgrounds. This concept, of an end product that appears with the right structure and appearance only because the parties using the system agree as to who supplies what, is increasingly coming into use. Companies and individuals who are required to file certain forms with the government, for example the Securities and Exchange Commission or the Internal Revenue Service, can use personal computer programs that contain within themselves the structure and arrangement of the form, but only the data are actually conveyed to the government, where an identical structure is used to view the document.

Another set of items on the Dataland plane were instruments such as a television, telephone, and calculator. When the user zoomed in on the graphic of the television, the large screen in front displayed a picture of a real television set in increasing detail, until the screen of the television filled the Dataland display screen. This would then show whatever was on the television set; for example, the signal feeding the television set would be feeding the display screen directly. In the demonstration system, the television programs that were available were not actually from live off-the-air television, but were segments of shows recorded on a videodisk. Because the videodisk could be controlled in an interactive manner, the left touchscreen contained graphically illustrated controls for frame access, freeze frame, slow and fast motion, and forward and reverse.

The other physical devices depicted in Dataland, the telephone and the calculator, were provided as suggestions of what might be done, as there was actually no dial-out capability for the telephone in the earlier versions of Dataland, and nobody really thought a calculator image on a touchscreen was a superior replacement for a real calculator. In later stages, users could not only dial out but could do so by voice command.

The content of Dataland was enhanced by the notion

that persons not only look and read things, but talk about them and jot notes on them. Thus the technical devices of the media room included an electronic stylus and a microphone. With the tablet, stylus, and an image of something projected on the front screen, the user could annotate the image with literally anything that could be printed or drawn in an optional selection of colors. As the annotations were assumed to be just that, and not a form of an electronic paintbox, the display was done so that they seemed transparent and did not obliterate the underlying image. The annotations were also stored so that the original image could continue to be viewed without them, or with them in a succession of layers. Spoken annotations could also be recorded and individually invoked when returning to specified spots within a document or image.

RESEARCH RESULTS

The Dataland experiments tested assumptions and produced a number of insights. The results reinforce the belief that people like to stick to familiar representations and quickly grasped concepts, and like to accomplish things as easily as possible. In addition, gadgets like joysticks are not necessarily the easiest way. Specifically, the more involved and complex arrangements of Dataland found less acceptance than the simple arrangement of a single plane containing everything that could be accessed. Of course, each item could also be increased in detail using the zoom feature, but that is a different effect than in the more complicated arrangements where users had to descend to subplanes containing their own sets of items, sub-subplanes, and so on. Users also did not necessarily like moving across the plane using the joystick, as if playing a video game. Instead, repeat users of Dataland tended to prefer the touchscreen on the right simply to touch an item to access it. For their part, beginners did use the joysticks to travel across the land, but relied on the overview monitor to give a constant picture of the entire collection much more than on the close-up images on the large front screen.

The researchers concluded that a spatial orientation was extremely advantageous but that it should not be much more than a "sufficient" idea of space, a minimum indication that would cause each user to form an individualized internal sense of orientation and relationships, rather than a fully detailed space. The more detailed and extensive displays defining a specific layout were believed to cause more trouble in that increasing detail and complexity would tend either to conflict with a given user's sense of how things should be, or would at least require more effort to understand.

One of the assumptions that guided the construction of the media room and that was, according to the researchers, reinforced by subsequent experiences, was that the items stored in Dataland should be eminently recognizable. A book should look like a book, a telelphone like a telephone, a slide tray like a slide tray. Because the essence of the project was to create a space in which stored information could be retrieved as immediately, comfortably, and efficiently as possible, users should not have to waste time learning what the visual symbols might mean or how to manipulate them. The assumption was perhaps proved correct in that novices, on their first time in the media room, were able to understand what they were looking at and how to use it in less than a minute.

The lessons of Dataland, created with interactive videodisks, digitized images, and extensive graphics along with sound, seem to have been incorporated into the design of the basic display of some computer systems. The Xerox Star and Apple Macintosh, and all related types of displays, use essentially a single-plane arrangement of graphically represented items, although there is also the facility for grouping items together into a collection. For example, documents can be represented by a graphic image or icon (icons are discussed in the next chapter at more length) and can also be grouped together into a "file folder" and represented by the single icon for the file folder. This does not really represent a different plane, though; like the final arrangement of Dataland, it is merely an instance of items being available for detailed inspection.

In addition to exploring the benefits of spatial orientation, Dataland examined ways to manipulate the display using voice recognition, gesturing, and eye-movement tracking. With voice recognition, the user could speak to Dataland, such as to give a name to an object, open a book, or move an item about the screen, and the system would respond correctly. This style of speaker-dependent voice recognition, of course, is no longer restricted to research laboratories and can be purchased for use with personal computers, especially for the relatively simple procedure of substituting spoken words for a selected number of usually typed commands. An example is replacing the MS-DOS commands available on personal computers using that operating system.

The Dataland system also could respond to gestures and eye movements. As noted above, users could do certain things such as turn the pages of a book by making a motion on a touch-sensitive pad. In later stages, users could move an item from one place to another by pointing at the object displayed on the front screen and then pointing to the preferred location for that item while saying something like, "Put that there." The pointing motion was tracked by a small device attached to the user's wrist and connected by a thin cord to a slightly larger stationary device, which in turn transmitted coordinates to a computer. As the orientation of the fixed-location device would be known to the computer, the movement of the user's wrist could be tracked by determining changes in the relationship between electromagnetic fields in both the wrist and the trans-mitting devices.

Along the same lines, eye movements were tracked and could be combined with voice commands to select and manip-ulate items in Dataland. Several methods of eye tracking were tested, including special glasses that bounced an infrared light beam off the cornea to measure eye movement relative to the glasses themselves. To complete the tracking capabilities, the motion-sensitive device that could be worn on the wrist also was attached to the eyeglass frames. This gave the wearer the ability to look anywhere around the large frontal display and select items or locations simply by looking at them, as long as items were far enough apart to cause the eyeglass system to detect a movement.

ADAPTATIONS

The concepts developed at the media laboratory have not been confined to MIT. A somewhat similar spatial data-management system was created by Computer Corporation of America (CCA), also during the late 1970s and also under a contract with the Defense Advanced Research Projects Agency, and used concepts borrowed from MIT's Dataland.

The CCA system, called View, was begun in 1977 and was initially designed to contain a data base of information on United States and Soviet ships, including an interactive videodisk containing maps of oceans and seas so that actual ship locations could be superimposed over detailed maps. The physical arrangement of View was more compact than the MIT media room in that there was no large screen display. Instead, three desktop monitors were used. The left monitor contained the overview, the middle monitor provided the detailed view, and the right monitor displayed commands typed on an attached keyboard.

The differences between Dataland and View can generally be attributed to the differences between a laboratory environment and a limited-resource working location such as on board a ship, as well as to the incorporation of an existing data base of textual information with existing procedures for using a keyboard to query the data base. Contrary to the conclusions reached at MIT, the View system also opted to contain a number of hierarchical planes whereby users could "pop" up or down among them rather than staying essentially on one surface. As a result, the overview monitor displayed only the overview of the plane currently in use, which might have been several levels below the topmost plane. On a given plane, the spatial orientation graphically depicted on the overview monitor was not necessarily elaborate. In fact, the display could be a very orderly set of tables, with horizontal and vertical lines dividing the tables like a tic-tac-toe screen. The entries in the tables could be words or perhaps icons for types of ships or other entities.

Access to the data involved both the joystick approach of moving and zooming, and more traditional keyboard queries. A typed request could be made for all items that matched a number of criteria, and the resulting set would be graphically displayed on the overview monitor. In this situation, the spatial orientation was dynamically generated, depending upon the collection of items matching the criteria in the query. This meant that the user had many spatial relationships among the items instead of one fixed orientation. To the extent that users felt comfortable with it, this represents a feature that should not be overlooked; namely, that the benefit of using graphics to depict a spatial relationship does not necessarily mean that the relationships must be fixed. Instead, we can use ad hoc spatial orientations to see the relationships among subsets of items, while adhering to only a very general spatial orientation for a data base as a whole.

Geographic Surrogates

The concept of spatial orientation for everything accessible within an electronic information system can be implemented in any number of imaginative ways, but the most obvious is in terms of real geographic location. The portion of Dataland that encompassed real locations, such as buildings within Boston within the coast of Massachusetts, represents only one of a great many uses of graphics and video, and especially inter-active optical disks, to create videobases that are geographic surrogates.

Geographic-based videobases have been accomplished in several different ways. At one level, geography can be a useful distinction in organizing information that is categorized by geographic boundaries. Census information is a good example. A map of the country can be used to represent the summary statistics, while zooming in or popping down to individual states, counties, townships, boroughs, and so on would restrict the statistics to the region selected. With interactive videodisks, motion video segments can also be selected at will to such an extent that the user experiences a sense of actually traveling, or at least of guiding a camera through a real space. Instead of visiting a location, the user of a geographic surrogate system is able to choose the direction of travel within the confines of the images contained by the system. Beyond that, these systems can stretch the reality a bit by combining video segments from several geographic locations, or depart from reality completely by portraying an entirely fictitious geography.

TRAVELOG

At the most basic level, video segments can be used to show a real location, such as a travelog. As mentioned in the first chapter, an early example was a demonstration videodisk created by Sony from video segments shot in Hawaii. The overall orientation is provided by a map of the Hawaiian Islands, and users can choose any island. This results in the display of a map of the designated island, with numbers and words indicating the locations of tourist attractions or general tourist information (Fig. 4.2). Choosing a specific tourist attraction causes the system to play a short video "commercial" or informative segment for that attraction. This is a useful way to arrange any type of travel information or data relevant to a geographic location.

Interactive videodisk systems have been used to link together mini-travelogs of all sorts. In the travel business, however, given the much greater popularity and lower cost of videotapes, travel videos are more likely to be video cassettes.

Figure 4.2. Sony's Hawaii disk. Four attractions are listed on the island of Hawaii. Selecting any one of the four leads to a motion video segment about that attraction. (Courtesy of Sony Corporation of America.)

DIRECTIONAL MOTION

One of the earliest and perhaps best known examples of an interactive videodisk system depicting directional motion was also mentioned previously, the so-called Aspen disk or interactive movie map produced by the same Architecture Machine Group at MIT that developed Dataland.

Aspen, Colorado, was chosen as the location to be immortalized, and cameras videotaped the entire town, capturing one frame every nine feet. In addition, slides were shot of individual buildings and of the interiors of selected buildings, even some in several seasons. Historical photographs of a few buildings were also gathered. All of these images were put on a videodisk under the control of a program that permitted the user, or viewer, to select which way to turn when moving down a street or approaching an intersection. The system gave the user the freedom to "travel" anywhere in Aspen, and to stop along a street at will and turn to the side to see a full view of a building. For certain locations, the many slides and historical photographs enabled the traveler to go inside and to travel through time, while staying in place, to different seasons and even to earlier years.

The spatial organization in this and similar systems is naturally geographic, as the intent of the interactive system is to represent faithfully the real thing. The systems succeed to the extent that you feel that you are actually in the filmed location, seeing it exactly as it really is, and perhaps imagining that you are guiding a camera at that very moment through and around the distant location.

There are several ways, though, to enhance the user's perception of the spatial arrangement, even given the obvious geographic basis. In the Aspen videodisk system, overviews were available in the form of aerial photographs, graphic maps, and graphic overlays indicating relative location. The driver at the console selected where to begin a tour by touching the desired spot on one of the maps or aerial photographs, and immediately was at street level ready to move. The subsequent movement was tracked on an overlay at the top of one monitor showing the driver's path relative to the main streets of Aspen. On a second monitor, a detailed graphic map of Aspen contained an expanded method of tracking progressive moves through the city. Even for persons who had never been to Aspen, the sense of knowing where they were was strong because of the visual summation of the locale—the maps—and the dynamic plotting of location relative to the whole.

The Aspen system also included some twists to the conventional sense of travel (beyond the relatively minor capacity for travel through time). Because the entire system was under computer control, it was not difficult to add preselected travel. Instead of using the touchscreen or joystick to drive through the city, users could preselect a path by touching a sequence of spots on the map. They could then sit back and be driven through Aspen along the selected route, with an option for interrupting at any point if desired.

There are now quite a few examples of geographically arranged videobases using interactive video, some of which evolved from earlier collections of slides, photographs, or other film images and were created for practical purposes. Most of the states in the United States, for instance, maintain libraries of pictures of the state road systems. In Connecticut, to pick one, all state highways and rail lines have been filmed every 0.01 mile in both directions, which is nearly one million images. In an effort to create a system that would simulate travel to the extent of reducing the number of field trips to check road sites, the images were put on videodisks to be viewed interactively with overlays containing details of the physical environment, the date of the photograph, and even graphic additions to the image, such as to highlight a trouble condition. The system has reportedly indeed achieved the goal of reducing field trips.[8]

While in this example and in the Aspen disk system users experienced a sense of motion by viewing frames in rapid succession, a geographic orientation is possible with data bases of still frames. A more recent example, using CD-ROM disks rather than the larger videodisks, is the Atlas disk from De-Lorme Mapping Systems. All of the frames are arranged hierarchically in terms of detail, with sixteen levels. At the top level, when the system is turned on, a map of the world appears. A user can then select an area and move to increasing detail, as essentially one quadrant of the previous level becomes the full screen of the next level. In recognition of the fact that experienced users of any information system are always looking for faster access, the DeLorme system also allows users to type in latitude, longitude, and desired scale in order to call up a map section immediately.

The preceding examples suggest several guiding principles that should be kept in mind, namely, the power of the familiar and keeping the focus on the functionality. For example, at first glance, it appears that the Atlas disk violates one of the conclusions of the Dataland experiments. The Atlas disk apparently has many more levels of zoom than might seem practical based on Dataland. The difference, though, is that the Atlas disk is restricted to a real and very familiar geographic orientation, while Dataland encompassed many forms of information and communication. Users of the Atlas disk know the exact spatial orientation at each level, either because they know the area or because they know in principle what to expect. In fact, the geographic orientation with increasing detail may not represent levels at all in the same way as in Dataland. It is quite possible to see the overall map as a single level, and the increase in details merely a way of taking a closer look at the one level. Thus the geographic nature of the Atlas disk may indeed be in agreement with the Dataland findings.

The second point to remember is that emphasis should be on the overall functionality, not only as it exists but as it could be. In the highway department application, as successful as the laser videodisk might be, it still has drawbacks given the current stage of development. The quantity of images, for one thing, means that at least fifteen disks must be used, and unless the disks are housed in some sort of jukebox arrangement or in a stacked arrangement with several reading mechanisms, an operator must still select the right disk, which is the same idea as selecting a role of microfilm or a file of photographs. More important, the ideal system would allow the highway department continually to update the videobase by taking a photograph or videotape of a site as soon as repairs are made or any other changes take place and adding the new images to the videobase. Such a capability may be possible with digital imaging systems or with optical systems that have either write-once or continuous read/write capabilities, but not with traditional videodisks. In any case, the technologies are just beginning to offer the full range of capability required.

MODIFYING REALITY

Moving beyond the geographic orientation of a real locale, interactive videodisks have been created that use real locations but assembled in a fictitious orientation.

Several years ago, Maritz Communications produced a videodisk for the Ford Motor Company that was intended to help car dealers become familiar with videodisk technology, with a disk that was essentially a golf game. The video displayed a person, showing only the shoes, walking up to a tee. Using graphics, the player was asked to select a club and determine the amount of force to use, how to swing the club, and a few other details of the game. The video next showed the ball being hit, and, depending upon the detail chosen—the ball landing on the fairway, behind a tree, in a sandtrap, or the like. Graphics were also used to show the layout of each hole and a player's progress. The video segments relating to each hole and the graphics diagramming each hole were taken from real locations, with each hole actually from a different golf course and chosen for its reputation as a noteworthy representative of its particular course.

Once again, the familiar was present. Users, or players, could readily understand the spatial orientation because the model was familiar and did not violate any assumptions about the golf course as a whole or how it should be arranged. The entire fictitious course contained the correct number of holes in the proper order, and with characteristics that could be found in any single golf course just about anywhere. The fact that the video displays and individual hole layouts were from real and famous courses did nothing to diminish the sense of familiarity with the arrangement. Rather than hinder the appreciation of the arrangement, the selection of parts of different golf courses added to the users' acceptance of the game. Players knew that the video segments were from different courses, and could look forward to seeing the different fairways and greens as much as to actually playing the holes. Moreover, the selection of courses and holes gave the player the sense of playing the best of the best.

IMAGINARY LANDSCAPES

Finally, taking the geographic orientation one step beyond the mixing of real locations, the geography of a videobase can be entirely fictitious.

Perhaps the most obvious examples in this group are from the games based on interactive videodisks. In many senses, interactive videodisks are only an extension of the video games using graphics and are only a temporary step in the progression of continually improving computer graphics. In any event, whether the display comes from a videodisk or a digitally created graphic stored on a hard disk or in computer memory, a game with spatial dimensions creates a logically consistent geography for the players, even when the geography includes black holes, time warps, magic movement, trapdoors, or other procedure for suddenly being in a different location.

A synthetic or imaginary geography can also be used in a more prosaic environment, and is often based on a sense of a real location or type of location that would be familiar. In a prototype interactive videobase for shopping, a unit of Warner Communications created in the early 1980s a shopping mall environment using graphics and interactive videodisks intended for display in the home by way of cable television networks. The overall arrangement of the mall, as well as the layout of each store, was done with simple computer graphics. Once within a store, several spatial arrangements were used to indicate specific items graphically, depending upon the number of items in that area of the store. Once an item was selected, the videodisk system would display either a simple picture of the item or a short video segment describing the item and its features in more detail.

One of the criticisms of this prototype was that it portrayed a small number of stores with relatively small numbers of items. The fictitious geographic arrangement was workable on that scale, but what would happen with more stores and many more items added to the arrangement? In 1981 Sears and Roebuck tested a videodisk catalog of over 5600 items and opted to structure it as just that, a catalog with no other spatial orientation. The question still has no definitive answer, primarily because not enough experience with very large videobases encompassing synthetic geographies has been accumulated. The answer may involve, once again, the notion of familiarity. As graphically oriented computer systems become more common, it is quite likely that visual procedures for arranging even the largest of imaginary spaces will be developed, albeit not necessarily in the same fashion as the early prototypes.

Interactive Video at Work

The previous section covered the general aspect of spatial orientation and the nature of geographic orientation made possible by interactive videodisks, compact disks, and the like. Most of the applications for existing videobases, however, and especially interactive videodisks, have been in areas where spatial orientation is not a significant factor, such as interactive training courses.

This section summarizes the applications that currently account for much of the work in interactive videodisks and other forms of videobases. Although most of the ones mentioned rely on videodisks for images, it should be noted that other storage media such as compact disks can be used. For example, in a somewhat unusual coalition, Apple Computer is working jointly with both National Geographic and film director George Lucas's Lucasfilm to research the possibilities of putting film on compact disks for educational purposes, games, or something similar.

Some of the applications listed are also being accomplished using more mundane media such as videotape. The once-bright future of the videodisk, proposed by a 1983 *Business Week* article[9] as the medium of the 1980s, has dimmed somewhat in the few years since. Achievements in manipulating video, voice, and data continue to merit study, however, as indications of the directions that are being pursued irrespective of an individual technology or type of machine.

TRAINING AND EDUCATION

The dominant single application for interactive videodisks in the recent past probably was in training and education, especially industrial training. There may be some good reasons why, other than the fact that industrial trainers have been more successful at finding funds and justifying the costs. According to one observer, interactive video as provided in a videodisk system is well suited to training programs because (1) the system can combine video, sound (alone or with video), and dynamic computer-generated displays; (2) students can be prompted or led interactively based on their responses; and (3) the system combines the well-known aspects of audiovisual aides with the now equally well-known capability of the computer.[10] Of course, many of the instructional videodisks that have been produced cover visual subject matter, from instructions on making paper airplanes to repairing a U.S. Army tank to adjusting a pacemaker for a human heart.

In the early years of interactive videodisk training, the cost of the systems was often justified as a means of providing an environment as close to the real thing as possible without using a much more expensive real piece of equipment or situation. In the military and in industry, for example, interactive videodisks can simulate to some extent the experience of using a hardware system that is costly in itself, costly in time taken away from production for training purposes, or costly because the system would be damaged or destroyed by a trainee's mistake.

Numerous subjects have been adapted to videodisk treatment, although some areas are more represented than others. One of the leading suppliers of interactive videodisks, Interactive Training Systems Inc. (ITS), has produced over ninety disks for standard training, most of which are on computer-related topics from understanding mainframe operating systems to using spread sheets on personal computers. For customized training, ITS created disks concerning such things as management techniques, financial planning, customer service support, helicopter flying, circuit board inspection, and the use of CAD systems.

On an industry basis, the automotive industry is reputedly the leader in using interactive videodisks for training.[11] Ford, General Motors, and Chrysler all use videodisks to train and educate employees on technical, managerial, and environmental topics. In one study involving 130 service technicians at Ford, the videodisk course reduced training time by 90 percent over previous methods, and the trainees scored an average of 89.6 percent on a postcourse test, compared to 67.2 percent on a precourse test. The statistics could have been affected by the novelty of the method, but the more compelling result of the study is that over two-thirds of the trainees said that they would prefer all training to be on interactive videodisks rather than other media. Thus for the near term, these may generally be more welcome as a training tool than other methods.

Videodisks are also being used for solving specific problems. At Chrysler, an interactive videodisk/computer system is being developed that can be brought to a defective piece of equipment so that the computer can analyze the problem and then use the videodisk to demonstrate to a technician how to repair it.

In addition to the multiplicity of topics in interactive videodisk training, a considerable variety of techniques, such as video, audio, computer graphics, graphics over video, and straight text, can be combined in numerous ways. For example, some instructional disks use only still frames of video, including pictures and text, and computer-generated text to provide the indexes and to ask the questions. At the other end of the scale, video segments with studio quality and Hollywood special effects are used to capture trainees' interest as completely as possible. In between are creative combinations of video, audio, and computer-generated graphics and text.

SALES AND PRODUCT DEMONSTRATIONS

Another major area for interactive video is in sales and product demonstrations, although the success of automated video vendors as applied to retail has thus far been mixed. In practice, interactive video fills much the same role as the videotape displays that have been used from supermarkets to high-fashion dress shops. The purpose of the display is to attract customers and promote sales. To the extent that the unattended videotape machine attracts passers-by while the interactive machine needs someone to use the device in order to display the depth of information within, the less expensive noninteractive display has the advantage. On the other hand, interactive video has been successful in retail applications where the videodisk can contain a much larger selection of items that is available on the shelves, and in situations where the customer tends to believe the videodisk but doubts the impartiality of a salesperson, such as perhaps in car sales.

Although it is hard to single out particular areas in which interactive video is being broadly used to sell products or services, the financial industry has been suggested as a good place to begin. Banks and financial organizations have been experimenting with a number of interactive technologies, including videodisks. They have used private locations such as bank lobbies and public locations such as shopping malls and airports to promote financial services, as competition has increased overall in banking and investing.

Two of the suggested benefits of videodisks in retail banking are the ability to educate customers on the intricacies of current products and the ability to cross-promote products. Both of these reasons stem from recent changes in banking and the fact the most customers still have traditional views about the industry. Banks now have many more products to offer to the average customer, but are not generally structured to lead customers from one to another. Moreover, in some cases, even bank employees do not fully understand the products enough to explain them readily to inquiring customers.

AREA DIRECTORIES

Although not widespread, area directories have appeared in the form of public information terminals or kiosks, such as guides to shopping malls, convention centers, and even cities. These kiosks sometimes use motion video to supplement computer graphics. In this application area, it is obviously possible to provide geographic information and use spatial orientation. The fact that these systems provide geographic information has not necessarily meant that they use a spatial orientation as the primary arrangement, though. Many use more commonplace lists, or menus, to categorize information, whether it is the textual description of a place, a graphic map, or a video message from the mayor. At the same time, some conference center systems are attempting to serve as primarily computer terminals for conference participants to send electronic mail, post messages on an electronic bulletin board, or access a computer at the home office. Therefore spatial orientation for the organization of the information, based on the building or the conference center, may not be the most useful arrangement.

REAL ESTATE

Another fledgling application area for interactive graphics and videobases is real estate. Because current real estate operations rely heavily on images and maps, almost all on paper, it seems natural that electronic versions should be welcome, especially if the images can be produced, managed, and distributed faster and more economically.

The costs of creating, managing, and distributing video images have not yet become attractive enough to convince real estate boards and agencies to substitute color video monitors for the multiple-listing books, however.

As is the case with most applications involving videobases, several different technologies have been tried, from analog to digitized images, laser videodisks, and laser film disks. Using more traditional analog video, for example, a number of real estate organizations are testing half-hour broadcast television shows to display properties, much as the cable television shopping channels seem to be much more successful than computerized shopping services.

Real estate images have also been stored in digitized form on conventional computer disk systems and displayed on video screens accompanied by computer-generated text and graphics. One national real estate company maintains a centralized file of photographs sent in by affiliated agencies. The data accompanying each photograph are keyed into a separate computerized data base so that other agencies can ask for properties matching certain criteria in a given location and eventually receive a facsimile version of the photographs for each property. Obviously, when economically practical, these same photographs can be digitized and stored in an indexed data base of images so that agents anywhere in the country can call up images at will.

VIDEO PRODUCTION

A somewhat different use of interactive videodisks, now that the time required to create the disk itself is diminishing, is in television and film production. Once a film or videotape is copied to a disk, each frame is immediately accessible to editors. Computer-controlled editing stations can be used to review and rearrange segments endlessly until the producer, director, or editor is satisfied with the results. The EditDroid is a videodisk-based electronic editing station that has been used for movie and television production. If a movie is being shot on film, the film is converted daily to videotape, and the tapes are subsequently copied to videodisk so that all available footage is on the disk. Editing is done on the EditDroid until the final arrangement is determined, which is then used to produce the completed film.

Eventually, interactive information and entertainment systems will also be able to mix and match images to create visual segments built from a collection of material depicting the same thing from a number of angles in a variety of ways. We might even develop an art form where each viewer really does see a unique version of a movie or videotape, depending on individual choices.

VIDEO COMMUNICATION

To complete the categorization, if video images can be stored as part of real estate or personnel files, product catalogs, and any of dozens of other applications and transmitted electronically, it is only a small step to include images that are captured, digitized, and transmitted in real time, or only slightly slower than real time. Ever since the earliest days of television, inventors have been working on ways to achieve two-way video communication. One of the drawbacks has been that the lines that are connected to most telephones cannot handle the band-width and the high data rates required for motion video. If images are transmitted at somewhat slower rates, however, digitized images from data bases or from live cameras can be moved readily along standard telephone lines.

There are a number of different approaches to such video communication other than increasing the bandwidth of the transmission path with, for example, fiberoptics, or decreasing the bandwidth requirement through digital compression tech-niques. Several products are available for microcomputers that transmit images in about a minute or so, and permit users at a distant microcomputer to see edits or changes made at the originating microcomputer.

Photomail from Chorus Data Systems supports such ac-tivities as well as alternate voice/data communication so that the changes can also be discussed by voice (Fig. 4.3). For digital image distribution on a wider scale, the Compuserve network offers subscribers the ability to transmit camera-fed images around the international network as long as the receiving per-sonal computers have the appropriate decoding software. For more local applications using networks with wider bandwidths, video communication with color and real-time motion is also available. Datapoint Corporation announced such a system in 1985 called Minx (Multimedia Information Network Exchange) with a somewhat overstated advertising campaign saying, "Fi-nally. Someone's put it all together. Voice. Video. Data." Also, there continue to be videophones or picturephones, with or without complete video such as full motion in real time, from companies such as PicTel, Luma Telecom, and Image Data Corporation.

While the uses for two-way video communications are yet to be established firmly in the marketplace and the rela-tionship with visual data bases or videobases is still evolving, the videophone concept does represent an aspect of videobases that will eventually be accommodated in one form or another. In fact, an established procedure for image transmission in the business world—facsimile—is becoming part of the personal computer and videophone environments. Facsimile images can be converted for display on personal computer screens, dupli-cating the effect of other procedures for transmitting images

Figure 4.3. Chorus Data Systems' Photomail™. Photomail is an interactive telecommunications system allowing users to send and receive images over ordinary telephone lines. (Courtesy of Chorus Data Systems.)

among microcomputers. Facsimile machines also have been offered with integrated telephones, such as the Canon Faxphone, giving users a desktop voice and document-image capability similar to some forms of videophones.

Electronic Publishing, Storage, and Distribution

On a broader note, the combination of images with text in digitized formats is being accomplished across a sea of activity in the areas known as document-image processing and electronic publishing. The expanding field of electronic publishing, from the desktop level to mainframes, is primarily concerned with an ultimate print product, while document-image processing is primarily concerned with converting paper into (or back into) digital formats for storage and distribution.

PUBLISHING

On the surface, electronic publishing might seem only a tangential issue in interactive videobases, as in its present form electronic publishing seems dedicated to reproducing the appearance of paper-conveyed information, whether text or pictures. In at least two ways, however, the swarm of electronic publishing systems can affect the eventual design and use of information systems using graphics and video. First of all, the mere fact that the electronic publishing and document-imaging systems combine text and graphics in a single page, or frame, within a data base of such entities exhibits a similarity of display if not of technique. Second, as electronic publishing comes increasingly into use and users increasingly have the terminals to access the pages or frames electronically, the necessity to adhere to the structure of a printed page lessens and the opportunity to borrow manipulation techniques from the interactive videobases expands.

The overall impact of electronic publishing and document-image storage systems is to enhance the integration of text and graphics in single data base systems. While the videobases of the previous sections certainly combined text, graphics, and video into unified information systems, the starting point was not the traditional arrangement of printed pages. With electronic publishing and document storage, however, the starting point is specifically the printed page. Eventually, the text and images of electronic publishing systems will be distributed and used without ever going to paper, and then there will be a real confluence of text, graphics, and images of all kinds in a broad class of visual information systems.

The obvious and important contribution of electronic publishing to visual data bases is the on-screen mixture and manipulation of text, graphics, and images (Fig. 4.4). This ability to display on a computer screen exactly what would appear on a typeset page is known by the acronym WYSIWYG (what you see is what you get), pronounced "wizzy-wig." A measure of the sophistication of an electronic publishing workstation is often in terms of how close the display is to true WYSIWYG. Of course, many other aspects of electronic publishing systems are important, and some argue that WYSIWYG capability is not an indispensable feature. The fact remains that a new generation of publishing systems is striving to combine and display text, graphics, and images exactly on the screen as on the paper produced by the best typeset system.

Actually, in addition to WYSIWYG, the manipulation of the elements of a page is perhaps even more important for the usability of a system. To provide the full range of editing, rearranging, pagination, sizing, and cropping, as well as other capabilities of paper-based manual or computerized systems, the electronic publishing systems are attempting to perfect procedures to accomplish all of this while hiding as much of the unnecessary detail as possible from the user. Both proprietary and industrywide standards, or "languages," have been developed to facilitate the arrangement of text and graphics, and the transfer of page images from one device to another. As mentioned in the last chapter, one of these standards is the Standard Generalized Markup Language (SGML). Document files created with SGML codes can be converted automatically to typesetlike displays. Although one of the reasons that SGML was originally developed was to allow keyboard entry of gen-

Figure 4.4. Desktop publishing. The Xerox Desktop Publisher integrates text and graphics and allows nontechnical users to create manuals, reports, and proposals in the office, eliminating the need for an outside typesetter and printing service. (Courtesy of Xerox Corporation.)

eralized codes as part of text files (e.g., by authors and typists), the codes can still play a crucial role even if the author does not realize that a mark-up language is involved, such as when using a full screen WYSIWYG display. The mark-up languages and output codes of electronic publishing are one more piece to the puzzle of how effectively to manipulate text, graphics, and images in general across the many devices that will be part of visual information systems.

The most dramatic aspect of electronic publishing in recent years has been the proliferation of page make-up capabilities at the personal computer level, leading to the designation of desktop electronic publishing as an industry in its own right. The phenomenon has been fueled by the combination of bit-mapped screen displays such as the Apple Macintosh and relatively low-cost laser printers that can produce fonts and images in finer detail than on the WYSIWYG screen. The features of desktop publishing systems are not limited to the Macintosh and similar microcomputers, though. With the appropriate software, IBM PCs and compatible machines can perform the same functions with the similar attributes, such as WYSIWYG, windows, and icons. PageMaker from Aldus Corporation, when used with Microsoft Windows, presents on a PC a graphic interface that is almost identical to PageMaker on the Macintosh (Fig. 4.5).

Despite the current attention to desktop publishing, some observers have suggested that it is a fad, in that when the glamour fades, business publishing activities will be returned to a publishing department, away from desktops. That is certainly true to the extent that most office workers who produce documents do not have the time to worry about publication-quality formats. As it becomes easier to use graphic arrangements and distinctive fonts in documents that previously would be merely typed, a greater appreciation of format, layout, and graphic style may result, much as typewritten formats are preferred over handwriting for business documents.

DOCUMENT PROCESSING AND STORAGE

Document-processing systems are, generally speaking, systems for converting large paper files to digital form where any doc-

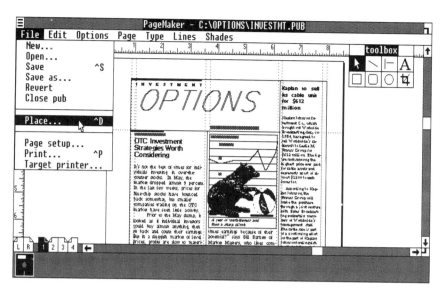

Figure 4.5. PageMaker on a PC. Under Microsoft Windows, the Aldus PageMaker for the PC features pull-down menus and a graphic user interface that is virtually identical to its Macintosh counterpart. (Courtesy of Aldus Corporation.)

ument containing text, graphics, handwriting, or whatever is captured as a complete image.

Some of the most active areas for conversion to digital format include collections of architectural and engineering drawings that in paper form are up to sixteen times the size of letter-size paper, and massive files of documents subject to retention requirements. In a way, document-processing systems could be considered just a digital replacement for microfilm except that they have a few added benefits. With digital representations, the document images can be distributed electronically to any workstation accessing the data base. In addition, if the documents entering the system are subjected to optical character recognition (OCR) techniques, text can be stored as identifiable characters and words, leading to the automatic generation of indexes so that searches of the data base can locate individual words within any document. Similarly, documents that contain graphic designs can be converted from pixel data to the drawing commands of CAD systems and edited at CAD/CAM workstations just as if the drawings had been created on a workstation in the first place.

There are several reasons to mention document-processing systems in connection with visual information systems. First, the systems do encompass computerized data bases of text and graphics. Even though the document images are for the most part mere electronic copies of paper displays, the processing of the images represents a step toward a somewhat different type of data base. The fact that the text can be processed and manipulated independently of the full image of a document's surface suggests that the graphics might also be processed to generate not just CAD/CAM drawing commands but also graphic symbol indexes. As this occurs, similarity will increase between these systems for storing paper files more efficiently and other systems for creating videobases with graphic-language capabilities that never did exist in paper form.

A second reason to consider the document-processing and -storage systems is that they use some of the same technology as other image systems. Videobases, especially those using analog video, began to be built when the capabilities of interactive laser optical systems became available. Now, certain document-processing systems are also building upon laser optical systems, although using digital recording rather than analog. The Library of Congress began using analog videodisks first, and later included digital optical disks to store images of printed material. The optical disk data base now includes the Congressional Record from 1985 to the present, articles and documents indexed by the Congressional Research Service, and a serials file of complete issues of selected journals.

Before considering the laser optical systems, it is worth mentioning that some document-image systems do in fact use microfilm in addition to digital representations. Kodak, as might be expected from its film background, announced a system in 1985 that combines autoloading microfilm devices with digital scanners and a local area network. When an information request is entered at a computer terminal, the correct reel of film is automatically loaded, the appropriate frame is scanned, and the result is transmitted electronically to the requesting terminal. On the display screen, document images can be scrolled, rotated, enlarged, and viewed four at a time in four separate windows or screen areas. The capacity of such a system approaches 3.5 million images stored on 240 microfilm magazines, and Kodak has said that eventually the same system could be used to read images from laser disks. For smaller data bases, Kodak offers a version based on an IBM PC/AT, with the index to the microfilmed documents contained on the AT's hard disk.

Using laser optics, the document-image processing system created by FileNet Corporation, to choose just one example, also exhibits some capabilities that go beyond the basic level of providing access to images of paper documents. Laser data disks are similar to videodisks in size—twelve inches—and construction. Each disk can hold 2.6 gigabytes, or 2.6 billion bytes, of digitized images. (Even larger disks are becoming available; Kodak and Philips have announced a fourteen-inch optical disk with a capacity of up to 6.8 gigabytes.) Unlike the consumer videodisks, laser disks are enclosed in a hard plastic jacket similar to the 3.5-inch microdisks, and their center is metal, similar to hard magnetic disks. Also unlike the consumer videodisks, the FileNet optical disks can be recorded in the same device that is used for reading them, although once recorded, the bytes are permanent, that is, a WORM system. The capacity of each optical disk, and the FileNet design of housing a jukebox-like arrangement of up to 204 disks in a box about the size of two refrigerators, means the system can hold a massive amount of data—up to four trillion bytes—that accommodates the high data requirements of digitized images.

The retrieval and display of document images in the FileNet system includes several features that, while not impossible using other retrieval technologies, represent improvements that have not yet been introduced in most other textual information systems. One such feature is the ability to see both the back and the front of a document image at the same time. Another feature is the use of the electronic file folder concept, with both logical and graphic implications. At the logical level, any document can be assigned to many file folders just as paper copies can be filed in several places. The difference is that in the FileNet system the image of the document exists only once. At the graphic level, file folders are displayed graphically such that users can flip through the documents in a folder by quickly seeing the top of each one. When the item of interest is found, the document is "pulled" from the folder and displayed in full. Yet another aspect of the FileNet system is that, to minimize retrieval time for document images, which can range from seven to sixteen seconds, once the first page is retrieved, subsequent page images are also sent to a magnetic hard disk in the workstation. Thus when the first page has been read, the second can be displayed in only four seconds.

All of these features are not particularly impressive in themselves and can be accomplished in other forms of computerized information systems. The point is that these and similar features have not been common in other systems, and yet seem to make sense in document-image systems using terminals and software designed for the electronic composition and manipulation of document images. Consequently, the current document-image–processing systems may presage some of the features we will eventually come to expect in graphically oriented information systems as a whole.

VIDEOTEX PAGES

A final note on the subject of electronic publishing, storage, and distribution is about videotex, a word that has been used to designate a broad class of electronic information systems to be used in home or office. Much debate has been generated about what videotex is and what it should be, including suggestions that perhaps the word is too vague, or has been used in too many ways, to be of any practical value. When looking back at the early systems that were called videotex, certain characteristics stand out that might mark the enduring contribution of videotex to visual information systems.

These characteristics were the integration of text, graphics, and color, and the organization of information into pages that matched screen constraints and not paper page limitations. As such, the videotex page or frame was not a replica of paper but was introduced with its own size and shape constraints. Also, unlike other computerized information systems, the information not only was displayed in discrete pages, a page at a time instead of a series of scrolling lines, but was stored in the same page units, rather than as large files of text and graphics that contained no internal correlation with the format of the display device. In the end, the early videotex systems may be recognized as providing a beneficial perspective on the use of color, graphics, and information organization that, together with interactive video and electronic publishing, helped form the eventual shape of visual information systems.

Summary

There is a merger of technologies and purposes among a number of different information-handling systems that seek to manage graphics and images, including video of one sort or another. From interactive videodisks to CD-ROM to optical data storage, and from digitized video to electronic publishing to document-image processing, common points of interest, and sometimes similar approaches, exist. All of these systems and technologies are confronted with the problems inherent in creating completely electronic information systems using graphics and video that are familiar enough in touch and feel to become as accepted as paper and yet offer functions that could never be possible in a paper world. In varying degrees, the characteristics and functions of each of these systems are influencing the others and helping to shape the future design of integrated data bases that go beyond the arrangements existing today by combining text and data, graphics, analog and digitized still-frame images and motion video, as well as analog and digitized audio.

5

THE GRAPHIC INTERFACE

The term graphic interface is not the best prose, but it does provide an abbreviated way of talking about icons, windows, graphically arranged menus of many kinds, highlighted options, diagrams and maps, and a multitude of other means for visually prompting users of computers and computerized information systems. In short, graphic interface summarizes the visual tools available.

The story of how a graphic interface evolved, in its many manifestations and with mistakes as well as successes, is fascinating in its own right and can be recapitulated only briefly here. We are now familiar with certain forms of the visual tools, but it is easy to forget that some types and designs simply did not survive. A wilted flower, for example, was once the visual indication of the procedure for removing files in a system called Okra at Xerox PARC.[1] In the future, some of today's visual tools may seem as quaint as that wilted flower.

Nevertheless, in one form or another, it seems certain that a graphic interface will eventually be accepted as the best way to make the fullest use of the human capacity for comprehension. The preceding chapters traced the developments and applications that have made graphic interfaces feasible. A confluence of forces from several disciplines has provided the means for accomplishing this different and in the end a very substantially different way of approaching computer systems in general and information systems in particular. This chapter focuses on the graphic interface itself, what it means, and what it does, beginning with a brief look at how the concept evolved.

The Groundwork

The decade of the 1980s may come to be recognized as a watershed for computer displays, from the days when almost all computer users faced screens or printouts of text and worked the system by typing commands, to the days — not yet here — when most users will usually see a graphically arranged display with a set of basic nontext procedures for taking action. The change has not been, and will not be, sudden. Despite the publicity of the Apple Macintosh and others, the pioneering work in using graphics and video as tools to command a computer was done years earlier, and the use of textual nongraphic procedures will persist for years to come.

A VISUAL ENVIRONMENT

The original work that led to the current graphic interface is commonly attributed to efforts at the Xerox Corporation's Palo Alto Research Center, Xerox PARC, at the beginning of the 1970s. It was based on even earlier work elsewhere, including research at organizations such as IBM and the Stanford Research Institute, and at universities such as MIT and Stanford. The Logo language, for example, was developed at MIT in the late 1960s and early 1970s, partially under funding from the National Science Foundation. It involved the movement of a graphic emblem, called a turtle, around the screen as the basic way of getting the computer to do something. As an interesting twist, the initial versions of Logo did not use graphics but instead sought to teach the use of commands by having the commands affect the movement across the floor of a robot device that resembled a turtle. The eventual manipulation of graphic images and the basic goal of finding more comfortable ways of getting a computer to react influenced later efforts including the work at Xerox PARC.

At Xerox, the concept of a graphic interface was incorporated into several efforts that resulted in a continual refinement of what to express graphically and how to do it. One such effort was a project called Dynabook, a computerized "book" that would be so simple that children could use it. A related effort was the development of a combination programming language and graphic environment known as Smalltalk, which even included a subset of Logo called Turtletalk. The ultimate goal of the Smalltalk projects, and there were a number of them beginning in the early 1970s, was to create a powerful information system that, as a user manipulated information, would grow together with the user's grasp of it.[2] The Smalltalk language/environment, as exemplified in Smalltalk-80, used windows or "views" extensively but did not rely very much on icons for normal interaction. In one of the instances where icons were used, the cursor could assume a different shape depending upon the process under way; if a program was calculating something to be looked at, the cursor would become a small pair of reading glasses, or if the user had to wait while a process took place, the cursor would become an ellipsis (. . .).

The programmers at Xerox PARC also incorporated the use of graphics as tools to manipulate information, and to present visually processes and relationships, into several products, including the Alto microcomputer, and the pioneering Star workstation introduced in 1981 (Fig. 5.l). The work at Xerox

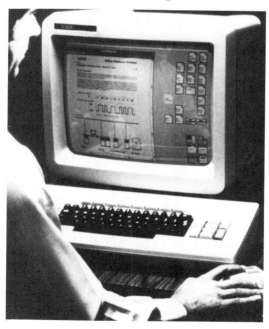

Figure 5.1. The Xerox Star. This was one of the first systems to implement fully the graphical interface. (Courtesy of Xerox Corporation.)

was certainly not done in isolation, and benefited from the sharing of ideas with other researchers, as well as contributing to the research being done elsewhere. As work on Smalltalk progressed, a manuscript was written to describe the concepts. The manuscript was offered to and reviewed by other companies also in the computer business, including Digital Equipment Corporation, Hewlett-Packard, Tektronix, and Apple Computer.

Despite the concentration of graphic interface activity at Xerox, it was not until Apple Computer began using similar techniques that icons, pop-up menus, and windows became popular. The first Apple product with a graphic interface was the Lisa, begun around 1978 and introduced in 1983. Xerox work notwithstanding, this is considered the first major effort by a computer hardware company to promote this particular use of graphics. The Apple Macintosh, begun in 1979 and introduced in January 1984, then made the graphic interface a decided success, being the first relatively low-cost machine to provide such capability. The Xerox Star, for example, initially cost $15,000, and the Apple Lisa cost $10,000, while the first Macintosh cost only $2500. The Macintosh was designed from the start for as low a cost as possible, and it was also helped tremendously by a general decline in the cost of component technologies.

PREGRAPHICS PROMPTS

To appreciate fully the magnitude of the move to a graphic expression of an operating system, it might be helpful to examine the way users operate computers that do not have a graphic interface.

The original development of the electronic computer as a calculating device and as a machine that could execute batched programs produced a "command" environment. To make the computer work, a user would type or keypunch a series of commands that constituted a program, and then additional commands to cause the program to be activated. Except for the replacement of keypunch machines with terminals, that is still the way computers are often used. Anyone who wants to direct the actions of the computer must know what commands to type and how to type them, with any prompting from the system usually consisting of a single character, such as a slash (/), right arrow (>), period (.), dash (-), dollar sign ($), and so on, to let the user know that a command is expected. As computers have become associated with large files of information as the means for access, users also have to know the commands required to retrieve information from the stored files. In general, therefore, the use of computers has traditionally encouraged a very strong orientation toward the meticulous typing of command characters and words, in prescribed order and in a sequential series of interaction, with a minimum of cues from the system.

SCREEN FORMAT

The introduction of screen displays as a replacement for paper-fed terminals began to change this. The character strings coming from the computer could include control codes to place text anywhere on the screen, instead of always on a line after the previous line. Other control codes and special characters could be used to draw lines and boxes. In a somewhat rudimentary fashion, such systems began to make use of visual arrangements of the display screen to make things more pleasant and perhaps easier for the person at the terminal entering commands.

Eventually, screen design became recognized as a serious concern. As demonstrated in Wilbert Galitz's *Handbook of Screen Format Design*, the most common computer terminal for quite a while has been the video display, and well-designed screens (e.g., in data entry applications) can "increase human processing speed, reduce human errors, and speed computer processing time."[3] The *Handbook* contains numerous details on where and how to arrange text for specific purposes with an emphasis on clarity, simplicity, meaningfulness, and balance. The text, published in 1981 and in revised form in 1985, is almost entirely devoted to screen formats that predate the icons and windows of graphic interfaces. Of the approximately 200 pages in the book, only 2 are given to pictorial descriptions, or icons, with the note that such graphics will open up new vistas in screen design. That is certainly true. In addition to all of the considerations for screen arrangements made possible by the use of video displays, an even greater number of considerations arises with the use of bit-mapped icons, windows, and other graphic techniques.

Together with the command environment, the complexity of computer systems and the increasingly vast amounts of on-line data available to users led to a concomitant proliferation of educational and training materials. A system of any size usually cannot exist without a pile of reference material and a cadre of knowledgeable individuals to guide others in the use of the system. To alleviate the problem, computer systems can include within their own structure various means for helping users discover the range of commands and the extent of any accessible files or data bases. For example, many interactive systems include some version of a "help" command. A user might type the word "help," or a question mark (?), and the system will respond with some text explaining how to do certain things and how to find out more about other features.

Conceptually, interactive computer systems have almost always included some means of prompting the user to take an action, albeit in a highly abbreviated form, and the elaborate prompts possible with a graphically expressed operating system are merely an extension of the past. The difference between the single-character prompt for a system command and the visual cues now being used is so substantial, however, that it must be recognized as a turning point in the use of computers and information systems.

Menus

One of the fundamental ways for systems to try to keep users aware of the actions possible is to present a list of choices, which for obvious reasons has become known as a menu. The menu has sometimes been presented as the antithesis of the command environment, as it presumably limits users to choosing one of a small set of listed items or actions, while virtually any valid command can be entered in a command environment. Aside from the fact that many systems today combine commands and menus, the difference between the two is essentially one of degree, not of kind. In all computer systems that accept commands, there is a finite set of commands; and it is also always possible to present a command as a menu option. Thus theoretically, all commands or command combinations could be displayed as menu choices, and only the physical problem of showing all the combinations determines that a system of menus shows fewer options than might be available by command. It also might be true that where a command such as "find" can be used with virtually any word to locate that word in a text data base, an action can be taken extremely easily, compared to selecting the "find" option from a menu and then selecting the desired word from a long list, or menu, of all words. Nevertheless, the result could have been achieved with either method.

The one advantage that menus have over procedures that do not display any list of options is that they let the user know what types of actions are acceptable at that time. Instead of the system blankly waiting for input, it gives the user some information about what to do next. Furthermore, when the user selects one of the options, such as by typing its number, there is no worry about spelling the command correctly or using the correct syntax.

In evaluating the difference between command-style input and menu selection, the former is sometimes characterized as user driven while the latter is system driven. This distinction is intended to highlight the fact that presumably a user of a command language can get a system to take any action by typing a command, while the user of a menu can only select an action if it is listed on the menu. In other words, the system controls and limits the options. The distinction is useful in that it focuses attention on the problem of presenting a range of options, but in an absolute sense the distinction is only a fuzzy one, because, as noted above, even a command environment is based on a limited list of possible options. To blur the distinction even more, that list of options is displayable in some systems, making it an accessible menu, while other systems freely mix a command format and any of a number of variations of the menu format. The challenge is to provide as much help as the user desires so that the system will react as intended, without ascribing control of the interaction to either the user or the system.

Another challenge when using menus within information systems is to avoid overwhelming the user with choices, and especially ones that cloud the user's concept of the organization of the information. Very often, as users are required to make a succession of menu choices in order to find some information, they lose track of which choices took them to the end point. They are therefore unable to avoid that series of choices again if it did not result in the desired information, or unable to duplicate the series of choices if it did lead to the right place. Moreover, when making the choices, users are dependent on the system designer's concept of what logically falls under one choice instead of another, and yet in practice, that logic is not always readily apparent. Finally, even when the choices are not confusing and are remembered, experienced users find a long series of choices to be tedious. The solution usually is to mix commands and menus for experienced users, or to organize the menus so that a short route is always available to the most used sections of an information file.

There are many ways to provide menus or to list options, whether presented as text alone or with the help of graphics. The text-only variations include binary menus (answer "yes" or "no" to a question), multiple choice from a short list, extended lists that are displayed on more than one screen, permanent menus always displayed, and others.[4] Additional variations are possible with different screen formats and with the addition of graphic procedures, with or without color, to present the choices. The following sections discuss some of the methods beyond the simple selection of one item from a vertically ordered list.

MULTICHOICE

Usually, menu arrangements are thought of as single-choice methods, where the user is to choose one option from the list. There are also various ways to allow users to select more than one item from a menu or a series of menus, whether or not a graphic arrangement is used.

If a list of items is displayed and the user can move a pointer or touch each item, several items can be selected before the user makes some choice that completes the selection process. Even in strictly textual systems, the user might have the option to select more than one choice. In some menu-based systems, a user can select any or all of a list of options by typing the numbers. If more than one option is selected, the system displays the selected screens in order, with a "next screen" option or function key used to move through the sequence. In other systems, where users know that a choice from one menu leads to a second menu, and a choice from that menu leads to a third menu, and so on, they can simply make all the choices at once, whether by typing numbers or letters, and immediately go to the lowest level selected.

In fact, in one particular menu-based information system that technically does not permit more than one-digit choices, system designers can still create two- and three-digit menu choices by adding "dummy," or intermediate menu pages in between. If a menu choice is sixteen, the designated page is choice one from the first menu and choice six from a dummy menu. Users who type the sixteen fast enough never see the dummy menu; if they type too slowly, the intermediate menu might appear, sometimes to users' surprise.

The success or failure of any given menu procedure is likely to depend much more on the relationship among the logic of the lists, their availability, and their reflection of users' desires than on the simple fact of their being in any particular form. Moreover, the ways to provide lists of options, especially with graphics and with selection devices such as touchscreens and pointers, are continually being refined.

STRIP MENUS

A strip menu is any arrangement of options presented as a strip, that is, a horizontal succession of choices perhaps outlined in little boxes. In practice, a strip menu usually appears along the bottom of a screen or along the top or vertically along the sides, rather than in the middle. Often it is fairly stable; that is, options given are the primary ones available in that application. The depiction of the options can be in numbers, words, or graphics. On the Xerox 6085, a strip menu appears across the top right of windows for individual applications, using both icons and words such as "close," "edit," "save edit," and so on, depending upon the application (Figure 5.2). Choosing either a word or an icon may actually lead to a pull-down menu, (discussed below), but the basic arrangement is that of a strip menu.

The strip menu is both an outgrowth of one-line-at-a-time text systems and a means of conserving space on a screen display. In text-only systems, some prompts from the system include a list of options, either abbreviated or spelled out, on the same horizontal line as the prompt or the request for input. The options might be enclosed in parentheses, for example, to indicate their status as ancillary information. With full-screen displays, the list of options can be arranged in a constant location that does not interfere with the basic activity of the system. The user always knows where to look for the options,

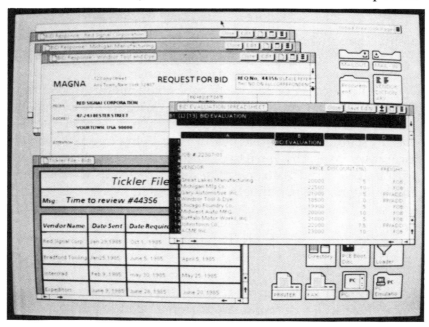

Figure 5.2. Strip menus on windows. On this Xerox workstation, each window contains a strip menu along the top on the right. The strip menu can vary from window to window, and contains both icons and words. (Courtesy of Xerox Corporation.)

even though, as expressed in words or icons, they can change depending upon a previous choice. Their location is by no means standard for all screen displays. Equally usable systems have options displayed across the top, across the bottom, centered, left-justified, right-justified, arranged vertically on the right side or the left side, or even appearing anywhere selected by a pointer such as a mouse.

The development of the strip menu has also stemmed in part from the efforts to install option selection in the input device, such as the keyboard, primarily to make the options more accessible while conserving screen space. Specific keys can be labeled and used to select specific functions. For example, a "print" key is included on many keyboards, so that "print" does not have to be included on a menu or even typed as a command. For most general-use systems, it is not possible to include a key for all the options that need to be expressed. On the other hand, the fact that at any given time within an application a user is likely to want to do only a small number of things has led to the inclusion of redefinable function keys. An available option can be invoked by hitting one of ten or twenty or so function keys, as long as the user knows which option is tied to which function key.

This in turn has led to procedures for labeling the function keys on the screen. On some keyboards, the function keys are arranged across the top, and therefore a strip menu along the bottom of the screen can be matched directly to them. As the activity on the screen changes, the labels in the strip menu can change as the function keys are redefined. Even some calculators come with a on-screen menu next to redefinable function keys. A Hewlett-Packard model has a four-row display above a row of function keys, and the row immediately above the unlabeled function keys contains the labels, (e.g., Calc, Insrt, Delet, Name, Get).

Systems designed especially for public use often include keys or buttons, or membrane-covered areas, arranged along the edges of the screen. These keys contain no specific labels, but when an option appears on the screen next to one, that key is pressed to make the desired selection. Some automatic teller machines use this technique quite successfully.

The introduction of the lightpen, mouse, touchscreen, and other means of selecting options means that there no longer needs to be a correlation between a strip menu and function keys, but the visual link between the two continues in some instances. The keyboards for some workstations not only contain function keys arranged across the top of the keyboard with labels like F1, F2, F3, and so on, but also a visual display of functions across the bottom of the screen. The latter are selectable by a mouse, in which some of the boxes are labeled with specific words and the others contain the same all-purpose F1, F2, F3 designations. On touchscreens, the strip menu similarly can be created to look like a row of buttons, so that users press the image on the screen just as readily as they would press the function key in a row along the edge of the screen.

In a way, the strip menu is a transitional step between early attempts to arrange lists of options creatively, and the more involved procedures made possible with better graphic capability. Strip menus will probably always have a place as a commonly accepted procedure for keeping a set of options in mind, but off to the side.

POP-UP, PULL-DOWN

The pop-up or pull-down menu is generally a vertical list of options that appears as an overlay on the existing screen display, disappearing as soon as a selection is made or the list is "closed" (Fig. 5.3). In addition, this type of new menu is usually a subset of the options from a previous selection. Using MacWrite as an example, a strip menu across the top lists "search" as one of the options. If the mouse's pointer is placed over "search" and the button pressed, a small box appears, like a window shade being pulled down, containing the additional words "find," "find next," "change," and "goto page #" listed vertically. This pull-down menu appears on the screen only as long as the button on the mouse is pressed. Once the button is released, the submenu disappears. To select one of the submenu options, the mouse's pointer is moved down the list, causing each option to become highlighted in turn. If the mouse button is released while a submenu option is highlighted, that option is selected.

The major intent of these types of dynamically appearing

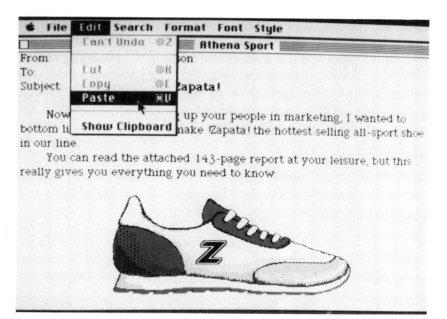

Figure 5.3. Pull-down menu. In this example from MacWrite, the "edit" pull-down menu is in view, and one of its options has been selected and appears in reverse video. (Courtesy of Apple Computer, Inc.)

menus is to use the graphics capability of the screen to provide option lists when desired only for as long as desired, and to keep them out of the way when not needed, while disrupting or obscuring the screen display as little as possible. The appearance of a submenu covers only a small part of the screen, and when the menu pops back to wherever it came from, that portion of the screen display behind the submenu reappears. This is a considerable change from the command language environment, although it does not necessarily preclude the use of commands or function keys. Using the same example, the "find next" and "goto page #" options can also be accomplished using a two-key command for those who are more comfortable with control-key actions. It is also a mark of the pervasive influence of the command environment, at least among the programmers of MacWrite, that the pull-down menu of English words includes "goto" instead of the proper spelling of the words, "go to." The single-word spelling is a command in some computer languages, but it is not found in Webster's dictionary.

The phrase "pop-up menu" is also used to indicate menus

that can appear and reappear anywhere on the screen and are not necessarily always a subset of a previous menu. The options in some electronic paint systems, for example, consisting almost entirely of icons, appear anywhere on the screen that the user selects by pointing a stylus at an electronic tablet.

Pop-up or pull-down menus can also be layered or overlaid. In a campuswide system created at Carnegie-Mellon University, with assistance from IBM, sets of optional commands are listed on a pop-up menu that appears to be five cards stacked on top of each other but slightly offset, so that only the heading for each card is visible.[5] If one of the five cards is selected, it appears as the topmost one in that its list of options is visible, although its position in the stack does not change (Fig. 5.4). Thus it becomes quite possible to give users visible access to large numbers of sets and subsets of options that are generally displayed in a minimum of screen space without disrupting the primary display.

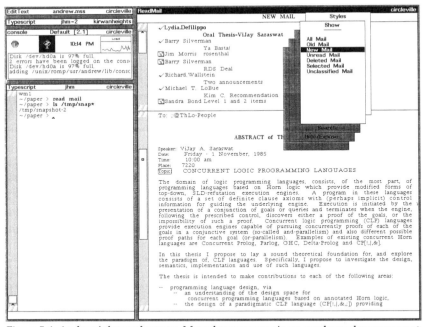

Figure 5.4. Andrew's layered menus. Menu boxes appear in an overlapped arrangement on the right, with one of the boxes showing a list of options. The menu in use appears to be on top, but does not change its position in the stack. (Courtesy of the Information Technology Center, Carnegie-Mellon University.)

IN CONTEXT

Another form of presenting options, which stretches the meaning of the word menu as a list of items, is the embedded menu, or the menu in context, sometimes also referred to as hypertext.[6] Instead of an obvious display of options in addition to the main display on a screen, the main display appears alone and certain parts of it may be selected by touch or by pointer to take an action or to access a new display.

The embedded menu can be accomplished with either graphic displays or with text. In the case of text, the display might contain a paragraph or two, and certain words or phrases might be underlined or otherwise highlighted. Any of these words can be selected to obtain more information on that topic. When the selection is done on a touchscreen system, the procedure has been called touchtext. In this way, a menu of additional topics is built into the wording of a more general statement. Obviously, the paragraphs in each screen display must be worded carefully so that the result is not only readable text but also contains appropriate words that will act as headings for the additional screens that can be selected. Studies of embedded menus have been somewhat inconclusive.[7] Some results indicate that they are preferred over traditional menus, but other research suggests that the embedded menus can be confusing and can cause users to take longer to find specific information, compared to alternate methods.

Other examples of menus in context rely on the traditional arrangement of books, with a table of contents, chapter headings and subheadings, and an index. The on-screen "help" information on Digital Equipment Corporation's VAXstation looks like a book. The first screen is a table of contents, and there is no indication that the entries are in fact selectable menu items. Only when the mouse-controlled pointer is moved over the display, and suddenly a box appears around the heading under the pointer, does it become apparent that these are selectable menu items. Further into the "help" text the process can be repeated with headings, subheadings, and tables. In all cases, however, the text display looks like the reproduction of a printed page, complete with printlike fonts, rather than a display of a computer-stored "help" file.

In graphic systems, any display in which parts of the display may be selected to get to another screen can be considered a menu in context, or an embedded menu. A common way to display options graphically with information that is based on geography is to use maps. An electronic city guide may display maps of the city with prominent buildings or places of interest highlighted. If a touchscreen is used, a tourist can touch any of the highlighted places and receive further information on that place and how to go there. This procedure of selecting a part of a display to obtain more information about it is functionally identical to the zoom feature on graphic workstations, where a user can select a portion of the screen to see finer graphic detail.

BARS AND DIALS

Other procedures for graphically indicating options include gauges, dials, meters, and bars that can be set to desired levels. Even DNA synthesis can be accomplished using a control program on an IBM PC that graphically displays gauges that can be set using a light pen. In a more consumer-oriented example, a real estate system presents a bar chart of price ranges, and clients electronically adjust the bar to select the one they prefer. In a variety of other systems, a scroll bar is used as a graphic way to move through a list or any ordered set. In MacWrite, a vertical scroll bar along the right edge is used to indicate the position of the current page relative to all pages in the document being written or edited. A fast way to move to another page is to use the mouse to "grab" the position indicator and slide it elsewhere on the scroll bar. In a number of systems, a similar style of scroll bar is used to present lists of files on a disk. Only a few files are listed by name at a time, but the position indicator on the scroll bar can be used to judge how long the complete list is, in either direction.

Overall, the menu concept has led from short lists presented as a way to select options or topics to a variety of procedures for giving the user hints without a traditional list. In the process, the value of visually presenting options, whether in a way that reflects the definition of a menu or one that begs the question, has been recognized as highly desirable across many types of computer systems. Graphically arranged menus, in fact, solve some of the problems of simple menu systems by keeping the user constantly aware of the range of options and where to find them on the screen, thus minimizing confusion about how to manipulate the system or find information. At the same time, the power of command-driven procedures has not been neglected, and computer systems increasingly are combining commands with menus or visual options of one sort or another.

Icons

Together with giving new meaning to menu, graphically expressed systems have made the word "icon" commonplace, as graphic symbols have been introduced to substitute for words in the display of options or topics. As is true for graphic interfaces in general, icons are still relatively new features, and there are more ways to use them than is evident at present. In fact, the use of icons for information retrieval is only beginning, even though in the 1970s researchers at Xerox PARC did envision them as a way to establish relationships visually in order to search data bases, instead of merely as a substitute for system command strings.[8]

PURPOSE

While the role of icons is still being established, their purpose and value are not necessarily accepted unconditionally. As mentioned in the first chapter, icons might seem like a return to the hieroglyphics that preceded alphabets, ignoring the good reasons why alphabets have been much more useful than hieroglyphics. To understand picture symbols, you usually must know something about the message already, and the number of picture symbols required to convey all thoughts is vastly greater than the number of letters required to convey thoughts in words.

These same considerations affect the use of icons in computer systems. Icons can be incomprehensible, or at best confusing, if the user does not readily relate them to a known action or object within the system. The exclusive use of icons can result in a system with more limitations on user action than a system that permits the typing of command words.

On the other hand, icons have been proposed as the beginning of a visual or graphic language that might even transcend national and cultural barriers. Such a language would not replace alphabets and text, but would provide the means to convey and comprehend some things much faster than possible with words. Aaron Marcus, a designer of graphic interfaces, suggested that the icons of today can lead to "higher-level abstractions which allow us to manipulate and really manage when we are dealing with gigabytes of data. Prose has its place, but we are beginning to need conceptual sign systems . . . to understand quickly what's there and what action should be taken."[9]

At present, icons are generally accepted as a way to save time, and this is expressed in several fashions. First, good icons can be recognized and understood more quickly than if the objects or actions behind them had to be expressed in words. Second, icons on the screen remind users of possible options or objects, and therefore users do not have to consult a reference text if they do not remember immediately what to do or how to do it. Finally, as an extension of that, some persons may require less training to use an icon-oriented system, and those who do not care to be trained at all might even use such a system. In a way, then, icons can be considered friendlier than the same concepts expressed in words. A 1984 article in *Datamation*, written when icons were new enough to require a definition, tentatively concluded that "icons are thought to save time in directing a computer's operation as well as making it easier for personnel with less training to use systems."[10]

A slightly different way to say that icons save time is to say that they capitalize on the fact that we can recognize something we see much more easily and quickly than we can remember something without a visual stimulus. A long history of studies of memory reinforces this notion. In fact, the classic commentary from Cicero on memory in *De Oratore* is that seeing is the most acute of the senses, so that memory can be improved by relating a list of things to be memorized to a real or even imaginary physical setting.[11] Cicero credited this argument to the "famous Simonides of Ceos" who had the reputation for being the inventor of the art of memory, and made it clear that the technique does work. Here, of course, Cicero advocated the use of mental images rather than images on paper or some other medium; but with actual images on a paper or on a screen, the ability to recall is even more enhanced.

As an aid for recall, the icon is simply a prompt. Therefore a system that uses words as prompts could presumably achieve the same ease of use as a system employing icons. There may be more to it than that, however. Obviously, in some cases an icon could just as easily be replaced by a single word, and the result might even be better than with the icon. In other cases, icons can reduce a fairly complex notion to manageable size. In these cases, they not only save screen space but also, and more important, can be grasped at a glance. This was, in fact, the primary intent of the groundbreaking work at Xerox. The creators of graphic interface techniques were not particularly worried about producing systems that could be used by persons without training, but were trying to use graphics "to make very complex tasks manageable . . . [and to use them to] communicate much more complex things to users."[12]

DESIGN

The design of icons for computer symbols follows in the tradition of the design of graphic symbols, or pictographs, for a wide variety of purposes. According to designer Gregg Berryman, pictographs first came into use in modern times on a wide scale in 1909, when they were used for national highway signs in Europe.[13] Now, highway, airport, and public signs in general are good examples of the degree to which concepts can be reduced to a well-known graphic with an obvious meaning.

The best of these icons are understandable by most people the first time they are seen. Airport signs are good examples in that they are designed for travelers who may not speak the local language and may not have been to an airport before. In fact, the signs designed under the auspices of the U.S. Department of Transportation for use at major airports are considered classics of good design (Fig. 5.5). Other public signs may not be as completely obvious on first sight, but they become well understood through constant use. Also, their meaning may be obvious, but they may not be examples of especially good design.

Pictographs used for public signs are difficult to design well because they are usually part of a set of symbols that should be balanced visually, and should be easily identifiable even though they often depict more than a single concept or action. In fact, Berryman provided a series of criteria including the following: the design should achieve the appropriate level of abstraction; eye flow should be internal rather than external; negative or white spaces must be carefully considered as a figure-ground relationship; the design should be capable of being reduced to a very small size and still be complete; and it should be quickly recognized.

The same concepts generally apply for icons used in computer systems. Some seem to convey an idea readily, while others are pretty much of a mystery until a reference manual is found to explain them. Because icons for computer systems have a much shorter history than traffic signs and other public symbols, no general consensus has been reached on the meaning of a wide variety of them. In addition, designers do not necessarily want to create something identical to what is used in another system. For example, several different systems use an icon to indicate that an action takes some time to complete,

Figure 5.5. Icons for public transportation. These are considered good examples of well-designed icons.

and therefore the user should be patient. The Apple Macintosh uses a little icon that looks like a wristwatch. When that symbol appears, replacing the cursor, the user must wait. An equally obvious icon, an hourglass, is used by Digital Equipment Corporation's VAXstation. Another hourglass, larger and in color, is used by some automatic teller machines. Still other systems use the face of a clock, complete with hour and minute hands.

Even when two or more systems use the same icon, there is room for individual differences. Several systems use the figure of a trash can to indicate the procedure for deleting or erasing files. Files are dragged by mouse and pointer to the trash can and the icon for the file disappears, although the actual deletion may not occur immediately. Of the systems that do use the trash can, the cans are not necessarily identical (Fig. 5.6). As a mark of the many ways such an item might be drawn, an early version for Macintosh was more like the type of can you would see in an alley, battered and dented and replete with buzzing files.[14] In the interests of simplicity, though, the trash can became a bit more sedate.

The similarity or individuality of icons used for similar purposes is not only a matter of creative design but also one of legal right. The legal constraints on icon design are summarized in the final section of this chapter.

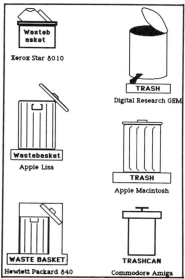

Figure 5.6. A Comparison of icons to delete files. The images shown represent icons from various systems. The images from the Xerox Star and GEM are early versions.

PRESENT AND FUTURE

At present, icons are well received in some systems and completely ignored in many others. Certain systems that use other elements of graphic interfaces such as windows and pop-up and pull-down menus do not use icons. In fact, there are still more computer systems and services that have no room for icons at all than those that do. Among the workstations and microcomputers that do use icons, the styles are mixed: icons with or without words attached, sometimes words and sometimes icons, as well as a mixture of good icons and bad ones. According to Aaron Marcus, icons should be judged on how well they represent an action or object; how they work together as a set; their shape, size, color, and how appealing they are; and how suitable they are for display.[15] If they do blossom as a graphic language, they will not only become more evident as time passes but will also be better designed as an appreciation for good icons accumulates.

Some newer implementations have symbols within symbols, and soon there may be procedures for linking icons into structures to express more complex relationships. Icons might also be rendered in three dimensions, and may have sound associated with them. This is not meant to imply that in the past no one thought to make a three-dimensional icon with sound. The designers of the Macintosh, as well as researchers at the MIT Media Room and others, considered and worked with those features specifically. In the final implementation, icons were given enough features to do the job without adding features that were technically available but logically unnecessary. Eventually, as experience expands, the more intricate icons may become necessary for practical purposes.

The broad acceptance of icons in computer systems is likely to follow the technical developments in both hardware and software that permit the use of small graphic images. Therefore, as long as individual computer terminals and microcomputers do not have the capacity for a reasonable display and manipulation of icons, the use of icons will be slow. Among those who have used icon-based systems, the appreciation of this feature seems assured. The next major step in development is likely to be the realization of the full power of icons for concisely expressing a complex idea, especially for information retrieval.

Windows

A large part of the current attention to the graphic interface is concerned with the use of windows. The word can be used in two different ways, however, and some implementations of a window may fall under one meaning or the other, or both.

In the more obvious meaning, windows refers to a procedure for graphically dividing the screen into areas, usually rectangular, so as visually to separate one activity from another. In the second meaning, the word implies that the computer can actually handle more than one task at the same time, such as multitasking, and usually the two or more activities can be viewed simultaneously in separate rectangular areas. Thus it is possible to have a system with windows that is not a true multitasking system, and also possible to have a multitasking system that does not use graphically separate rectangular display areas.

The term is also used to refer to specific products. For example, Windows (capitalized) is an operating system environment produced by the Microsoft Corporation for the IBM PC and compatibles, and X Windows is a proposed standard for window implementation particularly for workstations.

GRAPHIC VARIATIONS

A display screen can be divided into several areas to segregate activities visually. This can be done in many ways, with different impacts on the use of such windows.

In the least complicated arrangement, the rectangular areas are of equal size, do not overlap, and are either there or not but cannot be moved. For example, some display systems divide a screen in half vertically, and use one half to show a complete document page, for instance, and the other to show a more readable close-up of a section of the page. Alternatively, one side could show the results of a program running on the other side. For video displays in both analog and digital form, a single screen can be divided in half, into quadrants, or into even smaller segments of equal size to show many images at the same time. All of these examples can be considered rudimentary versions of the window concept.

On a slightly more involved level, the rectangular areas can be of arbitrary size and can appear anywhere on the screen. Once again, however, the areas are not permitted to overlap. This has been referred to as a "tiled" design, where, as in a mosaic, the tiles can be arranged in any way except on top of each other. If the system is a little more capable, the windows can be sized; that is, a given rectangular window can be shrunk or enlarged to reveal less or more of the text or images. In the Andrew system developed at the Information Technology Center at Carnegie-Mellon University, the windows do not overlap, but can be sized down to nothing to disappear, or perhaps only down to the header bar for the window identifying its contents (Fig. 5.7). The visual effect of closing and opening Andrew windows has also changed over time. Originally, the opening of a new window caused the largest existing window to be reduced in size, while the partial or full closing of a window automatically caused others to expand. Eventually, this automatic shrinking and expanding was abandoned in favor of keeping essentially two columns of windows, with blank space that might be filled or revealed by opening or closing them.

Together with sizing, a system might permit windows to overlap as well as enable the user to move the rectangular area elsewhere on the screen. Other systems permit windows to overlap and to be moved, but not to be sized. In any event, the combination of overlapping and movement means that users can keep a number of windows on the screen at the same time, with the areas arranged such that the edge of one might peek out here and the corner of another there, just as a reminder of what is going on or what is available. As a very simple example, one window might contain a clock image that displays real time, and it can be kept to the side and even covered by a document window just as a real clock might sit alongside the terminal and have a paper dropped on top of it. As another example, if the contents of two or more windows need to be compared, such as lists of files on separate diskettes, the windows can be sized

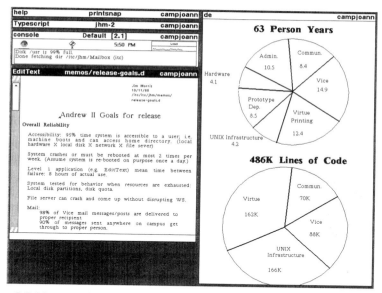

Figure 5.7. Nonoverlapping windows on Andrew. On the left side of the screen, two windows have been closed except for the headers, while one is slightly more open, and the fourth window on that side occupies most of the space. (Courtesy of the Information Technology Center, Carnegie-Mellon University.)

and positioned accordingly to provide the fastest visual comparison.

Going beyond simple manipulation is the use of graphic techniques to enhance the appearance and disappearance of windows. Motion can be suggested that even indicates where the window is coming from or what it looks into. As mentioned in the first chapter, the drawing of a window that results from "opening" or looking into a diskette can be accomplished by rapidly drawing expanding rectangular outlines that emerge from the diskette icon to become the window into the diskette. Similarly, the window for a particular file can expand out of the icon for a file folder. This merger of windows, icons, and simulated motion is a particularly clever way to establish spatial orientation.

DIALOG BOXES

Dialog boxes are difficult to categorize because they embody something of the window concept along with elements of the scrolling menu and the use of commands. Essentially, the dialog box is a rectangular windowlike area of the screen that appears when a certain action is chosen that might require some typed input from the user or in some other way cannot be accommodated by the existing array of menus or icons.

The action of naming a new file is a good example of a situation in which a dialog box appears. It has an area for the user to type a name, as the system could not possibly know what name the user might like to use. If the system can guess some or all of the input, based on what the user has been doing, this might be presented with the user having the option of deleting the guess and entering a new string of characters. Sometimes the dialog box combines a set of menulike options, with limited choices, with a free-form area for text entry. Other times, the dialog box is more for informational purposes and might contain only one option, such as returning to the state before the dialog box appeared. At the opposite end of the scale, if the system has a complete list of options but the list is extensive, such as a directory of files, the list can be scrolled within the dialog box using a scroll bar until the desired name appears for selection by a pointer device such as a mouse. In still other situations where the dialog box provides a way for a user to invoke commands not associated with a graphic environment, the user is able to type any commands understood by the system.

MULTITASKING

As mentioned earlier, the employment of windows does not necessarily mean that the computer system can actively handle more than one task or application at the same time. In a multitasking system, the computer does process more than one application at the same time, keeping track of all programs that are running simultaneously and separately storing all program-dependent values.

The popular Apple Macintosh is currently not a true multitasking machine in that essentially the computer can process only one application at a time. Users cannot run two programs simultaneously and view them in two separate windows.

On the other hand, the Macintosh does use windows to show several things at the same time, and does contain a few general-purpose routines that can be activated while another application is running.

For example, while using MacWrite, and keeping a document visible on the screen, a user can reach up — using the mouse — and select the general-purpose pull-down menu from the strip menu at the top and subsequently click the calculator on. A calculator image will appear on the screen in its own little window that can be moved, and calculations can be done. This is possible because the software routines for the calculator and a few other options are contained in an area of ROM and do not conflict with memory used for the active application. As long as both a MacWrite document and the calculator are on the screen at the same time, if their images overlap, the one actively being used is displayed on top of the other.

True multitasking, which used to be associated only with larger computers, is becoming more common for personal computers, and can be accomplished with or without a graphic interface. Multitasking techniques have been applied to existing microcomputers, and newer, more powerful generations of processor chips for microcomputers are becoming available with operating system software that can exploit them. The result is that multitasking will become a standard feature on personal computers without resorting to the simulated multitasking of the original Macintosh.

COMMON PROCEDURES

As in the case of multitasking, another feature is sometimes, but not always, associated with the use of windows and icons. That feature is commonality — the capacity of the window environment to include a common set of procedures for a variety of different application programs.

The mere fact that a screen can be divided into windows that may even permit two or more different programs to be run at the same time does not necessarily mean that each program would make use of a common set of procedures, whether commands or icons. For example, a business user might have a popular spread sheet package going in one window and a text editor active in another window, and perhaps be searching a data base in a third window. The user would have to know the particular commands and methods of using each program if the procedures were dissimilar. The fact that all three packages can be active and visible on the same screen at the same time is immaterial.

Alternatively, windows that are a true operating system environment might incorporate translation routines that present a common process to the user to reference the disparate capabilities of software packages from many vendors, and to transfer information easily from one application to another. The idea of presenting a common face for many different programs or systems is certainly not new, and has been tried in a number of different situations. The procedures for searching on-line data bases, for example, have long been subjected to attempts to produce a common means for searching within systems that use different command structures. Ideally, a user should need to know only one set of procedures, and this set would be automatically translated into the required commands for the individual data bases.

Another avenue that has been followed in providing a common set of procedures is to create programs that are designed from the start to work together, even though the applications might be different. These programs might be bundled into a single package, such as Lotus Development Corporation's Lotus 1-2-3, which combines a spread sheet with both a graph-generation program and a data base-management system. The more activities that can be built into a single set of programs that work in the same way, the more opportunity there is to provide a unified way of accomplishing any of the available tasks and sharing data among them. If all organizations producing software created all the software to work together using the same procedures, there would be no need to worry about finding a common ground for the usage procedures. That is not the case, however, and a more realistic approach is to place the structure for commonality in an operating system environment.

With windows and icons, the use of a common set of procedures for dissimilar software suggests that the software has been "integrated" into the system. The Apple Macintosh has three items called a Clipboard, a Scrapbook, and a Note Pad. All three can be opened as windows and used as repositories for text, graphics or images (the Note Pad is restricted to text), and all can exist outside of and yet be used with particular application programs such as MacWrite, MacPaint, or a host of other independently created programs. Regardless of whose software is used, as long as the program is designed for the Macintosh environment, exactly the same procedures can be used to move text and graphics into and out of the Clipboard, Scrapbook, and Note Pad. Thus, in this windowed environment, there is a common way to move data, text or graphics, among application programs.

The goal of integrated procedures that are valid across a wide range of software is an attractive one, and has been manifested in many ways other than windows. The graphic interface of the window has put new emphasis on integration, or common procedures, because the windows visually contrast different procedures when two or more programs have not been translated to a common procedure. The multitasking window environment may also make it more difficult for users to shift gears mentally when moving from one application program to another, because instead of tackling one set of procedures at a time, the user might be repeatedly jumping back and forth. On the other hand, an operating system environment with windows and a common set of procedures for using application programs makes it all seem so easy.

ADD-ON WINDOWS

All of the elements of a graphic interface, including graphically expressed windows, share the same problems of technical constraints and the weight of existing practices. Systems that have been created with the capacity for high-resolution, high-speed, bit-mapped graphics make windows seem like a natural way to use a screen, especially in view of the procedures for manipulating them. Many systems were not initially created with windows and icons, though, and reaction has been mixed to programs that have been sold to implement a windowed environment on microcomputers that did not originally include windows.

In the early 1980s, as the Xerox and Apple products with integrated windows were being singled out as the way of the future, other companies began to produce windows that could be added to existing personal computers. In late 1983, Microsoft Corporation, the originators of the MS-DOS operating system used by almost one-fourth of the then 4.4 million microcomputers in offices, announced the Windows product to run on computers using MS-DOS or PC-DOS, including the IBM PC. Other window systems being readied at the same time included VisiOn from VisiCorp, Desq from Quarterdeck Office Systems, and a revised version of the CP/M operating system — a rival of MS-DOS — from Digital Research. "Windows" became a popular topic.

It soon became obvious, however, that the window products to be added to existing microcomputers had problems, including slow speed, the requirement for high-resolution graphics, and some technical glitches. By the end of 1984 the experience with add-on window systems was disappointing enough to cause a *Datamation* article to be entitled "Broken Windows."[16] The slow acceptance of windows and icons as add-on features for personal computers has continued, affected in part by the delays in product introductions and in part by the fact that they are not incorporated within the microcomputer's operating system. Thus they appear to the user as just another piece of applications software with substantial memory requirements. A person already using a microcomputer for a specific task, such as spread sheet analysis, has probably learned enough to use the spread sheet sufficiently well so that it seems to make little sense to add another program on top just to get to the spread sheet.

STANDARD WINDOWS

Beginning in 1986, the future for windows as a basic standard for computer operating systems began to look better, as both hardware and software companies announced plans to integrate Microsoft Windows within their microcomputers and to implement the X Windows standard on workstations. Digital Equipment Corporation built Microsoft Windows into its VAX-Mate microcomputer, and in 1987 IBM announced that its new line of microcomputers would include a new operating system. This was Operating System/2 or OS/2, developed jointly with Microsoft and incorporating multitasking as well as a graphic interface called the Presentation Manager based on Microsoft Windows.

At the workstation level, the X Window System grew out of work done originally at Stanford University followed by a formal project, Project Athena, at MIT. Project Athena was backed financially by the leading computer manufacturers, IBM and DEC, and the resulting X Window System has gained industry support among workstation manufacturers, particularly for networked applications. In January 1987 a dozen manufacturers, including DEC and Apollo but not, initially, IBM and Sun, agreed to a joint effort to establish X Windows as a standard. Within months, Sun Microsystems agreed to combine its own window system, the Network Extensible Window System (NEWS) based on the Postscript language, with X Windows and to share window technology with Microsoft, and IBM has continued its involvement with the proposed X Window standard.

The future for windows generally seems assured in the long term as both workstations and microcomputers continue to incorporate some form of them. From a hardware standpoint, newer processor chips such as the Intel 80386 are making the multitasking windowed environment not only feasible but also desirable as a way to manage a computer's resources.

Metaphors

The words "window" and "icon," which are central to the concept of the graphic interface, are used figuratively in computer parlance, as we all know that a real window is not a drawing on a CRT screen. This use of a word to suggest an analogy with another object is known as a metaphor, and now even the word metaphor has been appropriated by computer system designers to say that the design of the interaction with the user is modeled on some other object or activity. Often, the entire concept of the graphically expressed operating system is called a metaphor of one sort or another, such as the desktop metaphor. To put it another way, the various metaphors that have been proposed act as the unifying theme for the graphic interface.

OBJECT ORIENTATION

Probably the most fundamental metaphor that has been expressed has been called the physical metaphor and has been attributed to Alan Kay, the source of inspiration for much of the work that led to Smalltalk, the Star, and the Macintosh.[17] The idea of the physical metaphor is that the computer system should present its capabilities to users as recognizable physical objects. In that way, persons would almost intuitively know what to do with things. To use the trash can example, if there is an icon of a wastebasket or trash can, it seems pretty obvious that anything placed "in" that area is to be discarded.

The power of the physical metaphor is the power of visual nontextual expression. All of the evidence regarding visual image processing by the brain and the way in which it complements text processing is behind the desire to exploit the visual, nonverbal appreciation of space, shape, texture, color, and relationships. The visual representation of what is "in" the computer and what the computer can do with it is a means of expression that has the potential for conveying more information faster than with words. Users can understand at a glance when looking at a well-designed icon, in less time than it would take to spell out the concept, even if it is the first time that they have seen the icon.

The physical metaphor is a way of saying that the visual displays of a computer system should present the images of real physical objects, with some degree of abstraction. Any number of themes can be followed in converting the activities of a computer system or information system to a cohesive set of visual displays. In practice, the physical metaphor is usually expressed as a more specific metaphor.

DESKTOP

Perhaps the most widely used theme to organize the visual display is that of the desktop. Especially for computer systems intended for workers who normally sit at desks, whether to read and write, analyze numbers, or draw pictures, the desktop seems to provide the appropriate level of familiarity.

The essence of the desktop metaphor is not, however, that the visual display contains anything looking like a desk or a desktop. Instead, the windows are displayed as if they are sheets of paper on top of each other, and icons look like things that might be on a desk. In practice, the word "desktop" should not be taken too literally, as the visual display may contain icons for things that are not usually on a desktop, like a wastebasket. Perhaps a more accurate term would be "office metaphor," because the visual display may show icons for the cabinets, desk drawers, and other things that are usually in an office but not necessarily in or around the desk.

The most dominant impression given by the desktop metaphor is not the desktop as such but the sense of a flat surface on which to work. Even though the CRT screen is most likely vertically positioned, the user accepts the visual display as representing a horizontal surface over which things can be moved, and icons denoting paper, file folders, calendars, and calculators can be readily positioned, stacked, and generally manipulated.

Unlike the real thing, though, the computer display can do things real objects cannot. Windows and icons can be sized to show just what the user wants to keep in mind. This is an important difference. A metaphor is just that, a suggestion of similarity, not a statement of identical properties. Any metaphor trying to adhere too strictly to the source of reference may do so to its own detriment. After all, its purpose in a graphic interface is to capitalize on the familiar while going beyond the limitations of the physical.

BOXES AND SPACE

It is not necessary to involve an elaborate scheme of icons, such as those in some desktop metaphors, to create a metaphor. One particular example of a simple idea, yet intended to do complex things, is Boxer.[18] There are two fundamental design elements for Boxer. One is that everything is simply displayed as belonging to a rectangular area or box, and the boxes, like windows, can be sized and moved, and can overlap or be entirely within another box. The second part of the design is that unlike windows, the very spatial relationships of the boxes define how they interact. Thus the basic metaphor is both box and, more generally, a spatial metaphor.

In essence, Boxer is a programming language because the manipulation of boxes, including adding text or graphics to them, can be used to direct the activities of the system. Figure 5.8 shows a number of boxes within boxes. Some of them are closed except for the header, and others contain statements made up of previous boxes that comprise a program, the results of which are shown in yet another box.

The boxes can also be used for information retrieval. A data base, for example, is a box containing other boxes (records) containing still other boxes (the record elements, or fields). A search of the data base is accomplished by entering the search request, such as a key word, in a box that might be named Keyword. The search is accomplished by a box that contains the programming code defining the search function. As might be expected, the answer arrives in the answer box. The data base is initially defined by the simple spatial arrangement of the field and record boxes, one set inside the other, for each record of data. Similarly, the search procedure is composed of subroutines that act like subroutines because they are inside a box that is within a larger box. Variables can be changed by retyping the data in the appropriate box, and routines changed by moving or removing boxes, as well as editing the content of boxes.

Like Smalltalk, Boxer is intended to be something more than just a metaphor for the visual display by incorporating the idea that users can manipulate the metaphor, in this case the boxes, to modify or even create applications. Boxer also borrows

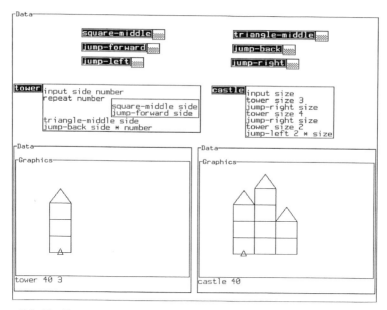

Figure 5.8. The Boxer environment. Boxes can contain other boxes, and can contain text and graphics. Some of the boxes are closed except for their titles. (Courtesy of the School of Education, University of California, Berkeley.)

from the work done at MIT on spatial data management, and on the educational software known as Logo, thus representing the long line of research that has generally fed the development of the graphic interface. Regardless of Boxer's ultimate fate as a programming language based on the spatial relationships of the boxes, the very use of the word boxes instead of windows or some other word shows that there are other ways to refer to the relevant areas of a flat screen. Those areas do resemble boxes much more than windows. The fact that spatial relationships are key to Boxer functions is an indication that we are only beginning to exploit the capability of the screen to display spatial relationships and the ability of the brain to interpret spatial relationships.

OTHER METAPHORS

Some metaphors have been suggested for computer systems that will never be implemented, at least seriously. It does not hurt to consider them at least briefly, however, to emphasize the point that the desktop metaphor is not the only one in existence, and that many other arrangements are possible.

A 1983 article in *Byte* magazine suggested metaphors based on a kitchen with, among other things, a refrigerator icon representing storage; an elevator, where each floor is an application; a cave, in which graphics are done on the walls; a cocktail lounge, with a bouncer to remove (delete) files; and a video gamelike battlestation in which the word processor is a "phraser" beam.[19] The article also suggested that a desktop metaphor may be fine for the near term, but wondered what would happen when widespread electronic systems take over real desktop activities to such an extent that workers no longer have any experience with that part of the metaphor. Such an event is not likely even in the forseeable long term, but perhaps the desktop metaphor will eventually be replaced for other reasons.

USEFULNESS

Given the wide range of unifying themes, even serious ones, that could be used for the visual display of information systems, it is not at all clear that the desktop metaphor is the best. Other metaphors may come along that will strike an even more responsive chord. Beyond the question of which metaphor, is a more basic question involving the usefulness of any of them.

Like icons, metaphors for the visual organization of the capabilities of a computer system can be misused to the extent of causing confusion or at best being less than helpful. Some researchers of screen formats and system design speak of "metaphor-induced troubles," and liken the problem to the psychological notion of functional fixedness.[20] Users take the metaphor too literally, and cannot see the differences between the real thing and a suggestion of it. Instead of being helped by the metaphor to grasp the capabilities of the system because of the reference to a well-known arrangement, the unfortunate users are kept from realizing the full capabilities of the system because they attribute limitations of the original concept to the system employing the metaphor.

Even if the metaphor does not result in such confusion, there still may be a mismatch between the capabilities of a system and the metaphor used to express them. A particular visual arrangement, or even a single icon, may not suggest to some people exactly what the system designers thought it should suggest.

It is dangerous, therefore, to push the value of one metaphor or another too hard. The use of a desktop metaphor does not mean that a computer display has to look exactly like a desktop or behave exactly like a desktop. If a certain visual arrangement is found helpful by a wide variety of users, and if there is something about the metaphor that leads people to call it a desktop, or boxes, or whatever, its value can be accepted and refined. As visual arrangements are used increasingly and experience accumulates, we can expect to see even more responsive metaphors for computerized information systems.

Information Maps

Another concept that has the potential for being a powerful guide in using systems to enter into worlds of information is the map. To the extent that a map for an information system has the properties of a map but does not actually chart a physical terrain, it is a metaphor. Yet a map to an information space also meets the definition of a real map as a representation of an area, even though the area in question is an abstraction of the arrangement and storage location of the actual binary digits. In what might be considered a preliminary step toward full-function maps, some information systems currently use the word "map" to refer to an outline organized as a table or a tree-structured menu.

If the concept does become accepted, information maps will take their place along with icons and windows as a standard part of the graphic interface.

VISUAL ORGANIZATION

A map is an inherently visual representation, and would appear to be a natural addition to information systems that have the technical capacity for a graphic interface. Previous chapters emphasized the point that for thousands of years information has been located spatially. Then, in the matter of a few decades, vast amounts of information became stored in coded form in a virtually invisible manner, and the only means of access continues to be a computer display. The information is organized, to be sure, such that logical procedures can be followed to search for specific things, but at least one step removed from the actual location of the binary digits. Now, the situation is changing once again, as visual means for representing the stored information are becoming more practical. The long history of relating to spatially located information can once again be realized with on-screen maps to the data in many logical arrangements rather than just one.

The desktop metaphor with icons is a reasonable way to present visually the capabilities of a system, but it does not solve the problem of letting the user know visually what the extent is of any and all accessible data bases or information files. At the application level, some programs have been developed that do use graphics in the form of icons to represent the information in a data base. Filevision for the Macintosh, from Telos Software Products, is one such attempt to bring the visual dimension to information retrieval. The contents of the data base (the records, in traditional terms) are created by establishing icons for them, and the whole can be organized visually as a real physical space. A click of the mouse on a specific picture or icon might result in the display of a more detailed view with its own collection of icons or with text displayed in a pop-up window.

The Filevision product has a number of other capabilities for enhancing the display, and has even been used with maps of the United States to display data that relate to specific geographic locations, but Filevision is not at its core a mapping procedure. There is a difference between using visual representations, and providing a standardized visual guide, or map, to the location of information.

MAP FORMS

The forms that information maps can assume are many, and some do not require very sophisticated graphics. A data base that is organized very simply as a series of subsets, the familiar inverted tree, can be depicted as just that, an upside-down tree with a single point at the top and a hierarchical series of branches. The tree's drawing becomes the map. Because tree-shaped data bases are also often menu based, the term "menu map" has been used to refer to the picture of the tree's organization. It is not unusual for the builders of such data bases to provide a drawing of the tree in which each node corresponds to a frame of information that can be accessed and viewed. Some studies have concluded that, at least in some restricted examples, users with menu maps perform retrieval tasks better than those without.[21]

Another form of a map that can be drawn relatively easily is the network, or an arrangement of the pieces of information, or topics, with interrelationships that are not strictly hierarchical or tree structured. The basic difference with regard to the impact of the network map is the suggestion that the user can get to a given piece of information by a number of paths, and not only by starting at the top and working down through some logical hierarchy.

Using a more graphic procedure, but with a similar arrangement, the data base can be represented as a collection of areas that, for ease of recognition and recall, can be distinguished graphically. The areas might even be arranged on the display surface such that no hierarchy is implied. This can be an improvement over the menu maps that, by virtue of the fact that a numeric order might be imposed, may suggest that some items are more important than others. With a more visual arrangement instead of the numerically ordered list, topics assume a certain amount of independence. One user might judge the relative importance of the topics in one manner, and another could see the same display in an entirely different light.

Other graphic forms that specify the location of information do have some value but do not quite match the normal understanding of the map concept. For example, information can be represented by document icons, arranged in file folder icons, placed in file drawer icons, and so on. This is similar to the Filevision product mentioned above, except that rather than individualized icons for specific data bases, such as a wine bin for a data base on wines, a standard set of icons can hold any type of information. Such an arrangement is unlike a map in that it has no encompassing spatial arrangement that shows locations and relationships in a single view as a real geographic map would. On the other hand, the sense of a map is conveyed as icons are opened to reveal the spatial relationships.

The problem with many information maps is that they quickly become unwieldy as the data base grows to any size. It becomes difficult to represent everything on a single map. The result is that the map then becomes a set of maps, hierarchically arranged, and it becomes even more difficult to keep everything in mind or to find something. An exception, of course, is when the map is based on real geography and thus the relationships of the detailed levels to the whole is well known. If the display device can show the set of maps quickly and in juxtaposition, such as with windows, and the user can easily click in and out of levels, the problem is not as severe. There is no common form for such maps, however, and no consensus that they should be more graphic than not, or might even be graphically arranged words, like entries in a thesaurus.

If information maps are to be successful, a standard system must be developed to provide two things: a consistent and recognizable way to express the extent and arrangement of information in data base; and an easily followed route to the desired "location" of information. It will not be easy to create such maps. They must have the same familiarity as real maps and yet not be limited by characteristics of real maps that do not apply to data bases. Information maps, for example, should provide several arrangements of the same information, as the power of the computer has released stored information from the restrictions of physical proximity. They also must provide a complete overview, or world map, of all the information that is available through the system, which can be enormous, as well as the detail necessary to navigate to a chosen spot. It is quite likely that information maps will have some hierarchical properties or relative detail, as we are used to using maps that have varying levels of resolution. We use a state map to follow the highway to a city, but we may need a city map to follow the streets.

Geographic maps have a long history and are well understood. Moreover, the reality behind them — streets and roads, cities and countryside — is what we see every day. We know very well what to expect and how to use the map to find our way. Information systems and the organization of data bases are not that familiar. Procedures for visually representing the contents and artificial arrangements of data bases are even less familiar. Eventually, information maps, in a design perhaps yet to be developed, should make their way into the information system environment as natural navigational aids.

Proprietary Graphics

The usefulness of the graphic interface is based in part on the extent to which objects and actions can be represented in the same way across different systems. Icons or pictographs used in airports and on highways are most readily understood if the same ones are used to mean the same thing regardless of location. In the computer world, there is some doubt about the right of any organization to sell a product using a graphic interface similar to that of another organization.

When Xerox developed a set of icons for the Star workstation, the company secured copyrights for them. Subsequently, those icons have been used in similar form without any action by Xerox to prevent their use. Apple Computer, on the other hand, threatened to sue Digital Research in 1985 because the latter's GEM (Graphics Environment Manager) was deemed to be too close to the Macintosh graphic interface. The threat of the lawsuit was withdrawn in late 1985 after Digital Research agreed to change some things such as the location of icons and to let Apple review the new version of GEM before its release, as well as to pay Apple a sum of money. The immediate result of the action by Apple, and the agreement by Digital Research, was to make system designers a little less inclined to borrow features of a graphic interface directly from another company, even though the public good would probably be served best by consistency.

The legal uncertainty has continued, revolving now around the question of whether one piece of software copies the "look and feel" of another. In one case, a freelance programmer sued Jaslow Dental Laboratory for creating a program that did the same thing as the freelancer's program, which was being marketed by Jaslow. The suit was decided in the freelancer's favor because the Jaslow product was similar in "structure, sequence and organization." In mid-1985, two software firms, Broderbund Software Inc. and Pixellite Software, filed suit against Unison World Inc. (now called Kyocera Unison) charging that the latter's design and sequencing of screens in a software package called Printmaster violated the copyright of the suitors' product called Print Shop. In October 1986 the suit was upheld in federal court, on the basis that the general appearance of a product, including the design, structure, and appearance of screens that constitute the user interface, is subject to copyright protection. After all, screen designs for video games can be copyrighted. Thus, the "look and feel" test was established.

In early 1987 another suit was filed, this time by Lotus Development Corporation against two competitors, charging that the look and feel of Lotus 1-2-3 had been copied. Subsequently, Lotus itself was sued for copyright infringement, among other things, by the company that developed VisiCalc. In yet another case Digital Communications Associates won a court test of the copyright for its Crosstalk screens. Eventually, a series of legal decisions may be required before a direction is established, but the current uncertainty suggests that firms will not lightly use the elements of another company's graphic interface.

Summary

As visual display devices displaced paper printouts, the possibilities for visually arranging the elements of interaction with a computer system began to expand. With the arrival of the technology to use graphics, and particularly bit-mapped graphics, the visual organization of the interaction became a multifaceted graphic interface. Menus are depicted on all portions of the display screen, including within the context of text or graphics presented, and can dynamically appear and disappear as pop-up or pull-down menus. The menu form of choices can also be expressed in a number of graphic ways for setting levels or moving along a continuum, such as a scroll bar. Icons or pictographs have been designed to represent objects and processes within a system to allow users to visually grasp the concepts much faster than if expressed in words, as well as providing a constant reminder, or prompt, of the options. The graphic interface also encompasses windows in which the screen is divided up into areas that can be moved, sized, stacked, or otherwise manipulated to keep track of several things at once. Some windows are primarily a means of graphically segmenting the screen, while others display the effects of multitasking, where the computer is in fact handling two or more processes at the same time. Metaphors such as the desktop have been created to provide the unifying theme for the graphic interface. In the future, an extension to the graphic interface, the map, may be required to provide a uniform way to travel to the depths of extensive information systems.

6
SIGHT AND INSIGHT

One of the more tantalizing promises of visual information systems is the ability to spark understanding, insight, imagination, and creativity through the use of graphic representations and arrangements. Especially in cases where the visual arrangement shows relationships that we might not have thought of before, there is the potential for evoking creative processes similar to those fleeting moments of instant understanding that "just come" to us. A major power of visual display is its ability to cause us to say, "*Now* I see!"

The evidence supporting the notion that visual information systems may be a substantial improvement over text-based information systems is at the same time obvious and tenuous. On the obvious side, pictures have a long-standing reputation for encapsulating concepts that would take many words to explain. A well-conceived data graph, particularly, can quickly show the relationships of thousands and even millions of data points or observations. As Edward Tufte aptly demonstrated, "No other method for the display of statistical information is so powerful."[1] Perhaps the surprising fact about data graphic procedures, given their remarkable ability to reveal associations, is that civilized society took such a long time to develop them. According to Tufte, it was not until the 1600s that persons in any society began adding data points to geographic maps, and it was not until the mid-1700s that researchers finally advanced to the stage of creating relational data graphics — statistical plots — that were not based on the drawings of physical features or geographic maps. Graphics cannot do everything, of course, and words have their own power for conveying information and invoking a mental response. It belabors the obvious to say that visual techniques will only enhance, not replace, textual information, or words.

The degree of the enhancement is less obvious. Graphic symbols and spatial arrangements may, in the near term in many cases, appear to be only minor improvements on the process of information access. The very fact that information systems can be managed visually and information can be manipulated in nontextual ways suggests that these methods will tap the power of visual comprehension that extends beyond the range of reading words.

How and in what manner this can be done is based on what we know (and do not know) about the intellectual processes of acquiring and making use of information, including creativity and insight, and on how we currently acquire information through the use of information systems. If creative thinking is "seeing" things in a new or different light, for example, a system that can help assemble these new or different "pictures," or juxtaposing of information, may indeed represent a dramatic change in the capabilities of information systems. At the least, and as previously described, implementation of graphics in computer systems in general is already increasing to facilitate the operation of the systems. The newer systems of the next generation of computers, the so-called fifth generation, will incorporate graphics and visual techniques even further.

This chapter begins with an assessment of creativity and insight, and relates that to current work on calculating the meaning and interrelationships of stored information with graphic procedures for doing so. It concludes with a look ahead toward what might occur with the use of more advanced visual techniques.

Creative Thinking

It is no doubt possible to find discussions, and fair ones, of thinking, imagination, creativity, and understanding from just about any period of the recorded history of human society. Some of the earliest Chinese philosophers grappled with the notion that there exists an ability to comprehend that is more than just listening to or reading words. A third-century Taoist text summarized the ancient Chinese appreciation of this difference in saying, "Words are for holding ideas, but when one has got the idea, one need no longer think about the words."[2] In Taoism, this ability to understand without words is a fundamental principle, but it is also an expression of the more general experience we have all had of mentally grasping something without any conscious connection to a set of words.

In more recent times we have continued to delve into what it means to comprehend intuitively and to imagine in relation to how our senses are stimulated, and with each sense further subdivided, such as reading text or seeing images. In innumerable explorations and studies, researchers have identified some characteristics as indicative of intelligent and creative thinking. A common finding is the ability to see things in a different light, coupled with the ability to make something of that difference.

IMAGINATION

In the 1950s, as the construction of computers was just beginning, a number of studies were conducted at the University of California to determine the common characteristics of persons from many professions recognized for their creative and original thinking.[3] The purpose of the studies was to try to discover differences between individuals recognized by society as highly creative and those who were not. The conclusions are still valid today.

The studies examined artists and scientists, students, and professionals with a variety of techniques, ranging from written tests and drawing-completion exercises to arranging figures and articles on a miniature stage. In most cases, the results of the tests were compared against independent group judgments by peers, instructors, or society at large regarding the originality or creativity of those being studied.

One of the primary conclusions was that persons noted for their originality are able to make sense out of complexity, to look at an unusual or unknown complex arrangement and see something in it. Test subjects who consistently chose answers or completed activities that demonstrated this ability to resolve complexity in an unusual way turned out to be those who were independently evaluated by society as creative and original. In tests involving the completion of line drawings and the construction of mosaics, these individuals tended to create things that were more complex (and asymmetrical). In figure-preference tests, the same type of person often gave higher ratings to figures that were not only complex and asymmetrical but almost chaotic. In the inkblot tests, the creative people generally tried to synthesize a complex blot, which the authors of the study termed the creative response to disorder.

Upon reflection, these studies of creativity may not seem to be particularly revolutionary and may even be a confirmation of the obvious. The authors readily admitted that they were using fairly standard psychological tests, and were accomplishing only one small step in analyzing creativity and "constructive imagination." They also noted the often-cited thin line between genius and madness. The conclusions, however, if accepted as valid, do establish a base from which to work. If we start from the point that identifies creativity in part as a capacity for seeing something out of the ordinary in complex representations, the next step would be to devise ways to increase the likelihood that those normally less creative might be helped to make the same response as creative individuals.

What might evolve is a system for graphically expressed information that could display complex relationships in an interactive way so that the person who does not readily resolve complexity would be led to see that which others intuitively see. The critical factor is not that the system necessarily displays an answer, but that it leads the user along, nudging the creative response, without in fact having "the answer" itself.

At the very simplest level, we already have evidence that a graphic display can help people, from the use of color to highlight a key point to the relational power of statistical graphics. At a higher level, a "creativity-inducing" system becomes harder to describe, as it must respond in a way that mimics creativity while not claiming to be more creative and original than the user. By definition it is to spark creativity in the user, not take over in place of the user. On the other hand, this sort of capability is part of the realm of expert systems, discussed later in this chapter, in that the same approach to capturing the expert's actions might be applied to capturing the creative person's methods.

If such a system seems a bit beyond the range of current information-processing systems, the capability for showing relationships that can be grasped visually and not as a sequence of words is not. The promise lies in what the visual component, addressing different information-processing capabilities within the brain, can add to existing forms of computerized information processing in order to bring us closer to systems that can really help the majority of us to do things normally reserved for the creative few.

RECOMBINATION

The ability to make sense out of the unusual has also been expressed in other ways, and has been expanded to include the concepts of mentally taking apart the ordinary and recombining the parts in a new whole. These abilities have, in fact, been proposed as the key elements in much of the progress of civilization.

One theme in broad discussions of the development of society has been the effect of the environment on a given society. Specifically, the fact that a society learns to combine and recombine the known with the unknown has been proposed as a procedure that has led to the growth of knowledge. Karl Deutsch pointed to maritime and caravan civilizations as ones that were able to readily dissociate existing knowledge and then recombine it to build a new collection of knowledge about the world.[4] By dissociating and recombining concepts, these societies were able to build upon their past and their wide range of experience, rather than being bound by the past. He went on to say that "abstraction, dissociation, recombination and transfer" are the roots of "the boldness of modern thought."

In a similar vein, Daniel Bell attributed the growth of knowledge, or the creation of new knowledge, to the ability to put things together mentally in different patterns. He spoke of the fitting together of intellectual mosaics as the fruitful reordering, rearranging, and reorganizing of perceptions, experiences, and ideas.[5] This can be taken as a statement about the social as well as the individual development of ideas. While the rearranging and the recombination of ideas on the societywide level may occur as the result of the contributions of a number of individuals, the development of ideas on the individual level can also occur as the result of a person taking one thought or experience and making an uncommon association with something else, producing a new thought.

Without claiming to know just how some persons accomplish this abstraction and recombination, there does seem to be a potential role for an information system that can help the process along. By using a procedure for encapsulating ideas, recombining these into a new intellectual mosaic, and presenting the display as a visual association, the machine may help the person to make what we currently call a creative leap. At this point, the exact process used by the information system to find these new associations does not have to be known yet; the system might even make associations at random that still spark intelligent response.

Assuming, however, that methods can eventually be devised to come up with dissociations and recombinations that are better than random, there does seem to be ample evidence that such recombinations by visual information systems will be beneficial. The evidence comes from two areas: the importance granted by scholars to the human ability to abstract, rearrange, and recombine thoughts, which admittedly in the past has had nothing to do with computerized information systems; and the power attributed by researchers to the human ability to grasp information visually, such that this visual synthesis reflects the process of creative thought. In other words, original and creative thinking, in the sciences as well as the arts, has stemmed from the individual ability to imagine things and relationships, or to see something in the mind's eye. The very fact that we use a visual metaphor to express this reveals the close connection this has to physically seeing things. Obviously, we have no proof that a computerized system that creates pictures of conceptual relationships would be able to help initiate creativity and insight, but we do have the experience often enough of reaching a new conclusion because of a singular visual impression.

Measuring Relationships

The computer's potential for combining concepts or rearranging ideas in a fruitful way is based in part upon procedures to measure meaning, that is, techniques for quantifying the relationships among words.

In information systems, and particularly the great majority of existing systems that store and retrieve text, various procedures have evolved to retrieve information based on some measure of closeness in meaning among the items retrieved. These procedures have been developed in the effort to go beyond the level of simplistic searching, where a person asks the system to find information matching a search request fairly exactly. For example, if we have a data base of items with dates stored and ask for all items matching a given date, or even within a date range, the system can do an excellent job of retrieving all the items, barring any clerical errors in putting the information into the system at the start or any gross system failures.

The retrieval task becomes more complex as we deal with information that has been stored with less structure, and as the request becomes a phrase, sentence, or paragraph that, taken as whole, represents an idea that may be expressed in myriad ways in the stored information. The presence of more or less structure in the information stored in a data base or information system has, in fact, been used as a means of distinguishing between traditional data base-management systems and text-based information retrieval systems. The data base-management systems were, and still are for the most part, characterized by the storage of data in well-defined fields in very specific ways. As a common example, an employee data base might contain fields for name, social security number, date of hire, salary, and the like, and each field contains only the defined type of entry. An on-line information system containing lengthy text, such as all issues of a daily newspaper, would also have some structure, such as specified fields for dates, but might also permit searches on any word within entire articles. With some measures of closeness, articles may be found that are about a desired topic but yet do not contain the actual word or words used by the information seeker to describe that topic.

Thus procedures have been developed to bridge the gap between the expression of what is sought and the expressions of what is stored. A very common practice is the use of descriptors. When an article or item is stored in a system, one or more descriptors are chosen (either by a person or sometimes by an automated procedure) from a carefully organized list, whether or not the descriptive terms actually exist in the article. A story concerning a congressional action might be given the additional tag of "federal government," even though that term did not appear in the story. Someone looking for material on the federal government would therefore be presented with this story as a possible item of interest. This process of classifying items according to a predetermined set of relationships is an extension of the practice begun in the earliest collections of written material, where like things were either grouped together physically or on lists or indexes. The process has, of course, continued in the organization of subject indexes of all kinds, from the document level to the largest libraries. Such organizations of material are obviously useful, but always limited by the terms permitted in the classification list and the judgment of the person doing the classifying.

CO-OCCURRENCES AND COUNTS

Many of the procedures developed to go beyond the limits of the traditional classification schemes are based on counting and matching words and word stems in relation to each other within the entity being stored and within the mass of stored information in general. These procedures are of interest because they represent a desire to go beyond individual words to concepts in a textual environment, and they may provide a starting point for the development of more visually oriented procedures.

One of the earlier, more well-known systems to use word counts and word frequencies as a retrieval method was the SMART system developed at Cornell University in the late 1960s. All words except common ones such as "the" in both the stored information and the multiword search were first reduced to word stems, for example, by removing normal suffixes. A value or weight was then assigned to each word stem based on its number of occurrences in any single document and in the search request. Thus a set of weighted word stems would represent each document as well as the request. A way to establish weight mathematically, for example, could be the number of occurrences of a term in the document (or search statement) divided by the number of all terms in that document (or search statement). The weighted set for the request was then compared to the set for each document and a correlation coefficient computed for each pair, which is a procedure for producing a measure of the similarity of two sets of data. The higher the correlation coefficient, the more likely that the document matched the idea expressed in the search request. This method is also known as the vector space model, as the set of terms can be considered as vectors, and both documents and search statements are represented as combinations of vectors.

In one of the many tests of the SMART system in the automated retrieval of stored text, the rather simple method of measuring similarity was not as good as a more traditional classification scheme used by humans to predetermine the descriptors to be attached to articles or items.[6] The system could be improved, however, with additional measures using word frequencies. Certain words could be identified as "nondiscriminators" because they occurred in too many documents. In computing the correlation coefficients for all pairs of documents, if by adding a given word it tended to increase the average similarity among documents, that word was a nondiscriminator because it caused all documents to look alike. In a data base of scientific material, the word "result" is a nondiscriminator. By ignoring the nondiscriminating words, the results of the fully automatic retrieval process became quite close to that of the search of a traditional data base prestructured by experts. A few more techniques were added, such as intermediate searching where a collection of documents is presented to the searcher, the more pertinent ones are selected, and that set of weighted term stems is used to search the data base again. Also, automatic reference to a thesaurus or list of synonymous and related terms was added. Thus the results of the fully automated procedure were judged to be equivalent to the nonautomated method.

MULTIDIMENSIONAL RELATIONS

During the past 20 or so years, information system researchers have explored variations on the notion that the closeness of terms can be measured and used as an indication of meaning, especially when compared to a set of terms that constitutes a search request, and perhaps presented graphically. The system, of course, does not actually determine meaning, but matches items that might mean the same thing based on the words used. Some of the variations are minor adjustments in the measures used and others represent a distinct change, making use of the notion of information as existing in an imaginary area.

In the late 1970s at Syracuse University, another system was proposed in which documents or concepts could be represented by a set of words (or word stems) plotted in a multidimensional space.[7] To be specific, concepts could be said to be points in space, and a document — or collection of concepts — would be located at the point most central to all the concepts, plotted as points, expressed in the document. When an information search request would be plotted into the same multidimensional space, the points closest to the plotted point containing the desired concepts would be chosen as the documents most likely to satisfy the request. In a suggested alternative version of the system, a circle or loop could be drawn around the specific points or documents identified to enclose points that had not been previously identified because they did not contain any of the concept terms, although they still might be related in some way.

Conceptually, the system was attractive as a means of using spatial dimensions to categorize information, but some mathematical difficulties arose in computing the location of points. More recent work continues to support the proposal that documents can be located in multidimensional space at the mean, or average, location of the concepts involved.[8] The idea is that both individual words and documents containing those words can be located in an imaginary space at some average distance from all concepts that constitute the terms or documents. The mathematical support for such a model is argued to be an improvement over the procedures known as vector space models in that it takes account of some of the inconsistencies and difficulties of the vector space models caused by assumptions about the similarity, and nonsimilarity, of terms.

A problem remains in trying to determine the relationships of concepts simply by counting the frequencies and co-occurrences of words. One suggestion is that at least two concepts can be said to be completely unrelated, or independent of each other, with respect to a given data base if they never appear together in any document in that data base. Given the flexibility of language, that is not necessarily true. Even if it were, that still does not lead to a measure of the closeness of concepts that are related.

Currently, even though a lot can be determined by the frequency of words used together, human effort still is often necessary in establishing sets of words that are related. Such sets can be formal arrangements, such as a thesaurus with "broader terms," "narrower terms," and "related terms," or a less formal clustering of terms without specifying a hierarchical relationship.

DISTANCE AS A MEASURE

Another way to try to establish the relationships among terms, documents, and queries is to concentrate on the concept of distance, specifically the mathematical concept of distance among abstract sets. During the last half-century in mathematics, abstract distance has gained acceptance as a way to unify various theories, and is believed by some information researchers to be one of the most fundamental concepts in information retrieval.

An abstract distance measure is useful as a means of calculating relationships but at the same time is difficult to represent graphically in two or even three dimensions. A simple example can be shown graphically as a tree graph, where "distance" is not the physical separation of nodes but the number of operations required to change one tree, or structural representation, into another.[9] The differences between two trees can, in fact, be seen visually, however. In the simple example in Figure 6.1, two books are represented in a data base by the set of terms: computer science, pattern recognition, text, syntactic pattern recognition, applications. Book A, however, shows a different relationship among the terms than book B. As mentioned above, the abstract distance concept as used here refers not to the separation between the nodes of a tree, but to the differences between the trees as measured by the effort to make one look like the other.

If a data base contains documents in which all the terms are structurally related, the abstract distance among all document pairs might be calculated, as well as the distance between a search statement and all of the documents in the data base. Unfortunately, for data bases of any size, the amount of calculating required is still far beyond the capability of modern computers in a reasonable time. Therefore procedures have been proposed to approximate the impossible exhaustive distance calculations.

One procedure again uses the idea of a tree graph where each node represents a cluster of documents. The starting node is the entire data base and the branches of the tree lead to successive subsets. To find the document that is closest to the search statement, the abstract distance between it and a given

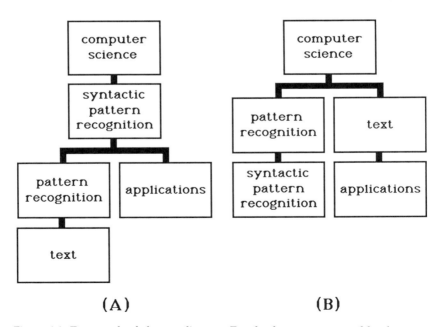

(A)   **(B)**

Figure 6.1. Tree graph of abstract distance. Two books are represented by the same keywords, but the relationships among the keywords are different. (Adapted from Lev Goldfarb, "Metric Data Models and Associated Search Strategies," *SIGIR Forum* 20 [Spring-Summer 1986]:7–11.)

node should determine which subnode is the next closest. As successive subnodes are reached, the clusters of documents grow smaller until the document or document cluster that is closest to the query is found. This, of course, assumes that the data base has already been clustered according to the distance calculations.

In all of the above models and similar procedures, there is an overwhelming acceptance of the usefulness of representations in real or abstract space, with notions of the closeness and relative distance of terms as indications of similarity in meaning. The problems encountered revolve around the need to find procedures to process and calculate the relationships when dealing with very large collections of words and documents, and the persistent gap between concepts as expressed in phrases, sentences, and paragraphs, and the reduction of that to any other form of representation.

SCREEN ARRANGEMENTS

With the availability of technology for displaying the relationships of terms and concepts on a video screen, graphics are being exploited to enhance these current information retrieval models, despite their shortcomings. If concepts, words, and documents can be mathematically located in imaginary space and statistically compared, to the extent possible the obvious next step is to depict the spatial orientation visually. This gives the user the advantage of literally being able to see the web of relationships, depending, of course, upon the success of the visual display in encompassing all of the relationships.

As a beginning, the display can keep the relationships to a two-dimensional representation, but can mix graphics and spatial arrangements with alphabetic organization. A simple example where the organization of terms has a real geographic basis can be drawn from the process of searching for a telephone number in a computerized telephone directory. Assuming that all telephone numbers in the country can be made available, perhaps on a disk for a personal computer such as a compact disk, the first display can be a literal geographic map of the country or any subset of that as chosen by the user to be the starting point. Using a mouse, a person could select a general area, causing a window to pop up showing an alphabetical breakdown similar to the headings on the top of each page of a paper telephone directory (Fig. 6.2). When the user selects one of the subheadings, the next window to pop up shows a column of listings pretty much as on a printed page. The user could move up or down the listings and click on the desired name, and the microcomputer could place the call.

At each step of the above process, the directory listings shown would be related directly to the geographic area chosen, so that expanding or shrinking the area would immediately affect the quantity of listings potentially viewable in the window; that is, the spatial organization and the alphabetic organization are dynamically related. There may be times when we are not sure of a person's geographic location and would type a name as a query, but in general the geographic orientation gives us a way to narrow an information search to a manageable size based on an understood spatial relationship among the items.

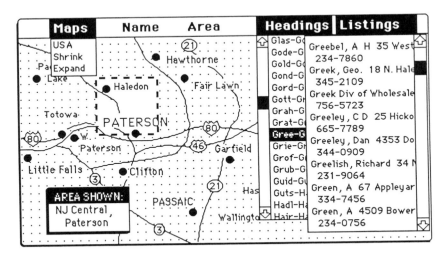

Figure 6.2. Mapping telephone directories. Various windows are shown open at the same time for illustrative purposes. Shrinking or expanding the geographic area selected would cause the listings to be modified appropriately.

Many other information searches have no geographic relationship, but still can have a perceived organization that yields to spatial arrangements. Assuming that we have a data base of articles and we want to locate information on a given topic, one procedure would be to start with a thesauruslike arrangement of terms surrounding the term given as the topic. The location of related terms, as well as the size of the lettering used, on a visual display, could indicate the closeness and quantity of related articles based on both an analysis of word frequencies and co-occurrences of words in the documents actually in the data base and on an intellectual analysis of topic relationships by a human expert (Fig. 6.3). The searcher could then select a number of the related areas, either by drawing a circle around the selected terms or by clicking on the related terms. The next pop-up window could display the titles of articles in the areas selected together with the context of the articles, such as the journal title. Ideally, the subsequent window would show the full text of the chosen article, complete with illustrations. Once again, changing the view of the spatial

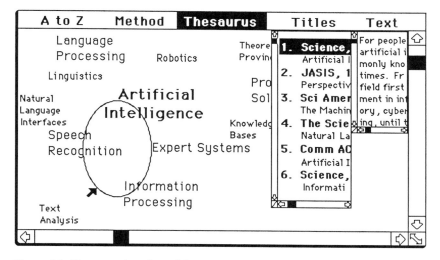

Figure 6.3. Thesaurus-based spatial arrangement. Again, several windows are open for illustrative purposes. The windows showing the titles and the text would be sized to show more or less of their content.

organization, the thesauruslike structure, would immediately change the listings and text in arrangement, quantity, and content.

This example was presented without specifying exactly how the relationships among concepts would be determined in order to produce the visual display, so that the potential value of the visual arrangement would not be clouded by attention to one particular method or another of calculating the relationships. Now, however, it might be helpful to look at the details of a given procedure.

In one system designed to plot visually the relationships of terms in a multiple-sentence request, a measure of lexical distance was established based on the co-occurrence of words right next to each other, within the same sentence, or within the same paragraph.[10] Specifically, each word is paired with each other word, and a score is assigned using a formula that includes a rating of 1 of the words are adjacent within a sentence, 2 if the words are within a sentence but not adjacent, and 3 if the words are in adjacent sentences within the same paragraph. The values for all word pairs then form the basis for a two-dimensional plot of the strength of the associations. Figure 6.4 shows a plot of 13 word pairs from a four-sentence request for information on the use of espionage to gain competitive business information. The word "espionage" was used in three of the four sentences in the request, and is shown as one of the more central concepts. Similarly, the phrase "proprietary information" was used in two sentences, and the fact that the words were used adjacent to each other is reflected in the plot.

This plot may give an overall view of the concepts in the information seeker's statements, but some problems do exist. The word "competitor" is not near "information," but the focus of the request is on competitor information. A much greater problem is the confusion that might occur when trying to apply this plotting technique to a very large number of word pairs.

Thus the difficult task of determining how to measure the closeness of concepts remains, together with the secondary task of finding the best visual representation. These examples have assumed a two-dimensional display, but if the measures of closeness exist in multidimensional space, a representative display may need at least three dimensions. The information

Question: I am doing a group project for class. We are trying to design
an espionage information system to be used by a hypothetical
business to gain proprietary information from competitors.
I would like to know if anything has been written on the use
of espionage, that is, covert, illicit or illegal activities. To
obtain proprietary information, I have done a number of searches
on SULIRS using search words such as: espionage, corporate
intelligence; and have found a number of articles and one book.

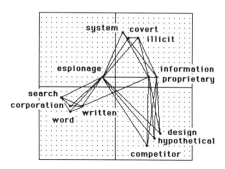

Figure 6.4. Plot of term relationships. Values for word-pairs have been calculated and plotted relative to each other. (Adapted from Ruth Ann Palmquist and Michael Eisenberg, "Testing a Text Analysis Metric Using Magnitude Estimation," *Proceedings of the 47th ASIS Annual Meeting,* vol. 21 [White Plains, N.Y.: Knowledge Industry Publications, 1984], 231–36.)

seeker could move in and around the information space studded with clusters of concepts, and be able to see different relationships by changing the viewpoint. The visualization of the information space does not, however, have to be a rather abstract multidimensional space of floating dots. Instead, the space could be a much more concrete arrangement based on familiar ways of organizing information, such as the metaphors of the previous chapter. In fact, as experience and research have shown, it is not usually helpful to make the visual display too complex or unusual. If it has too many levels of organization, or the implied movement through the information space is not obvious, users can feel confused and hindered by the system, rather than helped.

In the near term, there are several ways in which the existing procedures for finding information by assessing the similarity or closeness of concepts and terms, documents, and questions can be represented visually. As they evolve, they will make use of the theoretical underpinning provided by the continuing research on measures of closeness, abstract distance, and related concepts.

Dynamic Arrangements

In addition to the problems of devising programs to measure the relationships among words and planning the visual displays that contribute to our mental capacity for visually grasping information relationships, there is the notion that such relationships do not and should not remain static. In the first section of this chapter, creativity and insight were linked to the ability to assemble mentally, in a productive way, ideas or concepts that had not been normally associated with each other, that is, to see things in a new light. That is certainly an argument for developing information systems that can contribute to progress by prompting the production of these creative associations; but there are other ways that a notion of dynamic associations has had an impact on information retrieval.

At one level, the meanings of words can change over time, and new words and phrases are constantly introduced that incorporate concepts previously embodied, in whole or in part, by other words or phrases. Therefore, word associations have to evolve to reflect changes in language. On a more immediate scale, there can be a mismatch between the words of the information seeker and the words in the data base, even though both may be expressing the same or related concepts. In these cases, the information system could adapt to the seeker's vocabulary, rather than the other way around, in order to make the associations that the seeker is looking for. On an even more immediate level, the information seeker could be changing and modifying his or her own idea of the relevant associations as an information search is in progress. The last two levels have customarily been addressed by the use of feedback techniques.

RELEVANCE FEEDBACK

In information retrieval, procedures allowing the user to evaluate retrieved terms or documents and then to use these terms or documents as the basis for further searching are described as feedback techniques, or relevance feedback. The retrieval process is adjusted on the basis of judgments by the user regarding the desirability or usefulness of a preliminary set of retrieved items.

One early program was structured as a continuing dialog between the information seeker and the system in which the seeker could not only repeatedly evaluate the quality of the response but could also make contradictory judgments as the search evolved.[11] To begin a search in this system containing a data base of references to technical material, the user would type a word or phrase as the topic of interest. The program would respond with a description of an article, listing the title, journal name, authors, and descriptive terms. The first article would be chosen based on the system's measure of how close the article matched the request, relying on an internally stored thesaurus of related terms as well as the actual terms used. The user would then respond to this article, either accepting it or rejecting it as an example of the type of information sought. In addition, the user could select any word from the article summary, whether the author's name, title word, or descriptive term, as being particularly helpful or definitely not helpful, and could even add new terms. The entire response, which could range from a simple yes or no to a string of numbers indicating helpful or unhelpful words, was then used to find another reference, preferably more to the user's liking. (The string of numbers in this premouse system was a result of the fact that each word in the retrieved reference was numbered on the assumption that it was easier to select words by number than to retype them.) As the process continued, the user was presented with, and judged, one reference after another, and the terms selected as helpful or added were fed back into the program's procedure for picking the next most likely reference. The use of such feedback from the information seeker, which can be supplied to the system in any number of ways, is generally considered to be very helpful, especially in cases where the data base is large and the information request has any degree of complexity.

Methods for enhancing the feedback process through a graphic interface can be built upon the existing foundation. For example, in the system where citations or sample texts are retrieved and presented for judgment, the user can use a mouse to select the helpful words and phrases, thus eliminating the distracting need for numbering all terms in the retrieved citation and the need to type a string of numbers.

In fact, the use of a mouse and a graphic interface can be helpful with even a very straightforward method of relevance feedback. A recently created system for searching text data bases using a large-scale parallel processor can display the full text of a retrieved article alongside the list of article titles and two graphically expressed option buttons: good and bad.[12] After using a few terms to obtain the first list, any article on the list can be tagged as good or bad, relevant to the purpose of the search. All of the terms in the tagged articles then go into the next round of searching, producing subsequent articles and lists until the search is deemed complete. The parallel nature of the processor permits extremely rapid scanning of the data base even when the search "statement" now contains hundreds of words. Initial indications are that the use of hundreds of words from articles judged to be near the mark produces extremely good results in finding just the right kind of information without missing any articles that could be relevant.

In a more complex graphic interface, the mouse could be used to do more than select options such as good and bad. In systems where word associations in the request are plotted on a two-dimensional display, the user could select terms and move them about, thus graphically stressing particular associations in order to see what each new arrangement might retrieve. In the latter case, the user would presumably understand what such a rearrangement of terms would mean to the system. That is, both the user and the system would be communicating in a graphically oriented language based upon the spatial relationships of words in two or more dimensions, rather than in the one dimension of written sentences and paragraphs. As a further development, the concepts in both the information request and the data base conceivably could be represented by icons rather than words, and a true graphics language might evolve. Once again, stored information is commonly expressed in words and information requests are even more commonly expressed in words. Therefore visual representations will only be successful to the extent that they readily make sense to the user.

THE SPREAD SHEET MODEL

The success of electronic spread sheets (Fig. 6.5) in the business world has been attributed in part to the fact that such products make it easy to ask, "What if?" The financial analyst can ask innumerable such questions by changing the data in one cell of the spread sheet or a formula for a calculation to see immediately how the effects ripple throughout the spread sheet. There is a similar potential for "what if" exploratory analysis in information retrieval as soon as users are able to alter the relationships of concepts just as easily and dynamically. Just how this might be done is open to question, but a possible model to examine is the electronic spread sheet experience.

Electronic spread sheets have three aspects that seem pertinent. First, they are merely newer versions of earlier paper spread sheets, with the same basic concepts and the same basic organization of data. They did not begin by changing the way accountants segregate data in rows and columns, but simply

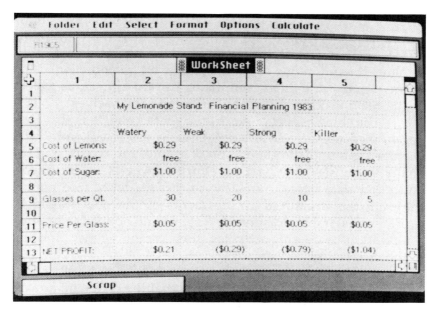

Figure 6.5. Electronic spreadsheet. General arrangement of electronic spreadsheets. The version shown is from an early Macintosh screen. (Courtesy of Apple Computer, Inc.)

created a digital version. In information retrieval, a similar basic organization should exist for specifying the relationships of concepts. Unfortunately, there is no well-accepted visual structure for organizing the relationships other than the sentences and paragraphs of the text itself, with the possible exceptions of thesaurus structures that show hierarchical and lateral relationships among terms, and the sentence diagrams used in elementary school.

On the other hand, the basic tabular arrangement of spread sheets is indeed very common. It can be used simply and easily to show relationships among concepts as well as numbers, even concepts that might be expressed with conditional statements, as will be seen in later sections in this chapter.

Second, electronic spread sheets made it very easy to explore hypothetical situations based on the simple substitution of one entry for another. The simple substitution, of course, could have radical effects on the relationships among the individual entries. In an information retrieval system, the same sort of simple maneuver is desirable. The information seeker should be able to gain an insight into an information problem by dynamically making a simple alteration in a structure entry in order to see what the effect will be on the relationships among the concepts. Assuming an acceptable structure for arranging an information request, in something like a tabular spread sheet, a changed word in one cell could trigger an immediate revision in the number of entities comprising the answer set, as well as in the relationships of the entities among themselves.

The third aspect of electronic spread sheets is that they began to encourage activities not normally associated with them, such as the automatic generation of graphs and charts, and the ability to transfer data back and forth between text documents and other data bases. Similarly, in this model of information retrieval, the structured arrangements of concepts should be readily transferable to different systems and adaptable to other information-processing activities, such as report generation and graphics creation.

One more aspect of electronic spread sheets hardly needs to be mentioned, and that is the fact that the dramatic growth in their use stemmed from and encouraged the proliferation of personal computers in offices. An electronic spread sheet for information retrieval will also almost certainly be a part of the personal computer phenomenon, whether the information files are stored at the microcomputer on some high-volume device such as a compact disk or in some remote computer facility accessible by telecommunications.

The practice of information retrieval would be helped immensely if some product for organizing and evaluating information relationships could achieve the kind of success that certain electronic spread sheets have, such as Lotus 1-2-3. An accepted way of arranging the concepts in a request as well as the concepts in a data base would become widespread. The greatest value would be in the dynamic manipulation of the relationships in an easily understood graphic structure, with the potential for finding more information of the desired kind, and the even more intriguing potential for gaining insights based on new conceptual relationships. To an extent, a tabular spread sheetlike approach to information retrieval has already been implemented, with pull-down menus and dialog boxes in some relational data base management systems. Perhaps the approach taken by these systems will provide the basis for future expansion, and we will return to this notion again in the next section.

Expert Systems

In a more general sense, improvements in information retrieval are taking place within the framework of expert systems and knowledge-based information systems. There are several ways in which expert system methods can be brought to bear on the information retrieval process, but the one mentioned most often is as a replacement for a professional searcher or intermediary.

THE EXPERT INTERMEDIARY

In the history of computerized information retrieval, the development of large sophisticated information systems led to the rise of a class of professional searchers who knew how to make the most of a system's features to find requested information.

Thus searchers act as intermediaries between the various on-line systems and the unstructured requests by persons who may know very little about the kinds of information available and the proper procedures for accessing it. This came about for a number of reasons, ranging from the diversity and complexity of the systems themselves, making it difficult for the casual user to keep up with the systems, to the costs for using large systems, making it economically better for an organization to have a only a small number of employees actually searching the systems. These professional searchers would be able to find information much faster, and therefore at less cost, than if all members of the organization had access to the systems.

A stream of studies has been directed at evaluating how intermediaries work and how they may assist a person in for-mulating and reformulating a request so that it best matches the constraints of the relevant data bases, while at the same time educating the information seeker on the ways in which the data bases might be of use. The role of the intermediary seems to lend itself to conversion to an expert system, as expert systems function in areas where the expertise or specific knowl-edge of a human expert can be captured within a framework and applied to all similar cases. The decisions made by the professional intermediary in the process of satisfying a search request can, perhaps, be captured as a combination of knowl-edge about the process and a set of rules to apply in given circumstances.

Not all information system researchers believe that ex-pert systems can indeed be built in the forseeable future that will function in the way described. One veteran researcher, for instance, maintains that a great gulf exists between what is required and both the available technology and the available knowledge about representing meaning.[13] Moreover, he be-lieves that information retrieval is basically an unstructured environment encompassing many dissimilar tasks, and is there-fore not amenable to a structured expert system methodology. Others are not quite so pessimistic, but do agree that significant problems must be resolved in the design of retrieval models and in compiling the massive knowledge base that may be required.[14]

Various Approaches Nevertheless, a good deal of activity is centered on the creation of expert systems to simulate the work of the human expert intermediary. One system for information retrieval is designed with three basic modules: (1) an information module that contains knowledge about the user and the user's performance; (2) a specific demand module that tries to interpret an information request, making it as specific as possible; and (3) a resource module that contains data on all the resources available to the user that the expert system knows about.[15] In each of the modules, the expert system asks the user a number of multiple-choice questions. Some answers may lead in turn to another multiple-choice question, although the questioning does not go much beyond that.

The first module asks questions about how much time the user wants the search to take, how much money the user is willing to spend, and whether the user is looking for written information. If the user prefers written information, a second question concerns the type of writing (e.g., journal articles or books); if the preference is for personal contact from a human source, the second question asks for a preference between a telephone call and a visit. In addition, the module asks the user to clarify the request; for example, two possible answers are as a search for general information or as a way to confirm a decision. The second module tries to narrow the request based on built-in knowledge about the data bases available. The first question asks the user to relate the request, if possible, to one of five general categories of information within the data bases. Depending upon which category is chosen, a follow-up question presents a list of subsets of the category. The third module then relates the details of the request to the known resources, including but not limited to on-line data bases, and formulates a search statement according to a set of rules governing the process. In the pilot version, this expert system did not then take the next step of automatically dialing into an on-line data base and running the search, although that would be the next development.

Other expert systems for information retrieval put more emphasis on the subject knowledge and the way it is expressed, by descriptors or keywords, in a given data base. In the chemical industry, for instance, an expert system is being developed to assist users in searching the massive *Chemical Abstracts* data base.[16] In designing the system, human experts were questioned regarding the knowledge required to handle difficult search requests, and the two primary areas of knowledge that emerged were (1) the professionals' acquaintance with the indexing terms that are applied by indexers and the manner in which indexing is done, and (2) the searchers' professional chemical knowledge. For example, if someone is interested in the "uses of alkaloids," the best search would not use any of those three words, as "uses" is not a keyword in that data base, "of" is not considered at all, and "alkaloids" is too general. To satisfy the search, the correct terminology would have to be used, suggesting that the searcher would already have to know some of the terms designating the uses of alkaloids.

An expert system based on some rules regarding relationships could provide some assistance, and it might be implemented in a matrix arrangement similar to the electronic spread sheet model. The system being developed relies on a number of abstract statements of relationships called scripts or "deep structures." A sample script is:

SUBSTANCE (class) is used as USE in some FIELD because of some PROPERTY.

The capitalized words are replaced by specific terms; for example, "GLYCOALKALOIDS are used as PESTICIDES in AGRICULTURE." The system designers intend to use the deep structures, or abstract scripts, and a set of inference rules to reorganize the data base automatically such that documents are represented by a number of specific scripts. This would enhance the existing data base structure of key words and descriptive terms by allowing searches that depend on the relationships among types of terms. In a matrix arrangement on a screen used to formulate a search request, the columns could be the categories from the abstract structures, such as substance, use, field, property. The rows in the matrix would be the abstract scripts, or sample statements of relationships. After selecting a script type, the searcher could enter terms into one or more of the columns. Help in choosing terms could be available in pull-down boxes for each column that would be relevant to the abstract script chosen for that row.

The advantages of this arrangement are similar to some of the advantages associated with relational data bases, with the notion of a visually arranged search screen that simply but powerfully communicates the relationships that are searchable.

Given that a data base is full of sets of terms that do have a number of generalizable relationships, information can be found based on those relationships, instead of the mere occurrence of key words or co-occurrence of terms.

As in the case of relational data bases in general, the way information is physically stored in a system and the way it is represented can be completely independent. During the development of relational data base systems, and based on the fact that the presentation would not and should not show any relationships imposed by the physical storage, the tabular format was chosen as the least encumbered way of indicating logical relationships. The flexibility of relational data base systems stems from the fact that new relationships among tables can be easily created by users.

Because software to create expert systems has now become available for personal computers, the number of expert-system approaches to information retrieval continues to grow. At the National Archives and Records Administration, a pilot expert system for searching Bureau of Land Management records has been created on an IBM PC/AT using a knowledge base of 300 rules. The system is intended to mimic the process the archives' historians go through when trying to find the answer to a generally worded request. In one series of tests, the system on the personal computer came up with the same answer as the archives staff about two-thirds of the time.[17] When the answers differed, about half the time the computer found a better answer than the staff, but in 7 percent of the cases the computer was dead wrong.

Nontraditional Retrieval   In addition to retrieving information from data bases of documents, expert system techniques have also been applied to the retrieval of information from less traditional structures, such as computer conferencing systems and bulletin boards. One system, called CODER, is being developed to search through such collections of "composite documents." It includes an expert subsystem for analysis of the text to be stored, an ancillary knowledge base derived from several machine-readable dictionaries, and an expert subsystem for handling the retrieval.[18] Other systems that originally were designed to provide a common procedure for access to a variety of on-line data bases with differing search procedures, such as

CONIT at MIT, have also incorporated features that are considered part of the broad definition of expert systems.[19]

Natural Language   One of the primary areas of investigation in expert systems in general, and in information retrieval in particular, is that of natural language processing. Considerable effort has gone into the study of how a computer program can read text or recognize spoken words, and understand the relationships among the words that give meaning to the whole, especially when compared to a variety of other arrangements of the words or words similar in meaning.

Adequate natural language processing for all but very restricted environments is still in the future, but a number of procedures have been proposed that can be represented in a graphic way, including the tree graph of abstract distance presented earlier in this chapter. A similar approach diagrams phrases and sentences into subsets where there are usually only two entities at each level, and one of the entities is the dominant one modified by the other.[20] Two identical sets of key words may not mean the same thing, if, when put back into complete phrases, they have different dominant/dependent structures. For example, when diagrammed in this manner, "approximate matching of strings" does not have the same diagram as "approximate number of matching strings," but "approximate string matching" and "approximate matching" do have the same structure. This type of diagram has been chosen for its potential in automatic pattern matching to compare search statements against stored text.

Overall, the trend in information systems research to apply expert system techniques to the searching process, and specifically to the creation of an automated process that can replace the human (and sometimes expert) intermediary, has followed general expert systems procedures in designing the way the user communicates with the system. Often, that communication is in strings of text. As expert systems of any kind turn to more graphic techniques, including the very simple arrangement of rows and columns like a spread sheet or a relational table, those for information retrieval will similarly use the power of the graphic arrangement.

KNOWLEDGE WORKSHEETS

One promising way to use a graphic arrangement for manipulating an expert system is the procedure mentioned previously — the variation on the electronic spread sheet. One example is MacSmarts from Cognition Technology.

The MacSmarts program is a procedure for creating, and using, a knowledge base of facts and rules regarding the facts. The knowledge base is created using logic worksheets that are intended to be like spread sheets, with rows and columns. The headings for the columns during the building of the knowledge base include labels such as "facts," "rules," and "conclusions." In addition, examples can be added using both text and graphics. The rules are the statements of relationships, and especially conditional relationships. The MacSmarts product contains help on deriving and applying rules, and is based on Prolog inference software, a staple of artificial intelligence work.

The entire package is a cohesive combination of spatial arrangements, windows, and overlays, where text and graphics are used as tools in the process as well as the end result. Graphics, for example, can be used as easily to explain how a conclusion was reached as to show the conclusion, such as the proper place to make a repair to a piece of equipment. In an example provided by Cognition Technology, the fastest route to the airport can ultimately be displayed as a map, based on such conditions as the expertise of the driver, type of vehicle, time of year, time of day, presence of exceptional conditions such as an accident, need to meet a flight at a given time, and so on, not to mention the starting point of the driver. The same procedure could also be used in less graphic situations, such as locating particular types of clauses in a complex contract.

There seems to be a fairly close fit between procedures that can be used to create knowledge-based expert systems and the simple arrangement of the electronic spread sheet, offering further evidence of the potential for even a plain graphic arrangement. Beyond that, as MacSmarts shows, the inherent graphic capabilities of a system like the Macintosh can then improve the power of that arrangement.

An additional comment, is that the use of graphics and spatial arrangements, including the electronic spread sheet model, in an expert or knowledge-based system does not depend on the construction of specific categories such as rules and conditions. Currently, some researchers in artificial intelligence and in expert systems are suggesting that machine reasoning should be based on the recall of specific "best match" episodes or memories, rather than rules.[21] In the past, one of the influences in favor of rule-based expert systems stemmed from the limitations of the computer. For large amounts of data in a knowledge base, the computer needed the establishment of rules, inferred from the data, in order to arrive at a solution in a reasonable time. With the more recent development of large-scale parallel architectures, such computers can actually search through all of the data quickly, thus finding a best match, or a pattern, without relying on a set of rules to follow. If expert systems do begin to abandon or at least lessen the need for rule-based procedures, the value of the graphic interface remains secure, and may even be increased, as graphic techniques can be used to demonstrate just how close the best match is.

EXPERT DATA BASES

Aside from the role of spatial arrangement and graphics in expert systems, and particularly in systems for information retrieval, the separate areas of data base systems and expert systems are coming closer together. Even though the available expert system products and data base management products are designed for essentially different purposes and thus would outperform the other class of software for its own type of problems, there are several ways that the two systems can rely on each other. Very large data bases in the future are expected to require some sort of expert system just to be able to use them, and expert systems themselves that rely on large amounts of data may need data base management techniques as a prerequisite to applying the expert system process.[22]

The Fifth Generation

The phrase "fifth generation" connotes many things, including the ultimate in computer capability and economic dominance by the country winning the fifth generation race. The derivation of the term suggests a less ambitious stage. In the history of computer development, the first generation was characterized by computers built with vacuum tubes. The second-generation computers used transitorized circuits, the third generation used integrated circuits, and the fourth uses very large-scale integrated circuits (VLSI). The fifth generation will be marked by parallel processing computers. In some definitions of fifth generation, the distinguishing factor is that the systems are knowledge-based expert systems, though presumably built with parallel processors. We are currently not quite through the fourth generation, while the machines exemplifying the fifth generation are just becoming commercially available.

The promise of the fifth generation is not so much in the way that the computers are constructed as in the way that the systems — both hardware and software — will interact with people. A primary assumption is that the systems will communicate visually and audibly in ways that go beyond the computer graphics and synthetic voices of today.

JAPANESE PLANS

One of the reasons for the popularity of the fifth generation as a proposal for dramatically new and intelligent systems stems from Japanese planning for the future models of computers. In general, various Japanese organizations have long been involved in intellectual and technical efforts to make the most of computerization. In 1969, the Ministry of International Trade and Industry published *Toward the Information Society*, with the ambitiously stated goal of creating systems that would spark human intellectual creativity instead of promoting material consumption.[23] A few years later the Japan Computer Usage Development Institute, a nonprofit organization, presented to the government the *Plan for an Information Society — A National Goal Toward the Year 2000*. In a 1980 publication, *The Information Society*, Yoneji Masuda expanded on the emphasis on knowledge-creation systems and suggested sweeping social changes that might eventually occur. It is interesting that Masuda's section on the generations of computer hardware stops with the fourth generation of VLSI technology and makes no mention of a fifth generation or its representative technology, although Japanese planning specifically for these computers was already in progress at least as early as 1978.

Another 1980 Japanese publication, the "Preliminary Report on a Fifth Generation of Computers," did relate knowledge-based systems to the fifth generation of computer hardware, and stated that these systems would be intelligent ones that could not only learn and make conceptual associations but could also communicate in speech and pictures. This was followed by an expanded "Preliminary Report" and then in 1982 by the establishment of the Institute for New Generation Computer Technology (ICOT), with the mission of leading the Japanese effort to develop the fifth-generation models.

An important part of the Japanese plan is the development of picture and image processing as a means for a computer to gather information and to respond with information, although admittedly the emphasis on visual processing is slightly less important than the emphasis on language processing.[24] According to the plan, the work on image systems will be divided into three phases. The first phase is devoted to hardware issues related to image processing and machine vision, such as feature extraction, and hardware and software aspects of image data bases. The second phase will be a development phase, including a pilot project, and the third phase is integration of the results into the larger fifth-generation systems. Part of the work is to revolve around an image-understanding system with a knowledge base of over 100,000 images.

This concern for natural language processing and visual communication, while definitely a forward-looking approach, is more a necessity in Japan than in the West. In North America and Europe, the success of the microcomputer, particularly as a business tool among managers, has led to the assumption that a CRT screen with a keyboard and mouse is a perfectly reasonable way to communicate with a store of computerized information. In Japan, for reasons associated with the written language, the incompatibility of personal computer hardware, and social customs affecting decision making, there is no proliferation of personal computers and no burgeoning crowd of professionals and white-collar workers communicating with data bases and with each other by means of video screens and keyboards. It was therefore clear that to capitalize on computerized knowledge bases and information systems would require a more natural way of interacting with the machine, namely by voice and by images. Regardless of the arguments and assessments of where Japan stands in relation to other countries in developing fifth-generation technologies, the Japanese have done well to promote voice and image processing as key ingredients of the ultimate information system.

OTHER NATIONS' PROJECTS

Japan is by no means the only country with ambitious plans for the fifth generation. In North America and in both Eastern and Western Europe, numerous projects reflect different aspects of these new systems, such as projects devoted to expert systems, artificial intelligence (AI), parallel processing, robotics, natural language processing, voice recognition, and visual recognition.

In the United States, among many other activities, a group of computer and technology companies founded the independent Microelectronics and Computer Technology Corporation (MCC) to provide a multiorganizational approach to the fifth generation. In addition, the National Science Foundation (NSF) funded a Supercomputer Center program at four universities, and the Defense Advanced Research Projects Agency (DARPA) is supporting a large Strategic Computing project that incorporates almost all the components of fifth-generation systems.

The various projects naturally have their own specific goals and designs for reducing general theory to particular substance. Image processing, for example, is a key element in the efforts funded by DARPA with a particular instance being the autonomous land vehicle. This vehicle, now in existence but not perfected, is to contain a vision and image-understanding system that can see the terrain and resolve differences between the actual sight and a data base of imagery. Using expert system procedures to process incoming images, sound, and other waveforms, the vehicle should be able to navigate successfully around obstacles, detect danger, avoid being seen or incapacitated, and locate and destroy targets. The current version of the vehicle uses twelve interconnected computers and a combination laser scanner and television camera to process two images per second at a rate of about a billion calculations per second; but to be successful, it may need a processing speed of a trillion calculations per second.[25]

In a different vein, one of the NSF-sponsored Supercomputer Center projects is concentrating on picture creation rather than image understanding. Realistic three-dimensional, high-resolution color graphics generated in real time are expected to require 100,000 times the capability of current supercomputers.[26] Such images today can require hours to generate a single frame on even the best of computers. The fifth-generation supercomputers, with massive parallel processing, may eventually give computers the ability to generate on their own and in real time (e.g., at the sixty-fields-per-second rate of our television system), moving displays that are indistinguishable from — but are not — the real thing.

At MCC other specific programs involve graphics and images. The total MCC effort is divided into four major development areas, one of which is advanced CAD, a predominately graphic activity. A second major area is advanced computer architecture, which has a subgroup devoted to the human interface.

One of the graphic concepts being explored by MCC is a variation of the view of a fish-eye lens, where an extremely wide-angle view is presented, but objects at the center of focus are larger.[27] On a computer screen, the display would be designed to show the detail of an item of interest, but would also show that detail's relationship to the big picture. The actual display may not resemble a real fish-eye lens but could still embody the concept. In one version of an on-screen calendar, the activities of the current day are listed in a large box, while the rest of the week is represented by smaller boxes, with less detail, and the entire month is depicted in even smaller boxes. Other versions are being developed to apply the fish-eye approach to computer programming, where one module of a program is viewed in detail while at the same time the position of that module is shown in relation to a host of other modules that comprise a complex program.

Outside the United States, there is a similar range of activity. In the United Kingdom, the primary effort is known as the Alvey Program, half funded by the government and named after the chairman of the committee that recommended a program of advanced information technology in 1982. It includes vision, speech, and touch interfaces among other fifth-generation technologies. West Germany and France have smaller but similar projects, while a joint effort, the European Strategic Program for Research in Information Technologies (Esprit) is supported by the European Economic Community. In the Soviet Union fifth-generation activity reportedly places primary emphasis on artificial intelligence and language processing.

GRAPHICS AS A PROGRAMMING TOOL

Overall, the use of graphics and images as tools for communicating with computers is a very basic part of the development of "intelligent" fifth-generation systems. It was, in fact, the early work in artificial intelligence ten to fifteen years ago that led to the creation of graphic interfaces such as windows, icons, and pull-down menus. Given time, graphic procedures became more feasible and more refined, and eventually became the primary interface on a popular personal computer, the Macintosh, with increasing influence on other machines' procedures.

In a similar manner, graphic procedures for representing relationships and for creating and manipulating information, used now in more specialized areas, are migrating to general use in newer computer systems. The simple arrangement of a tree graph as a way to show relationships, for example, has long been used with AI languages such as Lisp and Prolog, and is proposed as a way to represent visually information contained in data bases of documents and articles. Windows and diagrams used to create expert systems are also employed as the display for end users of the expert systems.

On a more complex level, visual techniques for enhancing and even replacing the typing of long lists of commands are being developed in several areas, not the least of which is computer programming itself, or computer-aided software engineering (CASE). In addition to using spatial arrangements and connecting lines to organize a display, such as a computer-generated flow chart, the manipulation of graphic images by a programmer can be used to generate programs automatically, and the dynamic display of animated images, including graphs and charts, by a program can help a programmer to understand what the program is doing. Among the various types and prototypes of visual programming languages, some do rely on the traditional text of programming statements while others might use graphics, color, sound, and animation with no text at all.

The dramatic capabilities of graphic tools at the high end of the scale should not obscure the fact that even the simple spatial arrangement of an electronic spread sheet or the tables of relational data bases have substantial power to convey information based on visual organization alone. The designations of the rows and columns can express relationships that are easily grasped and readily manipulated, including conditional relationships among the entries. Graphically arranged tables are used by telephone companies as the procedure for creating the conditional branching associated with the 800 numbers for toll-free telephone calls.[28] The 800 number itself must be translated to a client company's own telephone number, but a client may have many telephone numbers that should be used, depending upon where a call is coming from, the time of day, day of the week, time of the year, volume of calls coming in, and so on.

Each new 800 number could be established in the telephone system, then, by writing a routine containing a series of conditional statements. Instead, personnel adding a new 800 number to the system use a tabular arrangement. The columns in the table identify types of conditions, and the entries across a row give the specific conditions that must be present to yield the telephone number in the final column. The tabular system, which is a presentational arrangement and not necessarily a reflection of internal structure, has the advantage of using a very common visual arrangement, making it easy for telephone company personnel to comprehend and accept.

At the other end of the scale, one of the directions in visual programming is to apply CAD technology and techniques to computer programming or software engineering. Using a highly graphic CAD-like approach at a workstation or personal computer, a programmer can graphically design programs using a drawing/pointing implement such as a mouse or stylus. In both experimental and commercially available visual programming systems, the use of visual techniques is credited with dramatic savings in time. Understandably, there are difficulties with visual programming languages, and a primary one revolves around the imprecision of pictures. While ordinary language may also be imprecise, programming languages are very specific, permitting us to create complex programs out of a small set of defined types and functions. Visual programming languages will require the same development of specific meanings for icons or pictures and the relationships among them.

As fifth-generation systems evolve, the lessons learned in the development of visual programming will doubtlessly be applied to interaction with computer systems in general and to the construction of the interaction with information retrieval systems in particular, as the construction of a search request can be very much like creating a small program to retrieve data from a data base.

Summary

Graphically oriented information systems — from the tabular electronic spread sheet model and relational data base systems to complex multidimensional representations — can build upon human ability to comprehend relationships visually. Because creativity and insight are directly related to the ability to associate and recombine concepts in meaningful ways, systems that can visually portray such associations, including dynamic associations, can potentially spark new creative thinking. The techniques that might make this possible could be based on the existing efforts to quantify the relationships among words. Other technical developments that might make this possible are in the forefront of computer systems research for the fifth generation of computers as part of the work on image processing, artificial intelligence, expert systems, visual programming, and graphic languages, not to mention the whole area known as the human interface. Graphic representations and procedures will not replace text and textual structures, but are likely to increase the speed with which we can perceive relationships and digest information.

7
LOOKING AHEAD

Most of us have seen the poster. New York (or any locality of choice in copies of the Steinberg original) is prominent in the foreground, occupying over half the area, with the background containing in diminishing perspective an abbreviated version of the rest of the country, and in even less detail, some foreign lands. The poster pokes fun at the myopic view, present to some degree in most of us, that things closer to home are disproportionately important.

Paradoxically, that poster has been cited by information system researchers as an example of how a graphic display for information "space" can open our eyes to the world beyond. The point is that, given the limitations of a video display terminal and the potential immensity of the information space, the video display should show the items of most interest in greater detail, but should also at the same time show the relationship of those items to the entire set of items, albeit in lesser detail. To use another analogy, this is the fish-eye approach, mentioned in the preceding chapter, being explored by MCC as a way to improve access to stored programs and data while taking into account both technical and human limitations.

The components of human visual perception, from the structure of rods and cones to the brain's processing of imagery, do put bounds on our capabilities. To the extent that we continue to learn more about sight and mental processing of visual input, we can find new paths to explore in the development of technical systems that can exploit the human potential.

In the short term, the technical and economic aspects change the most. Graphically expressed concepts that could only be realized on expensive workstations a dozen years ago are now commonplace on relatively low-cost equipment. If you are an avid Macintosh user, for example, the value of the graphic interface is beyond debate. The only aspect open to question is which software packages make the best, or cleverest, use of it. On the other hand, many users of computers and information systems do not use, and may not even appreciate, visual tools.

The intent of the previous chapters has been to demonstrate why the visual nontextual dimension is important for computerized information systems, how it is being developed and implemented, and where it might be heading. There is certainly room for a great many additional changes in what becomes feasible technically and economically, and what becomes most useful psychologically and physiologically. This final chapter sums up the trends in system development and suggests some directions for the near future.

The Physical System

It has become a truism to say that, for computer systems in general, more power and capability are increasingly available at less price in smaller packages. With regard to the graphic and video features of personal computers, the capabilities associated with expensive workstations five or ten years ago are now available on microcomputers for less than one-tenth of the cost. A facile extrapolation is that the trend will continue and five or ten years hence there will be an equally impressive increase in capability at a lower price.

A few other general statements can also be made about technology trends. First, in the short term, very few things are replaced completely by a new technology. Just as pencils, pens, and typewriters are still manufactured, purchased, and used, the alphanumeric CRT screen will continue in service for quite some time. Second, prices for components do not usually drop to nothing, but instead may level off at some point above the mass market level. In the foreseeable future, therefore, some hardware factors will continue to be of concern, and will not be just a temporary limitation to be overcome in the next season's products.

READABILITY

The basic appearance of the video screen, or CRT, as a device that generates light with a resolution less than that of ink on paper continues to affect the way the screens are accepted and used as gateways or viewports into the information universe. Studies repeatedly show that a CRT screen is not as easy to read for extended periods of time as a piece of paper.[1] Part of the problem is related to the physical attributes of the display screen, such as the type of phosphor used, refresh rate, and resolution, and part of the problem lies with the human ability to perceive and resolve the light waves, or streams of photons, generated by CRTs.

By varying the physical components of video displays, readability can be improved. There is certainly a trend toward higher resolution raster displays, but extremely high-resolution displays are still too expensive for the nonspecialist market, and increasing overall pixel resolution itself is not the entire answer. As mentioned in previous chapters, the size of a screen is just as important as the pixel resolution if pixels are counted for the total horizontal and vertical dimensions instead of per unit of measure, as on paper. A horizontal resolution of 512 pixels, for example, is about 100 pixels per inch if the screen is five inches wide, but only 50 pixels per inch if the screen is ten inches wide. The readability of a given resolution can also be improved if the refresh rate is sufficiently high; that is, a desirable rate is one that is higher than the eye's ability to see changes at close range under the best conditions, without using the interlace technique of television that was developed under an entirely different set of assumptions about screen size, viewing distance, the objects of the viewing, ambient lighting, and so on.

Screens with increasingly more pixels per inch and higher refresh rates are available, but the overall effect on readability across a wide range of tasks remains to be considered. Very substantial changes in the design and construction of display devices may be required before there will be a concomitant advance in the readability of the devices. For the near term, incremental improvements are bringing the discernable resolution of a video screen—which is only part of the readability question—closer to the range for printed material, at least in specialty areas such as computer-aided design and electronic publishing.

COLOR

When comparing color to monochrome displays and holding costs the same, a monochrome display still provides better quality, that is, better readability, than a color display at the same manufacturing-cost level. This has been true in the past and is likely to continue to be true for quite some time, as the hardware used to manipulate color is more complex than that for monochrome—as is our own ability to process color mentally. The trend of the past few years has been toward increased use of color, but still with color displays of some limitations. Color systems for the general market—limited by the monitor, the graphics controller, and the software for managing the color—exemplify the problems with creating a good color display on a computer screen. Some systems have only a limited number of displayable colors, may exhibit color artifacts when a pixel of one color adjoins that of another, or may suffer from a number of other related problems.

On the other hand, within the general trend of declining component costs, good, sharp color displays are increasingly available. Moreover, color seems to be highly desirable to most users even when it is not presented particularly well. Some persons believe that its addition is inevitable, and should be implemented just as soon as technically and economically feasible. Especially in the case of presentation and entertainment media, color is considered the natural condition, and monochrome merely an artistic effort or, in some situations, an economic necessity.

Therefore, the deployment of color displays for computer systems will proceed, although not too rapidly due to the inherent cost difference between monochrome and color. As systems with color capability expand, both in number and in display quality, attention given to the psychologically sound use of color should increase. The difficulty of evaluating all of the variables of the use of color on CRT screens, on both objective and subjective bases, is perhaps underscored by the fact that at least one expert system is being developed just to guide screen designers in the use of color.[2]

PROCESSING POWER

The inexorable drive to pack more processing power and more memory into less expensive chips is one trend that may hold direction for the near and medium term. There may be ultimate limits, but at least to date whenever a limit has been approached, a new development obliterates it.

Processing power and memory are key ingredients in the creation of screen displays. The features of the graphic interface are made feasible by the newer generations of graphics chips and general processor chips. One of the newer processor chips for microcomputers, the Intel 80386, which comes in several versions related to speed, is bringing the power of workstations to the personal computer. It is expected to have a considerable impact once an operating system and applications software that take full advantage of the 80386 are available. Another chip comparable to the 80386 in power, is the Motorola 68020, which is the heart of the Macintosh II. Motorola has also announced the 68030, with twice the performance of the 68020, and machines like the Macintosh II will be relatively easily upgraded to the 68030 when it becomes available. In addition, other new and powerful chip sets include the Fairchild Semiconductor three-chip Clipper and the Weitek Corporation three-chip Accel 8064.

Expanded memory chips also contribute to increased screen display capabilities. In 1985, memory chips that could each hold one million bits were introduced; by early 1987, dynamic random access chips, or DRAMs, that can hold 4 million bits were nearing production, and DRAMs with 16 million bits were announced. The capacity of DRAM chips has a direct effect on screen resolution and display functions because screen memory is required to contain the bits related to each pixel in raster displays. At least one industry commentator suggests that DRAM chips with 256 million bits, or even one billion bits, will be available by the end of the century.[3]

REALISM

The processing power available for video displays, from personal computers to high-end workstations, is not, however, near the limit of what is desirable. The more complex suggestions for graphic manipulation and graphic generation, other than the display of video images originally from cameras, in high resolution and in real time still considerably outpace the technology.

A good example of what is possible now and what is being suggested is in the world of video games. The original video games contained mosaiclike displays. Then they began to incorporate better graphics in two ways: analog images from videodisks could be accessed at the appropriate time, and the quality of the computer-generated images increased in color range and resolution. Eventually, game designers would like the screen to be as real and as sharp as a movie screen, with the display generated dynamically entirely by and under the control of the game's computer. A video game might ultimately have both the same visual quality and the same power to involve us emotionally as a good movie with engrossing characters. That sort of video game, or video short story perhaps, would only be successful if the nontechnical creative influence was also present, as in any good creation of literature or art, but the fact remains that the technology itself is not yet ready. In the future, though, as one source suggests, there may be little difference between video programming, such as current movie and television production, and the creations of computer software.[4] The end product would look the same.

The temptation is to suggest that as such realism eventually becomes both possible and feasible for microcomputers, it should be harnessed for the visual representation of information spaces. We would be able to move through a synthetic but very realistic world of stored information as we use a computer terminal to explore any and all forms of stored information. Perhaps that will be true, but only in a restricted sense. Ample evidence supports the notion that it is not helpful to deviate too far from the accepted way of doing things when building new systems. We seem to need to understand intuitively the systems we use.

If a synthetic information space is created in realistic imagery to represent billions of bits on magnetic and optical media, that imagery will most likely be successful only if it is familiar or taps a responsive chord because of some connection with a familiar arrangement. Much of the information space that we are familiar with in the visible world is evidenced by papers, books, bookshelves, and generally physical collections of documents. Therefore, systems to represent the spatial arrangements and physical attributes of these types of storage devices may rely on some very plain and commonplace images, such as the digitized version of the printed page.

The technical capacity for realism could, however, substantially change the way we think about stored information if we conceive of it as other than written material. Taped television, radio programs, and movies are examples of stored information and entertainment. Thus the ultimate in a computerized information system might be an information world that we observe and listen to, as much as read. The computer system with the capacity for creating complex realistic displays could create a person to explain to us, or a motion segment to demonstrate to us, the information we are seeking. We would only have to read a display if we chose to. Pushing this even further, and assuming an immense amount of processing power, the information terminal could become an electronic genie, assuming on screen the shape we desire, such as a person or persons, other animate and inanimate objects, and so on, to deliver the information in the manner we desire.

Practically speaking, processing power and memory for screen displays are likely to remain a continually improving part of the physical system, but still far behind the capabilities of what some would like in the name of realism. At the same time, the more prosaic merger of images and text, from electronic publishing to picture data bases and maps, using analog as well as digital technology, is becoming more widely accepted as part of the information system environment.

DIMENSIONS

The dimensionality of displays can be considered in at least two ways. First, the two-dimensional physical display can portray both two and three dimensions using the age-old techniques of perspective drawing and placing distant objects behind nearer objects. At this level, for displays used to organize information, the most acceptable arrangements are either two-dimensional or very shallow three-dimensional, sometimes referred to as two-and-a-half dimensions. Among examples are the displays where windows, menus, and icons can overlay one another. This layered effect is three-dimensional, but there is no real perception of depth other than the fact that two-dimensional objects can appear to be in front of or behind each other.

A more involved three-dimensional display, other than for displaying retrieved items such as photographs in a real estate system, may evolve but will probably do so slowly. As long as the two-dimensional display is used to the fullest and three-dimensional arrangements seem contrived or excessive, the two or two-and-a-half dimensional arrangement will prevail.

In another sense, the physical display could have a more real third dimension. This has been done in a number of ways, from the overlay of images in separate colors to be viewed with special glasses to the rapid generation of images on several planes that have a real depth of an inch or so. The most interesting technique remains the hologram.

Holograms in some forms are becoming widely used, and in other forms are still at the technical edge. A good example of the application of a three-dimensional hologram for traditional information dissemination was the November 1985 cover of *National Geographic* magazine. Filling most of the cover was a hologram of a prehistoric skull recently found, so that by tipping the cover the sides and top of the skull, as well as the front, could be examined. In this instance, the hologram presented a detailed picture that could only have been duplicated with a multitude of traditional photographs from hundreds of angles, but the hologram was used in a very traditional way, as a magazine-cover photograph.

Other forms of holographic displays are still being refined in the research laboratories. At the MIT Media Laboratory, with funding from General Motors, researchers have created a hologram that can be viewed from any angle within a 180-degree radius with no glass or plastic between the viewer and the image. The hologram, in this case of a car about nine inches long, simply floats in space in front of an alcove about three feet wide and a foot high. Moreover, the image is created entirely from computer-generated dimensions, not from a photograph of a real object as is normally the case in producing holograms. The process currently used at MIT, and which takes several days, starts with the computer generation of nearly 1000 views of the automobile based on CAD drawings. The various views are then computer-recorded on 35mm film and subsequently transferred to holographic film under control of a laser beam that produces the three-dimensional interference pattern. The holographic film is finally bent into the alcove shape and lighted from behind by a laser and a mirror.

At present, this image is somewhat grainy and is in one color, bright green. Eventually, the MIT group expects to be able to increase the resolution, add color, reduce the generation time, and increase the size of the hovering image. General Motors would eventually like to see an image the size of a real car. For GM, the purpose of the research is to develop a way to evaluate car designs that is an improvement over the already graphically sophisticated CAD/CAM techniques. The three-dimensional perspectives available on two-dimensional CRT screens and the ability automatically to manufacture scale models from computer-stored data are not considered as good as the eventual ability to rapidly generate a full-featured hologram. The speed of generation is therefore one of the key factors, and the processing power required for such rapid generation of the many views is expected to be available from parallel-processing supercomputers.

Given the expected improvements in technical capacity, the MIT vision is that "high-quality three-dimensional hardcopy output [i.e., a midair hologram, will become] a routine feature of advanced information processing systems."[5] In the interim, which may be quite a while, before holographic terminals are routinely used for information systems, exploration of the third dimension on two-dimensional displays is evolving from applications that are inherently dimensional, such as modeling real objects or displaying points on a graph with x, y, and z axes.

One final comment, which may or may not involve holograms, is that the dimensions of storage may be a factor in future systems. Present-day digital storage devices are essentially two-dimensional, which places some limits on the speed of access and, more important, on the ways in which stored bits can be related to each other. Eventually, our ability to manage and to access the mass of digitally stored information may require some form of three-dimensional storage.[6]

Presentation Level

The first half of the 1980s was a time of change for computer systems especially at the presentational level, the view on the screen. The desktop metaphor was introduced on a wide scale, and several related arrangements to convey information graphically were tested. The inclusion of graphic images and video frames as static pictures and as motion pictures became practical at even the personal computer level.

In information-retrieval systems, we have seen data bases organized at the presentation level by a range of schemes from the complexity of real geography to the simplicity of relational tables and electronic spread sheets. Without a doubt, the current crop of graphic procedures is tapping a previously underused capacity in human perception for visual, nontextual comprehension. The present is probably only a rough indication of what will become possible at the presentation level.

SPATIAL ORIENTATION

The exploitation of spatial arrangements for organizing information is just beginning. There is still a need to adapt the spatial arrangements that are technically possible on a screen or other display device to the strong areas of spatial information processing in the eye-brain complex as these become better understood.

A much larger question revolves around the fact that, despite the human capacity for perceiving spatial arrangements, the representation of information stored in a computer system does not portray the actual location and storage of the electrical, magnetic, chemical, or optical conditions comprising the coded information. It is true that for the brief history of computerized information systems we have lost touch with the visual spatial dimension of information organization and storage. It is not necessarily true, however, that the best solution now that visual displays are much more capable is to recreate the visual arrangements of pages, articles, documents, books, shelves, filing cabinets, and libraries. Information is, in fact, stored and manipulated in ways that were not possible in pre-computer times. Just as we adapted to the searching strategies of the past decade or so, we are probably ready to accept new strategies using the visual dimension.

The desktop metaphor is a good example of how, in practice, the refinement of visual cues leads away from a strict interpretation of the foundation for the visual metaphor. The electronic desktop in systems using such a metaphor is not much like a real desktop, but is more an environment for activities associated with desks. As instances of graphic interfaces appear more widely, designed by creative researchers looking for better arrangements, the refinements of the underlying metaphors will continue. It should not be surprising if in another five or ten years the desktop metaphor is even farther removed from the reality of desktops themselves, or perhaps even replaced by a more potent metaphor.

In the previous chapter, the electronic spread sheet was described as an example of the type of presentational arrangement that could do for information retrieval what it did for business analysis. The simple tabular arrangement for information retrieval is not new, of course, and is also a fundamental part of relational data bases. There are some differences, however, between tabular arrangements and the requirements of information-processing systems. The relationships among the row-column entries are much more difficult to express for words taken from normal language than for the mathematical formulas of spread sheets or the limited fields of current relational data bases.

The simple basic graphic arrangement for information retrieval that is sought may require a new but equally intuitive type of arrangement. Some candidate arrangements are tree graphs, scatter plots, and diagrams that look like something used to analyze a sentence in elementary school. Primary considerations are the degree to which the visual arrangement captures the richness of word relationships that we are so familiar with in written language and the extent to which that visual arrangement adds something to the manipulation of language. A related concept is that we need a standard map form for navigating informational data bases, and the evolution of graphs, diagrams, or tables for information retrieval may turn out to be functionally the same thing as information maps.

In considering images as objects in the retrieval process, there will be no turning back in the increasing incorporation of such images, eventually to the same degree that pictures and artwork are part of the world of print publications. A leading authority on computer graphics applications has been quoted as saying that, regarding the merger of digitized photographs and images with text on computer screens, "there are probably a zillion applications where this is appropriate," and that for the present the technology is ahead of the marketplace.[7] A great many product changes and product introductions will occur in the coming years as this capacity is indeed pushed to its technical limits.

TIME AND MOTION

Going beyond the reproduction of photographs and printlike images, video and graphic capabilities will be used in other ways to organize and enhance information retrieval. Two developments that in the end could be quite unlike anything at present concern time and motion with respect to stored information.

With the ability to generate visual displays that have all the best of special effects, a piece of information could be projected backward in time to explore changes in meaning. Our understanding of the eye, for example, could be presented with the most recent views juxtaposed or contrasted with earlier views, either by overlaying images of words and pictures (with windows, or fading techniques, or the like) or by spatially arranging the representations. Obviously, this would require an internal organization of the information such that historical retrospectives are retrievable. Given the existing graphic ability to take an image and simulate aging, it may also be useful to apply the same idea to the presentation of information generally.

Thus, exploitation of the graphic interface may lead to the addition of the fourth dimension, time, to the process of retrieving and evaluating information. In a way, that is already the case, and without graphics. In many retrieval systems, each item may be tagged by at least one date, such as the date of publication, and sometimes more than one, such as the addition of dates from the body of the publication and the date of entry into the computerized system. A search for information can be ordered by the actual dates or by categories of dates. The visualization of time, based on the capture of the time-dependent relationships of information items, will go far beyond the basic sorting by date. At the least, we will have systems like the videodisk of Aspen, where objects such as buildings can be seen exhibiting seasonal changes and historic changes, all in a matter of seconds.

Similarly, the concept of motion can, and does, play a role in helping to organize stored information and the relationships inherent in the information. We already have the suggestion of motion on the Macintosh screen where a collection of file icons appears out of the disk icon and an individual file emerges from a file icon. At a more complex level, motion can be used to explore the relationships among stored documents or information items. Information items could automatically emerge from other items to indicate the dependence of one idea on another. Motion in conjunction with spatial arrangements could be used as an exploratory device to look at the closeness of information items, to travel through information space, and to form requests by altering a spatial arrangement of concepts. The sense of movement on the part of the user to the location of information has been studied in environments such as MIT's Dataland and will no doubt continue to be examined as technology makes it easier to do so on a smaller scale.

The addition of concepts such as time and motion to basic information retrieval systems can be accomplished in ways both common and uncommon to information systems. In pursuit of the uncommon, the visual representation of time and motion that is very acceptable in the movies and on television may become the basis for variations in retrieval techniques. The result may be something new for information systems but still familiar in the total range of human experience. To put it differently, the concept of computerized information retrieval will begin to include a lot more than the idea of people sitting at terminals typing search statements.

For a start, the trend in information distribution is already toward the use of computer and video techniques to accomplish things usually done with paper distribution, thereby adding more to the message than was there previously. On the computer side, examples are sales "brochures" for Buick, Chevrolet, Ford, and Chase Manhattan Bank, among others, that are floppy disks. Consumers can request a floppy disk brochure rather than a paper one. With the floppy disk version, the brochure is interactive, allowing the potential customer to configure a car, make comparisons, perform calculations, and perhaps even play part of it as a game. On the video side, an example in corporate communications is the use of video cassettes to provide information to employees, clients, shareholders, and financial analysts. One estimate is that between 1974 and 1986 the number of companies using video to accomplish these information-dissemination tasks rose from 300 to over 8500.[8] Video messages can bring all the persuasiveness and high production values of the best of television.

It is not hard to imagine the potential as these separate forms of expression—computer programs (with graphics) and traditional video—merge into the mainstream of computerized information systems.

OTHER ATTRIBUTES

Although this book is about the visual aspects of computerized information systems, it must be admitted that other attributes can also play a role in enhancing the way people use computers. Synthesized voice and digitized speech and audio capability in general also contribute to the expanding way individuals can interact with systems and the number who feel comfortable doing so. From the sound effects in video games and the speech chips in children's toys to the acceptance of voice commands and the interpretation of natural speech by personal computers, a considerable amount of effort is devoted to making sound a part of the computer interface.

Perhaps smell, taste, and texture will matter too at some point for computerized information retrieval, but in the interim, it is certain that sound should not be ignored. Whether sound is more or less important than visual techniques is hard to say; some fifth-generation efforts do place the emphasis more on audible natural language than on graphic interfaces. The best that can be said is that the ultimate relative value of sight and sound in computer usage will be in the same proportion for individuals as their daily reliance on these senses.

Guidelines for Design

Throughout this book the various efforts to tap the power of visual information systems have been reported, together with suggestions of how the visual dimension has been and can be implemented. At the risk of oversummarizing, we can restate some of the more general guidelines for adding visual elements to the process of finding and evaluating information in computerized systems.

ENHANCE, NOT DISTRACT

It is easy to say and harder to abide by, but a primary principle is that the visual tools should help the retrieval process, and not confuse or distract users with visual elements that are there simply for their own sake.

Graphic designers and video artists have known this for a very long time, but when graphics are employed more and more by the general population, the guidelines adhered to by the professionals can become lost. A good lesson can be found in charts and graphs. As these became increasingly used in print publications and are now routinely generated by hundreds of thousands of microcomputers, it has become very easy to find examples of poor design in which graphics overwhelm or even distort the message. An expert on graphics for data presentations, Edward Tufte, has no difficulty finding examples of bad displays from precomputer days, but the quantity has now increased dramatically. He points out at least three problems to be avoided in creating graphs and charts: avoid the vibrations caused by moiré patterns induced by cross-hatching, closely spaced bars, and the like; avoid letting the grid dominate the chart; and avoid "chartjunk" such as fake perspective, weird dimensions, and unnecessary color.[9] His concern is specifically with the display of quantitative data, but his comments apply generally to graphically enhanced representations. The visual elements added to the picture should not interfere with the message.

SIMPLICITY

Along the same lines, the addition of visual tools should be done with attention to simplicity of design. The most powerful and effective visual tools can appear to be very plain.

In the design of symbols and logos, for example, which preceded icons for computer systems, a great amount of information can be conveyed with a few well-designed sweeps of ink. In cases where it is necessary to convey information quickly as well as accurately, such as in traffic signs and signs for travelers, the art of simple yet elegant and meaningful designs has been honed over years. The situation is fairly similar for computerized information systems. Graphic symbols or icons must be apprehended quickly by a large majority of the users in a clear and unambiguous manner. An added difficulty with computer systems, though, is the lack of a base of common experience across inexperienced users. A sign in a transportation area showing a knife and fork readily conveys the idea that a restaurant or cafe is nearby. The use of a knife and fork is a very common experience, but many of the aspects of computer systems are familar only to persons who are already experienced with computers. Icons that play to that knowledge are appreciated only by those with the appropriate background. Thus simplicity of design also includes another principle, familiarity.

BASE IN EXPERIENCE

The most effective visual information systems are based on reality and upon the experiences of everyday life. Graphic tools and video enhancements should strike a chord of familiar impressions, leading the user along because it feels right.

The researchers at MIT's Media Laboratory tried a number of different uses of spatial arrangements and motion, and not all were readily accepted by the users. Some arrangements or techniques felt more natural than others to a majority of the users. For example, in using a joystick to move a window around the large screen to see more of the information within the window, it was more natural to have text slide to the right as the joystick was pushed to the left, rather than to have the text slide in the same direction as the joystick. The former sensation is the same as when looking out the window of a turning vehicle. As more scenery comes into view on the left, it essentially slides to the right in relation to the window's boundaries. Perhaps that is why it felt better to the users of Dataland's windows.

A cautionary note, however, is that while displays ought to be constructed on a base of human experience, that does not mean that common human experiences do not change. We do indeed become familiar with new things over time. It is probably safe to say that techniques used in television production can be understood within information systems by users in any country with a substantial television set population, even though such techniques might be confusing to those without much experience with television viewing. As video cassette recorders become part of everyday life, with features such as fast forward, we will probably become equally accepting of visually fast-forwarding through information displays.

BALANCE

Overall, the visual nature of presenting computer-stored information should be balanced with the demands of language, whether as text or as sound. At the same time, concentration on the visual element as distinct from text can lead to an understanding of the effects of the creation and arrangement of textual characters on video screens. The technical capabilities now common in desktop publishing, the arena of what-you-see-is-what-you-get, have reintroduced to computer terminals used for information systems an appreciation of layout, fonts, page design, and, in general, the visual impact of a screen full of words.

For the design of information systems, a sense of balance means not only a careful mix of text and graphics or video, but also an appropriate arrangement of text on the screen using fonts for specific purposes.

PSYCHOPHYSIOLOGICAL AWARENESS

As technology advances, the construction of physical display devices and the use of the devices' capacity can be adapted better to what is known about human optical signal processing. The basic functioning of the eye has been known for quite some time, but we are continuing to learn more about the details of the process, and especially about the brain's handling of imagery.

Actually, at least three branches of pertinent research benefit the design of visual displays. At the perceptual level, studies of the relationship between reported perception and visual stimulus can shed light on the value of different displays without delving into exactly how the eye responds to light and the brain registers a sight. A large amount of knowledge has accumulated about the perception of shapes, colors, balance, perspective, and the other elements of the visual aesthetic. With regard to computerized information systems, this knowledge must be adjusted to the specifics of the display device, such as the CRT. Some rules of thumb for print displays do not apply to video displays, for example.

Even among video displays themselves, the technical capabilities of one may reverse the rules of thumb applied to others. It has often been said, for instance, that for continued reading of text on CRTs, the lettering should be light against a dark background, unlike most print which is dark on a light background, because the CRT generates light while paper only reflects it. Newer CRTs and other display devices can, however, project a very comfortable dark text on a light background. The principles of design based on perceptual studies are therefore not absolutes, but evolve with technology.

Two other branches of research concern the functioning of the eye and the optic pathways, and the reception, storage, and retrieval of images in the brain. The former area has always been a part of the design and construction of video displays. Television was developed based on what was then known about the reaction of the eye to light sources, and on assumptions about the environmental conditions within which the light source and the light receptors would exist (e.g., the viewer would be a short distance from the screen). Monitors for computer systems, on the other hand, have to be designed for close viewing of detailed displays, such as text, where visual objects may need sharp edges. Because technical design is very often affected by economic constraints, the result is usually something less than the known upper limits of the human optical system. In other words, a video display does not need to have the finest resolution that is above the capabilities of the most discerning rods and cones under the best of conditions if the majority of users can and do use displays with lower resolution. For display hardware designers, the problem is more one of refining existing technology and incorporating newer technologies as feasible, rather than being limited by research in human optics. Nevertheless, we still do not know all there is to know about the human optical network, and as research progresses the findings will affect the future design of video systems.

It is in the area of image processing in the visual pathways and the cortex where there are many unknowns and where the potential effect on the design of information systems is considerable. If we knew how the brain associates images, for example, we might be able to devise systems that present information in ways that would appeal directly to a fundamental level of mental image processing, and skip levels of translation, thus speeding up our ability to grasp concepts in context. Just how this can be accomplished is still vague, as we continue to improve our understanding of human mental processes, including vision. Recent data suggest that the mental retrieval of images, and memory in general, involves cooperative processes among a host of neural elements, but it is much more complicated than just counting neurons and synaptic inputs. Mental awareness and memory may rely on properties of the neural system as a whole that are still not recognized or understood.[10]

Historically, the information technology of the day has often been invoked as an analogy for mental functions. In the days of wax seals, Plato suggested that the brain was like a block of wax on which ideas are imprinted like the stamp of a ring.[11] In this century, the computer has been promoted as a model of how the brain works, even as newer computers with parallel processors came along to change the analogy. The brain subsequently was characterized as a parallel processing system. To whatever extent the brain is understood, it is conversely used as a model for the development of information systems. It is hard to say which came first, the decision to develop parallel processing technology, or the recognition that the brain must do processing in parallel. More recently, brain activity is described as a vague cooperative process of neural networks, and the newest computer designs are called neural-net systems.

As neuroscience and biochemical research into the mental functions of vision increase our knowledge in that area, technology will adapt to the new understanding in ways that cannot be described fully at present. Thus awareness of the psychophysiological basis of vision is important, not only for all that has been discovered, but also for an appreciation of how much remains to be learned.

Finally, as we continue to explore the broader questions of creativity and insight, we may even be able to construct computerized information systems that will give us an assist in these activities.

The Larger Environment

Any evaluation of the potential for the visual elements that are or can be part of computerized information systems should be tempered by recognition of the larger environment.

MULTIDISCIPLINARY FOUNDATION

The expected benefits of visual information systems are supported by developments in a number of disciplines, some readily apparent and others less so. In the effort here to bring together the underlying evidence for the value of the visual dimension, it has not been possible to cover all topics in the depth that each deserves. At each phase of the visual process, from the creation of the light source, both physically and logically, to the reception of the signal, both physiologically and mentally, a host of variables affects how we see and what it means. At the very least, if some topics have not been covered sufficiently, it is hoped that the combination of the whole conveys the magnitude of the issue and the variety of influences.

CHANGING TECHNOLOGIES

Another difficulty with an examination of visual presentations, specifically as the interface between computer-stored information and humans, is that technology marches on. Statements made about technical issues, such as the resolution of a video screen or even the assumption that the primary display device is a video screen, can be rendered obsolete sooner or later by the advancement of technology. Keeping that in mind, an attempt has been made to concentrate on the technical issues that are expected to affect system design for at least the near future and to look at general conditions in addition to specific instances, in that as details may change, the overall considerations might remain the same. An attempt has also been made to take a reasonable look into the future by noting the trends in research and development.

In the longer term, current technical development may lead to visual information systems that are only dimly imagined today. We already have toys that react to inaudible signals from a broadcast television program. In an information system, we may have local personal devices not physically connected to a video terminal that will nonetheless be triggered by signals from remote data bases to help us respond in an individualized manner to the information system. Basic research into optical computers, SEED chips (self-electro-optic effect devices, i.e., chips that process light as well as electronic signals), superconductors, and lower forms of life such as worms and slugs to understand their information processing mechanisms may lead to even more unexpected configurations for information systems. Whatever these systems may be, they will build upon the existing appreciation of the power of visual tools and objects in computer systems.

TRANSITIONAL PERIODS

At a gross level, we are definitely in a transitional period between the alphanumeric displays of information systems of the recent past and the visually rich displays of information systems that are increasing in practicality and popularity. That is also an oversimplification of what is happening and what is likely to happen. For one thing, alphanumeric displays without graphic capability will continue to be used for quite a long time. In fact, there will probably always be a place for them. On the other hand, at some undetermined time in the future, the use of visual tools such as icons and windows and spatial arrangements generally, will also become so commonplace as to be considered almost essential for information retrieval.

Thus it may be helpful to see that there are really many stages to the transitional period. At first, there are suggestions that a real revolution is taking place, quickly and dramatically, only to be followed by the persistence of the existing methods. In the short term there is no wholesale replacement of one procedure by another. In fact, the newer procedures of visual information systems may be accepted as ancillary, but nothing more than that. Only after a longer period of time do we see by hindsight the changes that can be accepted as fundamental, and the way in which earlier methods or technologies may continue to exist, but perhaps in different roles.

A Visual World

Overall, most of us live in a very visual world where an understanding of the fundamentals of visual representations can be taken for granted. The general lack of graphics and video in computerized information systems, for the short period of time from the start of such systems in the late 1950s to the early 1980s, followed by the spread of graphics technology, has reawakened our awareness of what has been missing. For the future, system designers will no doubt build upon the traditional role of spatial orientation and graphic arrangements to add newer concepts made possible by the display technologies used. The newer concepts will also be necessitated by the very nature of vast amounts of information invisibly recorded and stored in computer data bases.

In the meantime, the development of visual information systems can proceed, based on the expanding technology for visual representations and on an amplified awareness of the human powers of visual comprehension.

NOTES

Chapter 1

1. William M. Newman and Robert F. Sproull, *Principles of Interactive Computer Graphics* (New York: McGraw-Hill Book Co., 1973), xxi–xxii.

2. David Olmos, "Panel Examines History, Future of Computer Graphics," *Computerworld*, 6 August 1984, 16.

3. Stanley Klein, "Established Corporations Move into the Graphics Market," *Computerworld*, 25 March 1985, SR/20.

4. Arthur W. Eve, "Graphics a Potentially Powerful Force in Business World Affecting Information Assimilation, Managerial Style," *Computerworld*, 24 September 1984, 60.

5. Charles P. Lecht, "Graphics Harmonizes Worlds of Art, Science," *Computerworld*, 18 March 1985, 43.

6. Rudolf Arnheim, *Art and Visual Perception* (Berkeley, Calif.: University of California Press, 1969), 323–59.

7. Stuart Sutherland, "Prestel and the User," research report of the Center for Research on Perception and Cognition, University of Sussex, Brighton, U.K., May 1980.

8. Brian G. Champness and Marco de Alberdi, "Measuring Subjective Reactions to Teletext Page Design," research report of the Alternate Media Center, New York University School of the Arts, September 1981.

9. Izak Benbasat, Albert S. Dexter, and Peter Todd, "An Experimental Program Investigating Color-enhanced and Graphical Information Presentation: An Integration of the Findings," *Communications of the ACM* 29 (November 1986): 1094–105.

10. Aaron Marcus, "The Ten Commandments of Color: A Tutorial," *Computer Graphics Today*, November 1986, 7, 12, 14.

11. *Computer Graphics* (a quarterly report of ACM Siggraph), 19 (July 1985).

12. Vannevar Bush, "As We May Think," *Atlantic Monthly*, July 1945, 101–8.

13. John D. Meyer, "Vision Systems: Technology of the Future at Work Today," *Computerworld*, 27 May 1985, SR-13.

14. P.T. Cahill, B. Kneeland, R.J.R. Knowles, L.F. Lunin, and O. Tsen, "An Intelligent Data Base for Image Analysis, Storage, and Retrieval in Radiology," *Proceedings of the Fourth National Online Meeting* (Medford, N.J.: Learned Information, 1983), 83–86.

15. Erik Sandberg-Diment, "Integrated Software for the Thin Mac," *New York Times*, 14 July 1985, F-11.

16. Oscar Ogg, *The 26 Letters* (New York: Van Nostrand Reinhold Co., 1983).

17. David Stuart, "A Maya Primer," *Science 86* 7 (March 1986): 55.

18. Jean Key Gates, *Guide to the Use of Books and Libraries* (New York: McGraw-Hill Book Co., 1962), 5.

19. George A. Miller, "Psychology and Information," *American Documentation*, July 1968, 286–89.

20. John M. Carroll, "The Adventure of Getting to Know a Computer," *Computer*, November 1982, 49–58.

21. Richard A. Bolt, *The Human Interface* (Belmont, Calif.: Lifetime Learning Publications, 1984).

22. Erik Sandberg-Diment, "Adding a Dash of Visual Sparkle," *New York Times*, 4 August 1985, F-10.

23. Jeffrey Cogen, "Graphics Pour into the Office," *Computerworld OA*, 5 December 1984, 21–23.

24. John A. Lehman, Doug Vogel, and Gary Dickson, "Business Graphics Trends," *Datamation*, 15 November 1984, 119–22.

Chapter 2

1. See, for example, Edwin B. Steen and Ashley Montagu, *Anatomy and Physiology*, vol. 2 (New York: Harper & Row, 1985), 178–201.

2. Jeremy Nathans, Darcy Thomas, and David S. Hogness, "Molecular Genetics of Human Color Vision: The Genes Encoding Blue,

Green and Red Pigments," *Science* 232 (11 April 1986): 195. See also, David Botstein, "The Molecular Biology of Color Vision," *Science* 232 (11 April 1986): 142–43.

3. Jeremy Nathans, Thomas P. Piantanida, Roger L. Eddy, Thomas B. Shows, and David S. Hogness, "Molecular Genetics of Inherited Variation in Human Color Vision," *Science* 232 (11 April 1986): 203–10. See also, Deborah Franklin, "Color Vision: Shades of Evolution," *Science 86* 7 (July/August 1986): 6.

4. David S. Falk, Dieter R. Brill, and David G. Stork, *Seeing the Light* (New York: Harper & Row, 1986), 394–96.

5. David H. Sliney, "Eye Hazards of Environmental Lighting," in *The Medical and Biological Effects of Light,* ed. Richard J. Wurtman, et al. (New York: New York Academy of Sciences, 1985), 114. See also, Michael F. Holick, "The Photobiology of Vitamin D and Its Consequences for Humans," in *The Medical and Biological Effects of Light,* 1–14.

6. John N. Ott, *Health and Light* (Old Greenwich, Conn.: Devin-Adair Co., 1973), 118–34.

7. Cathy Trost, "Study on VDT Use During Pregnancy Seen Lessening Concern of Health Risks," *Wall Street Journal,* 30 September 1986, 7.

8. Bill Grenawalt, "Screen Reflection: Its Glaring Effect on VDT Operator Performance," *Computerworld,* 7 July 1986, 18.

9. Hans Fantel, "The Competition for a Sharper Image Comes Up Against Realistic Limits," *New York Times,* 2 November 1986, H-32.

10. Gregory MacNicol, "Color Monitor Specmanship: Look Before You Leap," *Digital Design,* November 1985, 44–48.

11. William M. Newman and Robert F. Sproull, *Principles of Interactive Computer Graphics* (New York: McGraw-Hill Book Co., 1973), 13–14.

12. Conrac Division, Conrac Corporation, *Raster Graphics Handbook* (New York: Van Nostrand Reinhold Co., 1985), 48–49.

13. Karen Davis, "No Sacrifices with Raster Graphics Display," *Computerworld,* 28 October 1985, 96–97.

14. Andrew Wilson, "Flat-panel Displays: Still in the Future," *Digital Design,* December 1985, 54–58.

15. Dennis Allen, "Flat Panels: Beyond the CRT," *Computer Graphics World,* February 1986, 21–24.

16. More complete explanations can be found in various sources,

including the very understandable book by David S. Falk, Dieter R. Brill, and David G. Stork, *Seeing the Light* (New York: Harper & Row, 1986).

17. Deborah M. Barnes, "Brain Architecture: Beyond Genes," *Science* 233 (11 July 1986): 155–56.

18. Beverly J. Jafek, "Autoradiographic Imaging Improves PET Efficacy," *Diagnostic Imaging*, September 1983, 70–74.

19. Michael E. Phelps and John C. Mazziotta, "Positron Emission Tomography: Human Brain Function and Biochemistry," *Science* 228 (17 May 1985): 799–809.

20. Larry R. Squire, "Mechanisms of Memory," *Science* 232 (27 June 1986): 1612–19.

21. Joseph Alper, "Our Dual Memory," *Science 86*, July/August 1986, 44–49.

22. "The Many Faces of Memory," *Science 86*, July/August 1986, 48.

23. Betty Edwards, *Drawing on the Right Side of the Brain* (Los Angeles: J.P. Tarcher, Inc., 1979), 26–32.

24. William S. Cleveland and Robert McGill, "Graphical Perception and Graphical Methods for Analyzing Scientific Data," *Science* 229 (30 August 1985): 828–33.

25. See, for example, Stephen Monsell, "Representations, Processes, Memory Mechanisms: The Basic Components of Cognition," *Journal of the American Society for Information Science* 32 (September 1981): 378–90. See also, Stephen J. Ceci, "Memory Development," *Science* 231 (21 March 1986): 1452.

Chapter 3

1. Sheila Donoghue, "Industry Reps See Graphics Booming Commodity," *Computer Graphics Today*, May 1986, 3, 58.

2. John A. Lehman, Doug Vogel, and Gary Dickson, "Business Graphics Trends," *Datamation*, 15 November 1984, 119–22.

3. "Business Software: PC Applications in Use and Purchase Plans," *Computerworld*, 28 July 1986, 23.

4. Karen Sorensen, "Presentation Graphics Show the Big Picture," *Infoworld*, 16 December 1985, 27–28.

5. "Presentation Graphics Software," *Computerworld*, 23 June 1986, 64–67.

6. Erik Sandberg-Diment, "Adding a Dash of Visual Sparkle," *New York Times*, 4 August 1985, F-10.

7. Edward R. Tufte, *The Visual Display of Quantitative Information* (Cheshire, Conn.: Graphics Press, 1983).

8. Robert Rivlin, *The Algorithmic Image* (Redmond, Wash.: Microsoft Press, 1986), 16–19.

9. "Bringing CAE to the Mechanical World: Phil Villers' Cognition, Inc., to Automate Design Creation and Optimization of Parts and Systems," *S. Klein Newsletter on Computer Graphics*, 7 (18 October/8 November 1985): 1, 7–8.

10. Robert Rivlin, *The Algorithmic Image* (Redmond, Wash.: Microsoft Press, 1986), 166.

11. See, for example, Beverley J. Jafek, "Landsat Imaging and the Study of Volcanoes," *Computer Graphics World*, February 1984, 53–57. See also, Beverley J. Jafek and Ronald G. McLeod, "Solving Environmental Problems with Satellite Imagery, *Computer Graphics World*, February 1984, 75–78.

12. Abigail Christopher, "At the Frontiers of Medical Imaging," *Computer Pictures*, January/February 1987, 62–66.

13. See, for example, Shinya Inoue and Theodore D. Inoue, "Computer-aided Stereoscopic Video Reconstruction and Serial Display from High-resolution Light-microscope Optical Sections," in *Recent Advances in Electron and Light Optical Imaging in Biology and Medicine*, ed. Andrew P. Somlyo (New York: New York Academy of Sciences, 1986), 392–404.

14. Adapted from Raymond J. Offen, ed., *VLSI Image Processing* (New York: McGraw-Hill Book Co, 1985).

15. Robert Rivlin, *The Algorithmic Image* (Redmond, Wash.: Microsoft Press, 1986), 74–75.

16. Suzan D. Prince, "Television Stations Beam in on Computer Graphics Tech," *Computer Pictures*, March/April 1986, 20–28.

17. Karen Davis, "No Sacrifices with Raster Graphics Display," *Computerworld*, 28 October 1985, 96–97.

18. William Frentz, "High-performance and High-potential PC Graphics," paper presented at the Dataquest Display Terminals/Graphics Industry Conference, Monterey, Calif., 4–6 June 1986.

19. Peter R. Bono, "Software Standards: Which Ones Are Here to Stay," *S. Klein Computer Graphics Review*, inaugural issue (early 1986), 94–100.

20. American National Standards Institute, *Draft Proposed American*

National Standard, Graphical Kernel System, (New York: American National Standards Institute, 1984), 5.

21. John Lewell, "The Standardization of Standards," *AV Video,* May 1984, 18–21.

Chapter 4

1. "Home Movies from Phonograph Records." *Modern Mechanics and Inventions,* June 1932, 89.

2. See, for example, Mark Heyer, "Searching for Shakespeare," paper prepared for Reference Technology Product Introductions, September 1984, and distributed by Mark Heyer Associates.

3. Steven Greenhouse, "An Innovator Gets Down to Business—3M" *New York Times,* 12 October 1986, F-1, F-8.

4. Hans Fantel, "Digital Recordings—Beautiful Music by the Numbers," *New York Times,* 18 February 1979, D-19–21.

5. Peter R. Cook, "Electronic Encyclopedias," *Byte,* July 1984, 151–70.

6. John Durniak, "Kodak Boosts Electronic Pictures," *New York Times,* 27 October 1985, 75.

7. See, for example, Richard A. Bolt, *Spatial Data Management* (Cambridge: Massachusetts Institute of Technology, 1979); Richard A. Bolt, *The Human Interface* (Belmont, Calif.: Lifetime Learning Publications, 1984); and Richard A. Bolt, "Human Interfaces for Managers," *Computerworld,* 16 July 1984, ID-1–18.

8. "Laser Videodiscs, Computer Graphics for Road Evaluations," *Better Roads,* March 1985, 16–17.

9. "Videodiscs and Computers: A Dynamic Duo," *Business Week,* 7 February 1983, 109–11.

10. Greg Kearsley, "Instructional Videodisc," *Journal of the American Society for Information Science* 34 (November 1983): 417–23.

11. Ron Herman, "Detroit Gears Up with Videodiscs," *Corporate Television,* November 1986, 48–50.

Chapter 5

1. Kathleen Hemenway, "Psychological Issues in the Use of Icons in Command Menus," in *Human Factors in Computer Systems,* pro-

ceedings of a conference sponsored by the Institute for Computer Science and Technology, National Bureau of Standards, U.S. Department of Commerce, and by the Association for Computing Machinery, 1982.

2. Adele Goldberg and David Robson, *Smalltalk-80. The Language and its Implementation* (Reading, Mass.: Addison-Wesley Publishing Co., 1983).

3. Wilbert O. Galitz, *Handbook of Screen Format Design* (Wellesley Hills, Mass.: QED Information Sciences, 1981, 1985).

4. See, for example, Ben Shneiderman, *Designing the User Interface* (Reading, Mass.: Addison-Wesley Publishing Co., 1987), 86 ff; and Ben Shneiderman, "Designing Menu Selection Systems," *Journal of the American Society for Information Science* 37 (March 1986): 57–70.

5. James H. Morris, et al., "Andrew: A Distributed Personal Computing Environment," *Communications of the ACM* 29 (March 1986): 184–201.

6. Larry Koved and Ben Shneiderman, "Embedded Menus: Selecting Items in Context," *Communications of the ACM* 29 (April 1986): 312–18.

7. *Ibid.*

8. Kathleen Sullivan, "Icons Point to Changes," *Computerworld*, 20 August 1984, 87, 97.

9. "The Computerized Icon; CGW Interviews Aaron Marcus," *Computer Graphics World*, May 1985, 78–80.

10. Edith Myers, "Fingers Do the Work," *Datamation*, 15 August 1984, 58–61.

11. J.S. Watson, trans., *Cicero on Oratory and Orators* (Carbondale, Ill.: Southern Illinois University Press, 1970), 186–87.

12. Kathleen Sullivan, "Icons Point to Changes," *Computerworld*, 20 August 1984, 87, 97.

13. Gregg Berryman, *Notes on Graphic Design and Visual Communication* (Los Altos, Calif.: William Kaufmann, Inc., 1979, 1984).

14. "The Past, Present and Future of the Macintosh Desktop," *Semaphore Signal*, 12 March 1986, 1–7.

15. "The Computerized Icon; CGW Interviews Aaron Marcus," *Computer Graphics World*, May 1985, 78–80.

16. Irene Fuerst, "Broken Windows," *Datamation*, 1 March 1985, 46–52.

17. George M. White, "The Desktop Metaphor," *Byte*, December 1983, 220.

18. Andrea A. diSessa and Harold Abelson, "Boxer: A Reconstructible Computational Medium," *Communications of the ACM* 29 (September 1986): 859–68.

19. Tom Houston, "The Allegory of Software," *Byte* December 1983, 210–14.

20. John M. Carroll, "Presentation and Form in User-interface Architecture," *Byte*, December 1983, 113–22.

21. Ben Shneiderman, "Designing Menu Selection Systems," *Journal of the American Society for Information Science* 37 (March 1986): 57–70.

Chapter 6

1. Edward R. Tufte, *The Visual Display of Quantitative Information* (Cheshire, Conn.: Graphics Press, 1983), 26.

2. Fung Yu-Lan, *A Short History of Chinese Philosophy* (New York: Free Press, 1966), 12.

3. Frank Barron, "The Psychology of Imagination," *Scientific American*, September 1958, 150–66.

4. Karl W. Deutsch, "Knowledge in the Growth of Civilization: A Cybernetic Approach to the History of Human Thought," in *The Foundations of Access to Knowledge*, ed. Edward B. Montgomery (Syracuse, N.Y.: Syracuse University Press, 1968), 37–58.

5. Daniel Bell, "Teletext and Technology," *Encounter*, June 1977, 9–29.

6. G. Salton, "A New Comparison Between Conventional Indexing (MEDLARS) and Automatic Text Processing (SMART)," *Journal of the American Society for Information Science* 23 (March-April 1972): 75–83.

7. Matthew B. Koll, "WEIRD: An Approach to Concept-based Information Retrieval," in *Supplemental Proceedings of the International Conference on Information Storage and Retrieval* (New York: Association for Computing Machinery, 1978), 1–19.

8. Vijay V. Raghavan and S.K.M. Wong, "A Critical Analysis of Vector Space Model for Information Retrieval," *Journal of the American Society for Information Science*, 37 (September 1986): 279–87.

9. Lev Goldfarb, "Metric Data Models and Associated Search Strategies," *SIGIR Forum* 20 (Spring-Summer 1986): 7–11.

10. Ruth Ann Palmquist and Michael Eisenberg, "Testing a Text Analysis Metric Using Magnitude Estimation," *Proceedings of the 47th ASIS Annual Meeting*, vol. 21 (White Plains, N.Y.: Knowledge Industry Publications, 1984), 231–36.

11. R.N. Oddy, "Information Retrieval Through Man-Machine Dialogue," *Journal of Documentation* 33 (March 1977): 1–14.

12. Craig Stanfill and Brewster Kahle, "Parallel Free-text Search on the Connection Machine System," *Communications of the ACM* 29 (December 1986): 1229–239.

13. Gerard Salton, "On the Use of Knowledge-based Processing in Automatic Text Retrieval," *Proceedings of the 49th Annual Meeting of the American Society for Information Science*, vol. 23 (Medford, N.J.: Learned Information, 1986), 277–87.

14. Richard S. Marcus, "Design Questions in the Development of Expert Systems for Retrieval Assistance," *Proceedings of the 49th Annual Meeting of the American Society for Information Science*, vol. 23 (Medford, N.J.: Learned Information, 1986), 185–89.

15. Klaus K. Obermeier and Linda E. Cooper, "Information Network Facility Organizing System (INFOS)—An Expert System for Information Retrieval," *Proceedings of the 47th ASIS Annual Meeting*, vol. 21 (White Plains, N.Y.: Knowledge Industry Publications, 1984), 95–98.

16. Philip J. Smith and Mark Chignell, "Development of an Expert System to Aid in Searches of the *Chemical Abstracts*," *Proceedings of the 47th ASIS Annual Meeting*, vol. 21 (White Plains, N.Y.: Knowledge Industry Publications, 1984), 99–105.

17. Mitch Betts, "Archives Gets Expert System," *Computerworld*, 8 September 1986, 93, 95.

18. Edward A. Fox, "Expert Retrieval for Users of Computer-Based Message Systems," *Proceedings of the 49th Annual Meeting of the American Society for Information Science*, vol. 23 (Medford, N.J.: Learned Information, 1986), 88–95.

19. Richard S. Marcus, "Development and Testing of Expert Systems for Retrieval Assistance," *Proceedings of the 48th ASIS Annual Meeting* (White Plains, N.Y.: Knowledge Industry Publications, 1985), 289–92. See also ref. 14 above.

20. Douglas P. Metzler, Terry Noreault, Douglas F. Haas, and Cynthia Cosic, "An Expert System Approach to Natural Language Processing," *Proceedings of the 48th ASIS Annual Meeting* (White Plains, N.Y.: Knowledge Industry Publications, 1985), 301–7.

21. Craig Stanfill and David Waltz, "Toward Memory-based Reasoning," *Communications of the ACM* 29 (December 1986): 1213–228.

22. Bryan Wilkins, "AI Techniques Considered for DBMS Use," *Computerworld*, 3 December 1984, 57.

23. Quoted in Yoneji Masuda, *The Information Society as Post-industrial Society* (Tokyo: Institute for the Information Society, 1980), 3.

24. See, for example, Edward A. Feigenbaum and Pamela McCorduck, *The Fifth Generation* (New York: New American Library, 1984).

25. John J. Fialka, "Ambitious Computer Research Is Focus of Pentagon Program," *Wall Street Journal*, 15 August 1986, 17.

26. Kenneth G. Wilson, "Supercomputer Future: Scenario for 1990," *Computerworld*, 6 May 1985, Update/7, 22.

27. Bonnie Henson, "Complex Computer Systems May Use Fisheye View Approach," *Insight* 3 (2 April 1986): 4–11.

28. Wei-Ching Lin and Tsippora F. Dingott, "To Tree or Not to Tree: A Simple User Interface Design for Complex Decision Logic," *Proceedings of the 1986 IEEE International Conference on Systems, Man and Cybernetics* (New York: Institute of Electrical and Electronics Engineers, 1986), 617–21.

Chapter 7

1. See, for example, "VDTs Said to Slow Reading," *Computerworld*, 1 September 1986, 63.

2. Philip J. Gill, "AI, Graphics Launch New User Interfaces," *Computer Graphics Today*, September 1986, 3, 8.

3. Charles P. Lecht, "To Dream, Perhaps of DRAMs," *Computerworld*, 2 February 1987, 17.

4. John Marcom, Jr., "Movie-like Realism in Computers Could Put Sizzle in Home Market," *Wall Street Journal*, 4 June 1985, 35.

5. Stuart Silverstone, "GM Gets Holograms," *Computer Graphics Today*, 24 November 1986, 1, 24.

6. "Futurist Jonathan Post Explores Tomorrow's Databases," *Bulletin of the American Society for Information Science*, June/July 1986, 24.

7. Stanley Klein, quoted in Barbara Robertson, "Capturing Images in Databases," *Lotus*, January 1987, 13–15.

8. "Companies Use Video for Everything from Annual Reports to Stock Offerings," *Wall Street Journal*, 8 January 1987, 1.

9. Edward R. Tufte, *The Visual Display of Quantitative Information* (Cheshire, Conn.: Graphics Press, 1983).

10. E. R. John, Y. Tang, A. B. Brill, R. Young, and K. Ono, "Double-labeled Metabolic Maps of Memory," *Science* 233 (12 September 1986): 1167–175.

11. Robert Wright, "A Better Mental Model," *Sciences*, March/April 1986, 8–10.

BIBLIOGRAPHY

Alexander, James H., and Freiling, Michael J. "Troubleshooting with the Help of an Expert System." Technical Report no. CR-85-05. Artificial Intelligence Department, Computer Research Laboratory, Tektronix, Inc.

Allen, David. "Linking Computers to Videodisc Players." *Videography*, January 1985, 26–34.

Allen, Dennis. "Flat Panels: Beyond the CRT." *Computer Graphics World*, February 1986, 21–24.

Alper, Joseph. "Our Dual Memory." *Science 86*, July/August 1986, 44–49.

"An Alvey Survey: Advanced Information Technology in the U.K." *Future Generations Computer Systems*, July 1984, 69–78.

Amanatides, John. "Realism in Computer Graphics: A Survey." *Computer Graphics and Applications*, January 1987, 44–56.

American National Standards Committee. *Draft Proposed American National Standard, Graphical Kernal System.* New York: American National Standards Institute, January 1984.

Andersen, Richard A.; Essick, Greg K.; and Siegel, Ralph M. "Encoding of Spatial Location by Posterior Parietal Neurons." *Science* 230 (25 October 1985); 456–58.

Andrews, Nancy. *Windows.* Redmond, Wash.: Microsoft Press, 1986.

Ansberry, Clare. "Improved Photos Are Possible for Consumers, at a Premium." *Wall Street Journal*, 26 September 1986, 33.

Arnheim, Rudolf. *Art and Visual Perception.* Berkeley: University of California Press, 1969.

Aveney, Brian. "A Special Section on Micrographics." *Bulletin of the American Society for Information Science*, October 1980, 11.

Babcock, Charles. "Datapoint Unveils Color, Full-motion Video Unit." *Computerworld*, 5 August 1985, 4.

Babcock, Charles. "DBMS Image Processing Claim Seen Boosting Product Uses." *Computerworld*, 7 July 1986, p. 7.

Barnes, Deborah M. "Brain Architecture: Beyond Genes." *Science* 233 (11 July 1986): 155–56.

Barney, Douglas. "Intel Pits Graphics Chip against TI." *Computerworld*, 26 May 1986, 27, 34.

Barney, Douglas. "Quadram Focuses on Optical Mart with Video Data Bases." *Computerworld*, 21 July 1986, 37–38.

Barney, Douglas. "Windows Opens Up Micro Operating Environments Market." *Computerworld*, 3 February 1986, 10.

Barron, Frank. "The Psychology of Imagination." *Scientific American*, September 1958, 150–66.

Baskin, Yvonne. "The Way We Act." *Science 85*, November 1985, 94–100.

Beeler, Jeffry. "Optical Storage for Micros Will Upgrade Info Retrieval, NCR Chief Tells Conference." *Computerworld*, 28 November 1983, 34.

Beeler, Jeffry. "Software Offerings Reflect Windowing Craze." *Computerworld*, 5 December 1983, 7.

Bell, Daniel. "Teletext and Technology." *Encounter*, June 1977, 9–29.

Benbasat, Izak; Dexter, Albert S.; and Todd, Peter. "An Experimental Program Investigating Color-enhanced and Graphical Information Presentation: An Integration of the Findings." *Communications of the ACM* 29 (November 1986): 1094–105.

Bender, Eric. "Windows Finally Opens." *Computerworld*, 2 December 1985, 37, 39.

Bentley, Jon L., and Kernighan, Brian W. "GRAP—A Language for Typesetting Graphs." *Communications of the ACM* 29 (August 1986): 782–92.

Berg, Eric N. "CAD/CAM's Pioneer Bets it All." *New York Times*, 24 March 1985, F-4.

Berryman, Gregg. *Notes on Graphic Design and Visual Communication.* Los Altos, Calif.: William Kaufmann, Inc., 1984.

Betts, Mitch. "Archives Gets Expert System." *Computerworld*, 8 September 1986, 93,95.

Betts, Mitch. "Government PC Purchases Jumped in '85." *Computerworld*, 7 July 1986, 8.

Betts, Mitch. "Report Claims VDT Work Does Not Induce Miscarriages," *Computerworld*, 6 October 1986, 12.

Bolt, Richard A. *The Human Interface*. Belmont, Calif.: Lifetime Learning Publications, 1984.

Bolt, Richard A. "Human Interfaces for Managers." *Computerworld*, 16 July 1984, ID-1–18.

Bolt, Richard A. *Spatial Data Management*. Cambridge: Massachusetts Institute of Technology, 1979.

Bono, Peter R. "ANSI, ISO Approving Computer Graphics Metafile." *Computer Grahpics Today*, January 1987, 29.

Bono, Peter R. "Graphics Standards Migrating to PC Level." *Computer Graphics Today*, June 1985, 7, 11.

Bono, Peter R. "Meetings Resolve Formal Standards Issues." *Computer Graphics Today*," 12 August 1986, 12, 28.

Bono, Peter R. "Software Standards: Which Ones are Here to Stay?" *S. Klein Computer Graphics Review*, inaugural issue (early 1986), 94–100.

Borrell, Jerry. "Digital Paint Systems." *Computer Graphics World*, April 1982, 61–67.

Boulding, Kenneth E. "The Future of the Interaction of Knowledge, Energy and Materials." *Behavior Science Research* 13 (1978): 169–83.

Branscomb, Lewis M. "Information: The Ultimate Frontier." *Science* 203 (12 January 1979): 143–47.

Brodie, Richard. "Digital Readies Standard for Document Architecture." *Digital News* 29 September 1986, 1, 8.

Brodie, Richard. "For 5th Generation, the Language Just May Be Japanese." *Digital News*, 20 October 1986, 22.

Brown, Michael J. "The Complete Information-management System." *Byte*, December 1983, 199–207.

Bulkeley, William M. "Courts Expand the Copyright Protection of Software, but Many Questions Remain." *Wall Street Journal*, 18 November 1986, 35.

Bulkeley, William M. "Expert Systems Are Entering into Mainstream of Computers." *Wall Street Journal*, 5 December 1986, 33.

Burnett, Craig, and McFarlane, Gregory. "Sharp, Detailed Graphics Images Are Best Provided by Vector Graphics." *Hardcopy*, October 1986, 143–48.

Bush, Vannevar. "As We May Think." *Atlantic Monthly*, July 1945, 101–8.

Carroll, John M. "The Adventure of Getting to Know a Computer." *Computer*, November 1982, 49–58.

Carroll, John M. "Presentation and Form in User-interface Architecture." *Byte*, December 1983, 113–22.

Castagnoli, William G. "Videodiscs: A Leap Forward in Educational Marketing." *Medical Marketing & Media*, June 1982, 17–22.

Cavuoto, James. "Digitized Fonts in Postscript." *Computer Graphics World*, September 1985, 27–30.

Ceci, Stephen J. "Memory Development." *Science* 231 (21 March 1986): 1452.

Chafen, Rick. "Skills for Learning." *Data Training*, April 1985, 22–31.

Champness, Brian G., and de Alberdi, Marco. "Measuring Subjective Reactions to Teletext Page Design." Alternate Media Center, New York University's School of the Arts, September 1981. 59 pages.

Chin, Janet A. "Compatible Standards—Boon or Bane?" *Computer Graphics and Applications*, January 1987, 63–64.

Christopher, Abigail. "At the Frontiers of Medical Imaging." *Computer Pictures*, January/February 1987, 62–66.

Clanton, Chuck. "The Future of Metaphor in Man-Computer Systems." *Byte*, December 1983, 263–76.

Clarkson, Thomas B. "Device-independent Graphics Moves into Hardware." Paper presented at Display Terminals/Graphics Industry Conference, Dataquest Inc., Monterey, Calif., 4–6 June 1986.

Clarkson, Thomas. "Needed: Graphics Standards." *Computerworld*, 22 April 1985, ID-13–ID-16.

Cleveland, William S., and McGill, Robert. "Graphical Perception and Graphical Methods for Analyzing Scientific Data." *Science* 229 (30 August 1985): 828–33.

Coach, Ken. "Televisions as Monitors." *Byte*, July 1984, 170–76.

Cogen, Jeffrey, "Graphics Pour into the Office." *Computerworld OA*, 5 December 1984, 21–23.

Collett, Ronald. "Army of CAE/CAD Vendors Enrich PC Power." *Digital Design*, November 1985, 32–42.

Colmerauer, Alain. "Prolog in 10 Figures." *Communications of the ACM* 28 (December 1985): 1296–1310.

Computer Graphics 85. Proceedings of SIGGRAPH 85, San Francisco, July 22–26. New York: Association for Computing Machinery, 1985.

"The Computerized Icon. CGW Interviews Aaron Marcus." *Computer Graphics World*, May 1985, 78–80.

Conrac Division, Conrac Corporation. *Raster Graphics Handbook.* New York: Van Nostrand Reinhold Co., 1985.

Cook, Peter R. "Electronic Encyclopedias." *Byte*, July 1984, 151–70.

Cortes, Camila Chaves. "The Vital Statistics of Major Paint Systems." *Computer Pictures*, July/August 1984, 6–8, 54–56.

Cox, John. "Digital Adds DECWindows to Unify Its Desktops." *Digital News*, 26 January 1987, 6.

Crane, Ted. "Frame Buffer Architecture." Paper presented at Siggraph 85, Introduction to Color Raster Graphics, San Francisco, 22 July 1985.

Crecine, John P. "The Next Generation of Personal Computers." *Science* 231 (28 February 1986): 935–42.

Davis, Andrew. "Proprietary/Standard Graphics Software Mix to Give More." *Computer Design*, May 1984, 229–34.

Davis, Karen. "No Sacrifices with Raster Graphics Display." *Computerworld*, 28 October 1985, 96–97.

Daynes, Rod, and Holder, Steve. "Controlling Videodiscs with Micros." *Byte*, July 1984, 207–28.

"Despite Severe Limitations, PC-CAD to Become a $1 Billion Business by 1990." *S. Klein Newsletter on Computer Graphics*, 19 April 1985, 1–4.

Deutsch, Karl W. "Knowledge in the Growth of Civilization: A Cybernetic Approach to the History of Human Thought." *Foundations of Access to Knowledge.* Edited by Edward B. Montgomery. Syracuse, N.Y.: Syracuse University Press, 1968.

Dickinson, Diana M. "Computer Update: Graphics Processors." *Electronic Engineering Times*, 7 May 1984, 44.

diSessa, Andrea A., and Abelson, Harold. "Boxer: A Reconstructable

Computational Medium." *Communications of the ACM* 29 (September 1986): 859–68.

Donoghue, Sheila. "Industry Reps See Graphics Becoming Commodity." *Computer Graphics Today*, May 1986, 3, 58.

Donohue, James F. "Neatness, Low-power Drain Propel Flat-panel Displays." *Mini-Micro Systems*, April 1986, 41–46.

Dooley, Bill. "Lotus Readies CD-ROM-Based Financial Database Interface." *Management Information Systems Week*, 29 September 1986, 6.

Duke, Paul, Jr. "Powerful '386' Personal Computers Show Promise, but Software Lags." *Wall Street Journal*, 19 January 1987, 21.

Durniak, John. "Kodak Boosts Electronic Pictures." *New York Times*, 27 October 1985, 75.

Edwards, Betty. *Drawing on the Right Side of the Brain*. Los Angeles: J.P. Tarcher, Inc., 1979.

Elmore, William B. "UNIX and GKS in a New Age of Computer Graphics." *UNIX/World* 1 (1984): 50–57.

Eve, Arthur W. "Graphics a Potentially Powerful Force in Business World Affecting Information Assimilation, Managerial Style." *Computerworld*, 24 September 1984, 60–61.

"Face-to-face." *Audio-Visual Communications*, June 1986, 37.

Faff, Terry. "Optical Imaging Systems." *Journal of Information and Image Management*, November 1986, 22–25.

Falk, David S., Brill, Dieter R., and Stork, David G. *Seeing the Light. Optics in Nature, Photography, Color, Vision and Holography*. New York: Harper & Row, 1986.

Fantel, Hans. "The Competition for a Sharper Image Comes Up Against Realistic Limits." *New York Times*, 2 November 1986, H-32.

Fantel, Hans. "Digital Recordings—Beautiful Music by the Numbers." *New York Times*, 18 February 1979, D-19–21.

Fantel, Hans. "Enhanced TV Standards Still Elusive." *New York Times*, 11 January 1987, 30.

Fastie, Will. "IBM Images." *Creative Computing*, June 1985, 76–79.

Feigenbaum, Edward A., and McCorduck, Pamela. *The Fifth Generation*. New York: New American Library, 1984.

Fein, Alan. "Blockade of Visual Excitation and Adaption in *Limulus* Photoreceptor by GDP-β-S." *Science* 232 (20 June 1986): 1543–545.

Feldman, Steven. "Videodisk Boosts Mass Storage." *Systems & Software*, September 1984, 97–102.

Ferg, Stephen. "Data Independence and the Relational Database." *Datamation*, 1 November 1986, 103–6.

Fialka, John J. "Ambitious Computer Research Is Focus of Pentagon Program." *Wall Street Journal*, 15 August 1986, 17.

"Focus Vision Stores, Shows Color Pictures." *Computerworld*, 4 August 1986, 67.

Forney, Jim. "Video Wizardry with PC-Eye." *PC Magazine*, February 1985, 172–82.

Foskett, A. C. *The Subject Approach to Information*. London: Clive Bingley, Ltd., 1977.

Fox, Edward A. "Expert Retrieval for Users of Computer-based Message Systems." *Proceedings of the 49th Annual Meeting of the American Society for Information Science*. Vol. 23. Medford, N.J.: Learned Information, 1986, 88–95.

Freedman, Alix M., and Hudson, Richard L. "DuPont and Philips Plan Joint Venture to Make, Market Laser-disk Products." *Wall Street Journal*, 30 October 1985, 4.

Frenkel, Karen A. "Toward Automating the Software-development Cycle." *Communications of the ACM* 28 (June 1985): 578–98.

Frentz, William. "High-performance and High-potential PC Graphics." Paper presented at Display Terminal/Graphics Industry Conference, Dataquest Inc., Monterey, Calif., 4–6 June 1986.

Fuerst, Irene. "Broken Windows." *Datamation*, 1 March 1985, 46–52.

"Futurist Jonathan Post Explores Tomorrow's Databases." *Bulletin of the American Society for Information Science*, June/July 1986, 24.

Galitz, Wilbert O. *Handbook of Screen Format Design*. Wellesley Hills, Mass.: QED Information Sciences, 1985.

Galloway, Emily, and Paris, Judith. "Information Providers and Videodisc/Optical Disk Technology." *Journal of the American Society for Information Science* 34 (November 1983): 414–16.

Gill, Philip J. "AI, Graphics Launch New User Interfaces." *Computer Graphics Today*, September 1986, 3, 8.

Girill, T. R. "Narration, Hierarchy and Autonomy: The Problem of Online Text Structure." *Proceedings of the 48th ASIS Annual Meeting*. White Plains, N.Y.: Knowledge Industry Publications, 1985, 354–57.

Goldberg, Adele, and Robson, David. *Smalltalk-80. The Language and its Implementation.* Reading, Mass.: Addison-Wesley Publishing Co., 1983.

Goldfarb, Lev. "Metric Data Models and Associated Search Strategies." *SIGIR Forum* 20 (Spring-Summer 1986): 7–11.

Grafton, Robert B., and Ichikawa, Tadao. "Visual Programming." *Computer*, August 1985, 6–9.

Granholm, John W.; Robertson, Douglas D.; Walker, Peter S.; and Nelson, Philip C. "Computer Design of Custom Femoral Stem Prostheses." *Computer Graphics and Applications*, February 1987, 26–35.

"Graphics Systems, Form and Function." Special report. *Computerworld*, 25 March 1985, SR-1–26.

Greenhouse, Steven. "An Innovator Gets Down to Business—3M." *New York Times*, 12 October 1986, F-1, 8.

Grenawalt, Bill. "Screen Reflection: Its Glaring Effect on VDT Operator Performance." *Computerworld*, 7 July 1986, 18.

Grundberg, Andy. "At Photokina, Still-Video Cameras." *New York Times*, 5 October 1986, 74.

Guterl, Fred. "Design Case History: Apple's Macintosh." *IEEE Spectrum*, December 1984, 34–43.

Guyon, Janet. "Bell Labs Takes a Small Step Toward an Optical Computer." *Wall Street Journal*, 18 July 1986, 23.

Haber, Lynn. "IBM, DEC Threaten Apollo and Sun in Workstations." *Mini-Micro Systems*, April 1986, 21–22.

Hall, William. "An Imaging Revolution." *AV Video*, May 1986, 54–59.

Hamilton, Rosemary. "Chorus Unveils Image Data Base Management Packages." *Computerworld*, 23 December 1985, 17, 20.

Hartigan, John M. "History of Automotive Videodiscs." *Corporate Television*, November 1986, 50.

Heite, Edward F. "Presentation Graphics–Giving End Users the Power of the Palette." *Computerworld*, 23 June 1986, 57–67.

Hemenway, Kathleen. "Psychological Issues in the Use of Icons in Command Menus." In *Human Factors in Computer Systems.* Proceedings of a conference sponsored by the Institute for Computer Science and Technology, National Bureau of Standards, United States Department of Commerce, and by the Association for Computing Machinery, 15–17 March 1982.

Henson, Bonnie. "Complex Computer Systems May Use Fish-eye View Approach." *Insight* 3 (2 April 1986) 4–11.

Henson, Bonnie. "The Master Mediator." *Insight,* 19 March 1986, 2–12.

Herman, Ron. "Detroit Gears Up with Videodiscs." *Corporate Television,* November 1986, 48–50.

Heyer, Mark. "Searching for Shakespeare." Paper prepared for Reference Technology, September 1984. 17 pages.

Heyer, Mark. "The Video Consumer. Interactive TV in the Home." *Educational and Instructional Television,* April 1979, 56–60.

Hindin, Harvey J. "Graphics Standards Finally Start to Sort Themselves Out." *Computer Design,* May 1984, 167–80.

Holden, Constance. "An Omnifarious Data Bank for Biology?" *Science* 228 (21 June 1985): 1412–413.

"Home Movies from Phonograph Records." *Modern Mechanics and Inventions,* June 1932, 89.

Houston, Tom. "The Allegory of Software." *Byte,* December 1983, 210–14.

Howitt, Doran. "Digital Pictures May Boom." *InfoWorld,* 26 November 1984, 43–45.

Hudson, Richard L. "Erasable Optical Disk Comes Closer, but Problems Remain." *Wall Street Journal,* 5 September 1986, 21.

Human Factors in Computer Systems. Proceedings of a conference sponsored by the Institute for Computer Science and Technology, National Bureau of Standards, U.S. Department of Commerce, in cooperation with the Association for Computing Machinery, March 1982.

Hymowitz, Carol. "Kodak Unveils Data Retrieval, Publishing Gear." *Wall Street Journal,* 30 May 1985, 8.

Jafek, Beverley J. "Autoradiographic Imaging Improves PET Efficacy." *Diagnostic Imaging,* September 1983, 70–74.

Jafek, Beverley J. "Landsat Imaging and the Study of Volcanoes." *Computer Graphics World,* February 1984, 53–57.

Jafek, Beverley J., and McLeod, Ronald G. "Solving Environmental

Problems with Satellite Imagery." *Computer Graphics World*, February 1984, 75–78.

John, E. R.; Tang, Y.; Brill, A. B.; Young, R.; and Ono, K. "Double-labeled Metabolic Maps of Memory." *Science* 233 (12 September 1986): 1167–175.

Johnson-Laird, Andy. " 'Mac' for the IBM PC." *Software News*, January 1985, 21–22.

Kalowski, Nathan. "The Marriage of Video and Computer Graphics." *Computerworld*, 13 May 1985, ID-29–32.

Kearsley, Greg. "Instructional Videodisc." *Journal of the American Society for Information Science* 34 (November 1983): 417–23.

Kilgour, Frederick G. "New Information Systems." *Bulletin of the American Society for Information Science*, (February 1980) 13.

Kirchner, Jake. "Federal Computing: The Good and the Bad." *Datamation*, 15 August 1986, 62–72.

Klein, Stanley. "Coping with the Doldrums." *S. Klein Computer Graphics Review*, Fall 1986, 11–16.

Klein, Stanley. "A Year to Forget, Another You'll Remember." *S. Klein Computer Graphics Review*, inaugural issue (early 1986), 11–12.

Klopfenstein, Bruce C. "Forecasting Use of Home Information Technologies." *Bulletin of the American Society for Information Science*, October/November 1986, 16–17.

"Kodak Enters Documentation Market." *Seybold Report on Publishing Systems*, 10 June 1985, 15–16.

Kogan, Philip, and Pick, Joan. *The Cathode Ray Revolution*. London: Sampson Low, Marston and Co., 1966.

Koll, Matthew B. "WEIRD: An Approach to Concept-based Information Retrieval." *Proceedings of the International Conference on Information Storage and Retrieval, Supplement.* New York: Association for Computing Machinery, 1978.

Koved, Larry, and Shneiderman, Ben. "Embedded Menus: Selecting Items in Context." *Communications of the ACM* 29 (April 1986): 312–18.

Lach, Eric. "Court Backs 'Look & Feel' Copyright." *InfoWorld*, 20 October 1986, 1, 8.

Lambert, Steve, and Ropiequet, Suzanne, eds. *CD/ROM. The New Papyrus.* Redmond, Wash.: Microsoft Press, 1986.

Langhorst, Fred. "VDI Promises Graphics Software Portability." *Computer Design*, May 1984, 197–203.

"Laser Videodiscs, Computer Graphics for Road Evaluations." *Better Roads*, March 1985, 16–17.

Lecht, Charles P. "Graphics Harmonizes Worlds of Art, Science." *Computerworld*, 18 March 1985, 43–44.

Lecht, Charles P. "To Dream, Perhaps of DRAMs." *Computerworld*, 2 February 1987, 17.

Lefkowits, Robert. "Environment Software Marketplace Heats Up." *Computerworld*, 29 April 1985, SR-7, 14.

Lehman, John A.; Vogel, Doug; and Dickson, Gary. "Business Graphics Trends." *Datamation*, 15 November 1984, 119–22.

Leinfuss, Emily. "QuadVision System Combines PC, Video, Compact Disk Technologies." *Management Information Systems Week*, 28 July 1986, 21.

Levine, Terri. "The Off-the-shelf Revolution." *Corporate Television*, November 1986, 40–46.

Lewell, John. "The Standardization of Standards." *AV Video*, May 1984, 18–21.

Licklider, Tracy. "Windowing Software Shatters Users' Hopes." *Computerworld*, 6 October 1986, 87–100.

Lin, Wei-Ching, and Dingott, Tsippora F. "To Tree or Not to Tree: A Simple User Interface Design for the Complex Decision Logic." *Proceedings of the 1986 IEEE International Conference on Systems, Man and Cybernetics.* New York: Institute of Electrical and Electronics Engineers, 1986.

Lindamood, George E. "The Structure of the Japanese Fifth Generation Computer Project—Then and Now." *Future Generations Computer Systems*, July 1984, 51–55.

Liskear, Jack, and Wilson, Ron. "Sorting Out the PC Graphics Board Tangle." *S. Klein Computer Graphics Review*, Fall 1986, 38–47.

Lunin, Lois F., and Paris, Judith, eds. "Perspectives on Videodisc and Optical Disk: Technology, Research and Applications." *Journal of the American Society for Information Science* 34 (November 1983): 405–40.

MacNicol, Gregory. "Color Monitor Specmanship: Look Before You Leap." *Digital Design*, November 1985, 44–48.

Marcom, John, Jr. "Movie-like Realism in Computers Could Put Sizzle in Home Market." *Wall Street Journal*, 4 June 1985, 35.

Marcom, John, Jr. "Much More than Music Lies in Future for Compact Disks." *Wall Street Journal*, 24 January 1986, 27.

Marcus, Aaron. "The Ten Commandments of Color: A Tutorial." *Computer Graphics Today*, November 1986, 7, 12, 14.

Marcus, Aaron. "Users Must Establish Own Rules for Color." *Computer Graphics Today*, September 1985, 7, 9.

Marcus, Richard S. "Design Questions in the Development of Expert Systems for Retrieval Assistance." *Proceedings of the 49th Annual Meeting of the American Society for Information Science.* Vol. 23. Medford, N.J.: Learned Information, 1986.

Marcus, Richard S. "Development and Testing of Expert Systems for Retrieval Assistance." *Proceedings of the 48th ASIS Annual Meeting.* White Plains, N.Y.: Knowledge Industry Publications, 1985.

Marcus, Richard S., and Reintjes, J. Francis. "A Translating Computer Interface for End-user Operation of Heterogeneous Retrieval Systems. I. Design." *Journal of the American Society for Information Science* 32 (July 1981): 287–303.

Marsh, Fred E., Jr. "Videodisc Technology." *Journal of the American Society for Information Science* 33 (July 1982): 237–44.

Marshall, Eliot. "Library Cutbacks: An Information Deficit." *Science* 232 (9 May 1986): 700–1.

Martin, R. L.; Wood, C.; Baehr, W.; and Applebury, M. L. "Visual Pigment Homologies Revealed by DNA Hybridization." *Science* 232 (6 June 1986): 1266–269.

Masuda, Yoneji. *The Information Society as Post-industrial Society.* Tokyo: Institute for the Information Society, 1980.

McEnaney, Maura, and Warner, Edward. "Standards Let CD-ROM Disks Run Across Multiple Systems." *Computerworld*, 23 June 1986, 12.

Meigs, James. "Going Interactive: Menu for Success in Corporate Disc Production." *Videography*, January 1983, 24–25.

Metzler, Douglas P.; Noreault, Terry; Haas, Douglas F.; and Cosic, Cynthia. "An Expert System Approach to Natural Language Processing." *Proceedings of the 48th ASIS Annual Meeting.* White Plains, N.Y.: Knowledge Industry Publications, 1985.

Meyer, John D. "Vision Systems: Technology of the Future at Work Today." *Computerworld*, 27 May 1985, SR-13.

Miller, George A. "Psychology and Information." *American Documentation*, July 1968, 286–89.

Miller, Michael W. "Apple Enters Pact to Study New Uses of Compact Disks." *Wall Street Journal*, 3 June 1986, 24.

Monsell, Stephen. "Representations, Processes, Memory Mechanisms: The Basic Components of Cognition." *Journal of the American Society for Information Science* 32 (September 1981): 378–90.

Moore, Connie. "Image Processing Offers MIS a New View of Information." *Computerworld*, 23 June 1986, 69–84.

Moriconi, Mark, and Hare, Dwight F. "Visualizing Program Designs Through PegaSys." *Computer*, August 1985, 72–85.

Morris, James H.; Satyanarayanan, Mahadev; Conner, Michael H.; Howard, John H.; Rosenthal, David S. H.; and Smith, F. Donelson. "Andrew: A Distributed Personal Computing Environment." *Communications of the ACM* 29 (March 1986): 184–201.

Murray, John P. "Put Graphics in the Corporate Picture." *Computerworld*, 29 October 1984, 67–68.

Myers, Edith D. "In the Hands of Users." *Datamation*, 1 May 1986, 48–52.

Myers, Ware. "Computer Graphics: The Next 20 Years." *Computer Graphics And Applications*, August 1985, 69–76.

Nathans, Jeremy; Thomas, Darcy; and Hogness, David S. "Molecular Genetics of Human Color Vision: The Genes Encoding Blue, Green and Red Pigments." *Science* 232 (11 April 1986): 193–202.

Nathans, Jeremy; Piantanida, Thomas P.; Eddy, Roger L.; Shows, Thomas B.; and Hogness, David S. "Molecular Genetics of Inherited Variation in Human Color Vision." *Science* 232 (11 April 1986): 203–20.

Nelson, Harold. "Logo for Personal Computers." *Byte*, June 1981, 36–44.

Nemzer, Daniel E. "Chemical Structure Input Method." *Proceedings of the 48th ASIS Annual Meeting*. White Plains, N.Y.: Knowledge Industry Publications, 1985.

Newman, William M., and Sproull, Robert F. *Principles of Interactive Computer Graphics*. New York: McGraw-Hill Book Co., 1973.

Obermeier, Klaus K., and Cooper, Linda E. "Information Network Facility Organizing System (INFOS)—An Expert System for Information Retrieval." *Proceedings of the 47th ASIS Annual Meeting.* Vol. 21. White Plains, N.Y.: Knowledge Industry Publications, 1984.

Oddy, R. N. "Information Retrieval Through Man-Machine Dialogue." *Journal of Documentation* 33 (March 1977): 1–14.

Offen, R. J., ed. *VLSI Image Processing.* New York: McGraw-Hill Book Co., 1985.

Ogg, Oscar. *The 26 Letters.* New York: Van Nostrand Reinhold Co., 1983.

Olmos, David. "Panel Examines History, Future of Computer Graphics." *Computerworld,* 6 August 1984, 16.

O'Malley, Christopher. "Driving Your Point Home." *Personal Computing,* August 1986, 86–105.

O'Malley, Christopher. "Graphics." *Personal Computing,* October 1986, 105–113.

"Online Subscriber Count Tops 1 Million." *IDP Report* 6 (April 26, 1985): 1–5.

Orr, Joel N. "Visual Illiteracy Hinders Computer Mapping." *Computer Graphics Today,* February 1986, 8.

Ott, John N. *Health and Light.* Old Greenwich, Conn.: Devin-Adair Co., 1973.

Paller, Alan. "CAD/CAM and Business Graphics—Where the Twain Meet." *S. Klein Computer Graphics Review,* Fall 1986, 35–36.

Paller, Alan. "Million-dollar Graphics." *Computerworld,* 21 April 1986, 67–78.

Palmquist, Ruth Ann, and Eisenberg, Michael. "Testing a Text Analysis Metric using Magnitude Estimation." *Proceedings of the 47th ASIS Annual Meeting.* Vol. 21. White Plains, N.Y.: Knowledge Industry Publications, 1984.

Paris, Judith. "Basics of Videodisc and Optical Disk Technology." *Journal of the American Society for Information Science* 34 (November 1983): 408–13.

"The Past, Present and Future of the Macintosh Desktop." *Semaphore Signal,* 12 March 1986, 1–7.

Pezzanite, Frank A. "The LC MARC Database on Video Laserdisc: The MINI MARC System." *Library Hi Tech* 3 (1985): 57–60.

Phelps, Michael E., and Mazziotta, John C. "Positron Emission Tomography: Human Brain Function and Biochemistry." *Science* 228 (17 May 1985): 799–809.

Phillips, Brian; Messick, Steven L.; Freiling, Michael J.; and Alexander, James H. "INKA: The *In*GLISH Knowledge Acquisition Interface for Electronic Instrument Troubleshooting Systems." Technical Report no. CR-85-04. Computer Research Laboratory, Tektronix, Inc., Beaverton, Ore., 1985.

"Photomail Hits Market." *Computerworld*, 18 March 1985, 55, 60.

Pope, Andy; Kates, Geoff; and Fineberg, Dan. "Making Life Easier for Professional and Novice Programmers." *Byte*, December 1983, 155–60.

Powell, David, "Getting on the Air." *PC Magazine*, 19 February 1985, 190–95.

Price, Neel, and Flatley, Jay. "Opting for High Tech: Implementing Optical Disk Technology for Government Agencies." *Journal of Information and Image Management*, October 1986, 22–25.

Prince, Suzan D. "Number Nine's Revolution: PC Graphics Cards." *Computer Pictures*, September/October 1985, 51–58.

Prince, Suzan D. "Television Stations Beam in on Computer Graphics Tech." *Computer Pictures*, March/April 1986, 20–28.

Raeder, Georg. "A Survey of Current Graphical Programming Techniques." *Computer*, August 1985, 11–25.

Raghavan, Vijay V., and Wong, S. K. M. "A Critical Analysis of Vector Space Model for Information Retrieval." *Journal of the American Society for Information Science* 37 (September 1986): 279–87.

Raghavan, Vijay V., and Yu, C. T. "Experiments on the Determination of the Relationships Between Terms." *Proceedings of the International Conference on Information Storage and Retrieval, Supplement*. Edited by Robert T. Dattola. New York: Association for Computing Machinery, 1978, 20–52.

Raimondi, Donna. "Laser Disk-based Systems Offered." *Computerworld*, 25 November 1985, 41, 46.

Ratajczak, Jean. "Keyed Up on Color." *Hardcopy*, May 1985, 58–63.

Rhodes, Michael L.; Kuo, Yu-Ming; Rothman, Stephen L. G.; and Woznick, Charles. "An Application of Computer Graphics and Networks to Anatomic Model and Prosthesis Manufacturing." *Computer Graphics and Applications*, February 1987, 12–25.

Rice, John, and Schubin, Mark. "Conversation with Kerns Powers." *Videography*, April 1986, 101–22.

Rifkin, Glenn. "Toward the Fifth Generation." *Computerworld*, 6 May 1985, Update/3–23.

Rivlin, Robert. *The Algorithmic Image*. Redmond, Wash.: Microsoft Press, 1986.

Robertson, Barbara. "New Chips Spur PC Graphics." *Computer Graphics World*, January 1987, 42–43.

Rogowitz, B. E. "The Human Visual System: A Guide for the Display Technologist." *Proceedings of the Society for Information Display* 24, no. 3: 235–52.

Rose, Albert. *Vision—Human and Electronic*. New York: Plenum Press, 1973.

Rose, Denis. "Optical Disk for Digital Storage and Retrieval Systems." *Journal of the American Society for Information Science* 34 (November 1983): 434–38.

Rosebush, Judson. "New Choices and Challenges." *S. Klein Computer Graphics Review*, inaugural issue (early 1986), 49–57.

Rothchild, Edward S. "An Eye on Optical Disks." *Datamation*, 1 March 1986, 73–74.

Rothfeder, Jeffrey. "Bergen Company Enlivens TV Graphics." *New York Times*, 15 September 1985, NJ-23.

Salton, Gerard. "On the Use of Knowledge-based Processing in Automatic Text Retrieval." *Proceedings of the 49th Annual Meeting of the American Society for Information Science*. Vol. 23. Medford, N.J.: Learned Information, 1986.

Salton, G. "A New Comparison Between Conventional Indexing (MEDLARS) and Automatic Text Processing (SMART)." *Journal of the American Society for Information Science* 23 (March-April 1972): 75–83.

Salton, G., and McGill, M.J. *Introduction to Modern Information Processing*. New York: McGraw-Hill Book Co., 1983.

Sandberg-Diment, Erik. "Adding a Dash of Visual Sparkle." *New York Times*, 4 August 1985, F-10.

Sandberg-Diment, Erik. "A Data Base that Thinks by Seeing. *New York Times*, 17 February 1985, F-15.

Sandberg-Diment, Erik. "The In Crowd is Watching Apple." *New York Times*, 25 January 1987, F-16.

Sandberg-Diment, Erik. "Integrated Software for the Thin Mac." *New York Times*, 14 July 1985, F-11.

Sandberg-Diment, Erik. "Is Optical Memory Next from I.B.M.?" *New York Times*, 31 March 1985, F-14.

Sandberg-Diment, Erik. "Making Graphics Glitter." *New York Times*, 20 October 1985, F-14.

Sanger, David W. "Can Lotus Make Japanese Executives Love PC's?" *New York Times*, 30 November 1986, F-6.

Schubin, Mark. "CCD 4 U?" *Videography*, April 1986, 47–48.

Schubin, Mark. "How Sony Makes CCDs Work." *Videography*, April 1986, 48–50.

Schubin, Mark. "Pyramid Power." *Videography*, August 1986, 72–75.

Schubin, Mark. "Report on Graphics and Animation Systems." *Videography*, February 1985, 37–42.

Schubin, Mark. "SMPTE Convention: One Man's View." *Videography*, January 1987, 31–33.

Schubin, Mark. "The Tiniest Videodisc." *Videography*, April 1986, 51.

Schultz, Claire K. "Through the Looking Glass." *Bulletin of the American Society for Information Science*, December 1980, 30–31.

Schuyler, Cynthia. "Interactive Video Information Systems." *Computerworld*, 29 October 1984, ID-13–16.

Schwerin, Julie B. "Optical Publishing. Technological Breakthrough as a Marketing Challenge." *Information Times*, Fall 1985, 30–32.

Shneiderman, Ben. "Designing Menu Selection Systems." *Journal of the American Society for Information Science* 37 (March 1986): 57–70.

Shneiderman, Ben. *Designing the User Interface*. Reading, Mass.: Addison-Wesley Publishing Co., 1987.

Shuey, David M. "ANSI Standards Draw Attention of Graphics Industry." *Computerworld*, 25 March 1985, SR-10.

Smith, Bradford M. "CAD/CAM Data Exchange Leaps Beyond IGES." *S. Klein Computer Graphics Review*, Winter 1987, 79–80.

Smith, Philip J., and Chignell, Mark. "Development of an Expert System to Aid in Searches of the *Chemical Abstracts*." *Proceedings of the 47th ASIS Annual Meeting*. White Plains, N.Y.: Knowledge Industry Publications, 1984.

Somlyo, Andrew P., ed. *Recent Advances in Electron and Light Optical Imaging in Biology and Medicine*. New York: New York Academy of Sciences, 1986.

Sonenclar, Kenneth R. "Esprit Crucial to European Technology." *Computerworld*, 6 May 1985, Update/18, 24.

"Sony MVR-5500 Still Video Recorder Offers Floppy Disk Alternative to Slides." *Computerworld*, 26 May 1986, 85.

Sproull, Robert F.; Sutherland, W. R.; and Ullner, Michael K. *Device-independent Graphics*. New York: McGraw-Hill Book Co., 1985.

Squire, Larry R. "Mechanisms of Memory." *Science* 232 (27 June 1986): 1612–619.

Stanfill, Craig, and Kahle, Brewster. "Parallel Free-text Search on the Connection Machine System." *Communications of the ACM* 29 (December 1986): 1229–239.

Stanfill, Craig, and Waltz, David. "Toward Memory-based Reasoning." *Communications of the ACM* 29 (December 1986): 1213–228.

Steen, Edwin B., and Montagu, Ashley. *Anatomy and Physiology*. Vol. 2. New York: Harper & Row, 1985.

Stipp, David. "Lotus Suit Charges Two Software Firms Infringe on 1-2-3 Program Copyrights." *Wall Street Journal*, 13 January 1987, 8.

Stock, Rodney, and Robertson, Barbara. "New Chips Unleash Super Graphics." *Computer Graphics World*, June 1986, 24–32.

Sullivan, Kathleen. "Icons Point to Changes." *Computerworld*, 20 August 1984, 87.

Sullivan, Kathleen. "MIS Panel: Windows Not the Answer." *Computerworld*, 20 May 1985, 47, 54.

Sun, Marjorie. "Federal VDT Study Finally Wins Approval." *Science* 232 (27 June 1986): 1594–595.

Sustik, Joan M., and Brooks, Terrence A. "Retrieving Information with Interactive Videodiscs." *Journal of the American Society for Information Science* 34 (November 1983): 424–32.

Sutherland, Stuart. "Prestel and the User." University of Sussex, Centre for Research on Perception and Cognition, Brighton, U.K.: 1980. 134 pages.

Thompson, Richard F. "The Neurobiology of Learning and Memory." *Science* 233 (29 August 1986): 941–47.

Treurniet, W. C. "Display of Text on Television." CRC Technical Note no. 705-E. Canada, Department of Communications, Communications Research Centre, May 1981. 42 pages.

Trost, Cathy. "Study on VDT Use During Pregnancy Seen Lessening Concern of Health Risks." *Wall Street Journal*, 30 September 1986, 7.

Tufte, Edward R. *The Visual Display of Quantitative Information.* Cheshire, Conn.: Graphics Press, 1983.

Utz, Peter. "How the Heck Does Color TV Work?" *AV Video*, May 1986, 46–52.

van Overbeek, Thomas T. "Graphically Speaking: PC Business Graphics." Paper presented at Display Terminal/Graphics Industry Conference, Dataquest Inc., Monterey, Calif., 4–6 June 1986.

van Rijsbergen, C. J. "A New Theoretical Framework for Information Retrieval." *SIGIR Forum* 21 (Fall-Winter 1986/87): 23–29.

"VDTs Said to Slow Reading." *Computerworld*, 1 September 1986, 63.

Veith, Richard H. "Information Retrieval and Spatial Orientation." *Proceedings of the 48th ASIS Annual Meeting.* White Plains, N.Y.: Knowledge Industry Publications, 1985.

Veith, Richard H. "NAPLPS Demands Conservation Tactics." *Computerworld*, 25 June 1984, SR-2–8.

Veith, Richard H. "Using Form, Color and Spatial Dimensions in Information Retrieval Systems." *Proceedings of the Fifth National Online Meeting.* Medford, N.J.: Learned Information, 1984.

Verity, John W. "Graphically Speaking with Dr. Edward R. Tufte." *Datamation*, 1 April 1985, 88–92.

"Videodiscs and Computers: A Dynamic Duo." *Business Week*, 7 February 1983, 109–11.

"Videophone System Bows from Pictel." *Computerworld*, 31 March 1986, 73.

"Viewing a Data Base Through Graphics in Works at CCA." *Computerworld*, 13 December 1982, 79.

"Visage Boosts V:Station Videodisk Line." *Computerworld*, 26 August 1985, 55.

"Visage Ties Micros, Videodisk Players," *Computerworld*, 10 December 1984, 107, 126.

Voos, Henry. "Implications of Holography for Information Systems."

Journal of the American Society for Information Science 31 (November 1980): 449–51.

Waldrop, M. Mitchell. "Artificial Intelligence (I): Into the World." *Science* 223 (24 February 1984): 802–5.

Waldrop, M. Mitchell. "Artificial Intelligence in Parallel." *Science* 225 (10 August 1984): 608–10.

Waldrop, M. Mitchell. "The Connection Machine goes Commercial." *Science* 232 (30 May 1986): 1090–91.

Waldrop, M. Mitchell. "The Machinations of Thought." *Science 85,* March 1985, 38–45.

Waldrop, M. Mitchell. "Natural Language Understanding." *Science* 224 (27 April 1984): 372–74.

Ward, Alex. "Computer Graphics Enliven the Screen." *New York Times,* 22 July 1984, H-21.

Warfield, Robert W. "The New Interface Technology." *Byte,* December 1983, 218–30.

Warner, Edward. "Graphics Interface Spec Proposed." *Computerworld,* 7 April 1986, 33, 37.

Warner, Edward. "IBM Micro, Videodisk Aid in Training." *Computerworld,* 1 July 1985, 41, 50.

Warner, Jim. "Graphics Landscape." *Hardcopy,* February 1984, 142–43.

Watson, J. S., trans. *Cicero on Oratory and Orators.* Carbondale, Ill.: Southern Illinois University Press, 1970.

Watt, Peggy. "Apple Forces Rewrite of GEM." *Computerworld,* 7 October 1985, 2.

Watt, Peggy. "DRI Unveils Polished GEM." *Computerworld,* 25 November 1985, 31, 36.

Watt, Peggy. "Microsoft MS-DOS Strategy Features Windows Way of Life." *Computerworld,* 10 February 1986, 13.

White, George M. "The Desktop Metaphor." *Byte,* December 1983, 220.

Whitehead, Alfred North. *Science and the Modern World.* New York: (The Macmillan Company, 1925) The Free Press, 1967.

Wilkins, Bryan. "AI Techniques Considered for DBMS Use." *Computerworld,* 3 December 1984, 57.

Williams, Gregg; Edwards, Jon; and Robinson, Phillip. "The Amiga Personal Computer." *Byte*, August 1985, 83–100.

Williams, Martha. "Database and Online Statistics for 1979." *Bulletin of the American Society for Information Science*, (December 1980), 27–29.

Williams, Martha. "1977 Data-base and On-line Statistics." *Bulletin of the American Society for Information Science*, December 1977, 21–23.

Williams, Martha. "Transparent Information Systems Through Gateways, Front Ends, Intermediaries, and Interfaces." *Journal of the American Society for Information Science*, 37 (July 1986): 204–14.

Williams, Tom. "LCDs Lead the Assault on CRT's Dominance." *Computer Design*, 1 November 1986, 53–59.

Wilson, Andrew. "Flat-panel Displays: Still in the Future." *Digital Design*, December 1985, 54–58.

Wilson, Andrew C. "High-resolution Graphics—Implementing Software in Silicon." *Digital Design*, August 1985, 52–58.

Wilson, David. "Video DRAMs Shift Image of Graphics Systems." *Digital Design*, April 1986, 28–32.

Wilson, Kenneth G. "Supercomputer Future: Scenario for 1990." *Computerworld*, 6 May 1985, Update/7, 22.

Withington, Frederic G. "Winners and Losers in the Fifth Generation." *Datamation*, December 1983, 193–96, 200–9.

Wong, S. K. M., and Ziarko, W. "A Unified Approach for Artificial Intelligence and Information Retrieval." *SIGIR Forum* 20 (Spring-Summer 1986): 15–16.

Wright, Robert. "A Better Mental Model." *Sciences*, March/April 1986, 8–10.

Wright, Thomas. "Is GKS Powerful Enough for the Application?" *Computer Design*, May 1984, 211–14.

Wurtman, Richard J.; Baum, Michael J.; and Potts, John T., Jr. *The Medical and Biological Effects of Light*. Annals of the New York Academy of Science, vol. 453. New York: New York Academy of Sciences, 1985.

Zieman, Mark. "Compact, Affordable Picture Phones May Revive Once-heralded Technology." *Wall Street Journal*, 16 January 1985, 31.

INDEX

Frequency, 47, 71–73

G

Galitz, Wilbert, 173
Games, 105–7, 256. *See also* specific names of
Gas plasma panels, 67–68
Geographic surrogates
    directional motion, 147–49
    imaginary landscapes, 151–52
    modifying reality, 150
    overview of, 145
    travelog, 146
GKS (Graphics Kernel System), 115–18
Graphic interface. *See* Interface
Graphics. *See also* Graphics and video technologies
    and information retrieval process, 11–13
    technologies of, 17
    and video, 9–11
Graphics and video technologies. *See also* Applications; Graphics; Interface; Videobases
    categories of, 4–5
    and computer systems, 1–2
    design guidelines
        balance, 267–68
        base in experience, 267
        enhancement, 265–66
        overview of, 265
        psychophysiological awareness, 268–70
        simplicity, 266
    elements of
        color, 6–9
        form, 9–17
        graphics, 9–13
        motion, 17–20
        overview of, 5–6
        video, 13–17
    growth of, 2–4
    importance of, 251–52
    in larger environment, 270–72
    objects

    dynamic creations, 34–37
    overview of, 31–33
    stored pictures/graphics, 33–34
    presentation level
        motion, 262–64
        other attributes, 264–65
        overview of, 260
        spatial orientation, 260–62
        time, 262–64
    as programming tool, 247–49
    summary of, 37
    tools
        attractiveness, 27–29
        icons, 20–23
        overview of, 20
        spatial orientation, 23–27
        transformation, 30–31
    trends in
        color, 254–55
        dimensions, 257–60
        overview of, 251–52
        processing power, 255
        readability, 253–54
        realism, 256–57
    and visual world, 272–73
Graphics applications. *See* Applications
Graphics card. *See* Graphics controller
Graphics controller, 111–13
Graphics standards
    CGI, 117–18
    CGM, 118
    CG-VDI, 117–18
    Core, 115–17
    DGIS, 119
    GKS, 115–17
    IGES, 118–19
    other, 119–21
    overview of, 113–15
    STEP, 118–19
    window systems, 121–22

H

High-definition television systems (HDTV), 59

Vector CRTs, 63–64
Vertical resolution, 59–60
Very large-scale integrated circuits (VLSI), 243–44
VHD (Video High-Density) system, 129
Video. *See also* Graphics and video technologies
  and analog video signals, 15–17
  development of, 13–14
  and digitized video, 15–17
  and graphics, 9–11
  technologies of, 17
  use of, 14–15
Videobases and image bases
  contribution of, 123
  electronic distribution, 164–67
  electronic publishing, 160–63
  electronic storage, 164–67
  and form, 13–14
  geographic surrogates
    directional motion, 147–49
    imaginary landscape, 151–52
    modifying reality, 150
    overview of, 145–46
    travelog, 146
  interactive videodisks at work
    area directories, 155–56
    real estate, 156–57
    sales and product demonstrations, 154–55
    training and education, 153–54
    use of, 152–53
    video communication, 158–59
    video production, 157
  methods of
    capacitance systems, 128–29
    CDs, 130–33
    digitalized video, 133–34
    film disks, 129–30
    laser disks, 125–28
    in past, 123–25
    related, 135–36
    videodisks, 125–28
  spatial data management
    adaptations, 143–45
    Dataland concept, 136–41

  research results in, 141–43
  summary of, 167
  videotex pages, 166–67
Video communication, 157–59
Videodisks
  and CDs, 130–31
  for digital data, 16–17
  interactive
    area directories, 155–56
    real estate, 156–57
    sales and product demonstrations, 154–55
    training and education, 152–54
    use of, 152–54
    video communication, 157–59
    video production, 157
  laser, 14
  and videobases, 125–28
Video display terminal (VDT), 53–54
Video High-Density (VHD) system, 129
Video productions, 157
Videoshow, 85–86
Video technologies. *See* Graphics and video technologies
Videotex pages, 166–67
Video tubes, 53–56
View, 144–45
Vision, 76–77. *See also* Visual processes
Vision systems, 15–16
Visual environment, 170–72
Visual experience, 39–41
Visual pathways, 73–76
Visual processes, basic
  and assimilation in brain
    association, 79–80
    memory, 76–77
    right/left processing, 77–79
    vision, 76–77
    visual pathways, 73–76
  and computer systems, 39
  and display devices
    non-CRT displays, 65–68
    overview of, 52–53
    raster scan CRTs, 57–62

About the Author

Richard H. Veith is Director of Research and Development (Eastern Region) for Volt Delta Resources, a subsidiary of Volt Information Sciences. He is primarily engaged in projects that include audio, video, and graphics as components of information systems. Previously, he was with the National Broadcasting Company, Warner Communications, Logica Inc., and Informatics Inc., working with text, video, and graphics data bases. He holds a PhD in Information Studies from Syracuse University and an MA in Radio and Television from San Francisco State University. His three previous books are *Television's Teletext* (1983); *Multinational Computer Nets: The Case of International Banking* (1981); and *Talk-back TV: Two-way Cable Television* (1976).